C000241393

ULSTER'S LAST S

ULSTER'S LAST STAND?

Reconstructing Unionism after the Peace Process

JAMES W. McAULEY
University of Huddersfield

IRISH ACADEMIC PRESS
DUBLIN • PORTLAND, OR

First published in 2010 by Irish Academic Press

2 Brookside,	920 NE 58th Avenue, Suite 300
Dundrum Road,	Portland, Oregon,
Dublin 14, Ireland	97213-3786

www.iap.ie

copyright © 2010 James W. McAuley

British Library Cataloguing in Publication Data
An entry can be found on request

ISBN 978 0 7165 3032 9 (cloth)
ISBN 978 0 7165 3033 6 (paper)

Library of Congress Cataloging-in-Publication Data
An entry can be found on request

Printed by Good News Digital Books, Ongar, Essex

For Stephanie, Charlotte and Rowan,
and in memory of my mother,
Mary Ellen (Maisie) McAuley, 1923–2003

Contents

Abbreviations

AIA	Anglo-Irish Agreement
APNI	Alliance Party of Northern Ireland
CEC	Campaign for Equal Citizenship
CIRA	Continuity Irish Republican Army
CJR	Criminal Justice Review
CLMC	Combined Loyalist Military Command
CRJ	Community Restorative Justice Ireland
DUP	Democratic Unionist Party
EPIC	Ex-Prisoners Interpretative Centre
FAIR	Families Acting for Innocent Relatives
IICD	Independent International Commission on Decommissioning
IMC	Independent Monitoring Commission
IRA	Irish Republican Army (Provisional)
LINC	Local Initiatives for Needy Communities
LVF	Loyalist Volunteer Force
MLA	Member of the Legislative Assembly
NICRA	Northern Ireland Civil Rights Association
NILP	Northern Ireland Labour Party

NIUP	Northern Ireland Unionist Party
NUPRG	New Ulster Political Research Group
OIRA	Official Irish Republican Army
PrUP	Protestant Unionist Party
PSNI	Police Service of Northern Ireland
PUP	Progressive Unionist Party
RHC	Red Hand Commando
RIRA	Real Irish Republican Army
RUC	Royal Ulster Constabulary
SDLP	Social Democratic and Labour Party
TUV	Traditional Unionist Voice
UCAG	Ulster Community Action Group
UCUNF	Ulster Conservatives and Unionists – New Force
UDA	Ulster Defence Association
UDP	Ulster Democratic Party
UKUP	United Kingdom Unionist Party
ULDP	Ulster Loyalist Democratic Party
UPRG	Ulster Political Research Group
USC	Ulster Special Constabulary
UUAC	United Unionist Action Council
UUC	Ulster Unionist Council
UUCA	United Unionist Campaign Against the Agreement
UUP	Ulster Unionist Party
UVF	Ulster Volunteer Force
UWC	Ulster Workers' Council
WRUC	Women Raising Unionist Concerns

Timeline of Major Events 1985–2009

1985	The leader of the SDLP, John Hume, meets in private with representatives of the Provisional IRA leadership.
	United Kingdom prime minister, Margaret Thatcher and the Irish taoiseach, Garret Fitzgerald sign the Anglo-Irish Agreement, (giving the Dublin government a consultative role in the future of Northern Ireland).
1986	Widespread unionist protests take place against the Anglo-Irish Agreement.
	The Stormont Assembly is dissolved (June).
1987	An IRA bomb kills eleven people at a Remembrance Day Parade in Enniskillen.
1988	John Hume, leader of the Social Democratic and Labour Party, begins talks with Gerry Adams, leader of Sinn Féin, about the political future.
	The SAS shoot dead three IRA members in Gibraltar. At their funeral in Belfast Michael Stone kills three mourners.
1990	The UK secretary of state, Peter Brooke, declares that Britain has 'no selfish strategic or economic' interest in Northern Ireland.
1991	Round-table talks begin (without Sinn Féin) and continue until November 1992 with little progress made.
	The UDA and UVF call a ten-week ceasefire to coincide with the beginning of the talks (which does not hold).
1992	Amid continuing sectarian violence, further talks at Stormont are adjourned without any agreement.

The UDA is banned.

The Ulster Unionist Party agrees to hold formal talks with the Irish government.

1993 John Hume and Gerry Adams issue a joint public statement.

The IRA plants a bomb in a shop on Belfast's Shankill Road killing ten people. A wave of reprisal attacks by Loyalist paramilitaries follows, including the killing of seven people in a Greysteel bar.

The media expose a sustained series of secret contacts between the UK government (through MI5 and other intermediaries) and the Irish republican movement.

UK prime minister John Major and the Irish taoiseach Albert Reynolds issue the Downing Street Declaration.

1994 The IRA announces a complete cessation of military activity.

Six weeks later the Combined Loyalist Military Command (representing the UDA, UVF and Red Hand Commando) also calls a ceasefire.

The Forum for Peace and Reconciliation is established.

Albert Reynolds resigns as taoiseach following the collapse of his coalition government and is replaced by Bertie Ahern as Fianna Fáil leader.

1995 Civil servants representing the UK government meet with Sinn Féin – the first formal engagement between the two groupings for twenty-three years.

The re-routing of an Orange Order parade at Drumcree, near Portadown leads to widespread protests. Eventually as part of a huge security operation, the parade, with David Trimble and Ian Paisley at the fore, is forced through the predominately nationalist area of Garvaghy Road.

Daylight patrols by the British army end in most areas of Northern Ireland.

The Framework documents are published, including proposals for a devolved Northern Ireland Assembly and cross-border political and economic bodies.

1996   An International Body on Arms chaired by US senator George Mitchell sets out proposals on how to tackle the decommissioning of weapons.

The Mitchell report is published, proposing all-party talks if all those involved meet six principles of non-violence.

An IRA bomb in London's Canary Wharf kills two and causes millions of pounds worth of damage. After Sinn Féin's exclusion from inter-party talks the IRA bomb Manchester city centre causing vast economic damage.

1997   New Labour sweep to a landslide election victory and Tony Blair becomes prime minister.

The IRA renews its ceasefire and Sinn Féin re-enters talks, causing the DUP to lead a boycott.

1998   Further Anglo-Irish proposals are rejected by Sinn Féin and the IRA.

Mo Mowlam, the UK secretary of state, visits loyalist prisoners in the Maze to urge their support for planned talks.

The UFF issues a statement acknowledging that they carried out sectarian killings.

Serious negotiations begin after George Mitchell establishes 9 April as a deadline for a peace agreement.

The Belfast (Good Friday) Agreement is signed.

The Agreement is approved by referendums in both Northern Ireland and the Irish Republic.

June elections are held to determine the composition of the new devolved Assembly. The UUP and SDLP are elected as the two largest parties and David Trimble (UUP) and Séamus Mallon (SDLP) elected as first and deputy first minister.

For the first time since the protests surrounding the Drumcree Orange Order parade began, the march is not allowed through the Garvaghy Road. The decision precipitates widespread violence in loyalist districts and marks the first of several years of overt conflict around the issue.

Gerry Adams unequivocally condemns a Real IRA bomb in Omagh that kills twenty-seven people. Shortly afterwards he meets with David Trimble for talks.

The first paramilitary prisoners are released under the terms of the Belfast Agreement.

US president Bill Clinton makes his first visit to Northern Ireland to offer his support for the peace process.
The IRA rejects unionist demands to decommission its weaponry.

1999   The start of power sharing is put on hold amid continued disagreements between the political parties.

The nomination of Assembly ministers collapses because the UUP boycotts the meeting over lack of progress in the decommissioning of IRA weapons.

The Pattern Commission makes 175 recommendations concerning wholesale policing reform in Northern Ireland.

The IRA announces that it will send a representative to talk with the international arms decommissioning body.

The Assembly meets and nominates Executive ministers. Power sharing begins, but the DUP remains opposed.

2000   Peter Mandelson, the UK secretary of state, suspends the Assembly because of the lack of progress on arms decommissioning.

The IRA announces it will open up some of its arms dumps to inspection.

Unionists confirm they will return to the Assembly provided the arms issue is dealt with while it functions.

Sinn Féin and the DUP both make gains at the general election.

2001   Following the resignation of First Minister David Trimble, the UK government suspends the Assembly to allow more time for negotiations.

The IRA announces a first act of decommissioning, triggering a return to power sharing.

David Trimble fails to win the support of other unionists for his re-election. He is forced to rely on the votes of other parties, especially the Alliance Party.

Following adoption of the Patten report the Royal Ulster Constabulary becomes the Police Service of Northern Ireland (PSNI).

2002   The IRA announces further disposal of parts of its arsenal.

The PSNI raid Sinn Féin's offices in Stormont following allegations that they are running an organised 'spy ring'.

John Reid, secretary of state, suspends the Assembly as power sharing falls apart as unionists openly express their distrust of Sinn Féin.

2003   The London and Dublin governments propose a joint blueprint seeking to move the process forward.

An Independent Monitoring Commission is appointed to monitor paramilitary activity.

A third act of IRA decommissioning takes place, but Trimble rejects it as insufficiently transparent and claims he can therefore no longer deliver his end of the deal.

New Assembly elections see the DUP and Sinn Féin emerge as the major political representatives of their respective communities. Ian Paisley warns he will not sit in government with republicans until the IRA disarms and disbands.

2004   Another round of talks fails to find an agreed way forward.

Intensive party negotiations are held at Leeds Castle.

Tony Blair and Bertie Ahern set a September deadline to end the impasse.

A proposed political deal fails over the issue of photographic evidence of IRA decommissioning demanded by unionists.

2005   The political strength of Sinn Féin and the DUP is reinforced at the general election (see Appendix 1).

Sinn Féin calls on the IRA to end its campaign.

The IRA formally orders an end to its armed campaign. The IICD confirms that IRA decommissioning has been completed and its arms 'put beyond use'.

2006   Tony Blair and Bertie Ahern unveil their latest plans to restore devolution. Parties are given until 24 November to set up a working power-sharing Executive.

Three days of all-party negotiations in Scotland end with the announcement of the St Andrews Agreement. Although the outcome is far from definitive, the DUP signals a willingness to share power with Sinn Féin if they accept policing.

2007   At a specially convened árd fheis (conference), Sinn Féin votes to support the Police Service of Northern Ireland and to take its place on the Policing Board.

As new Northern Ireland Assembly elections are held, the DUP and Sinn Féin emerge as clear victors at the polls.

Ian Paisley and Gerry Adams hold their first public meeting to announce that the new Assembly will be delayed for six weeks.

Ian Paisley makes a public visit to the taoiseach, Bertie Ahern, in Dublin.

The UVF announces that it has renounced violence, its weapons have been put 'beyond reach' and it will disband.

Following elections, the Northern Ireland Assembly opens on 8 May, with Ian Paisley (DUP) elected as first minister and Martin McGuinness as deputy first minister (see Appendix 2).

The North/South Ministerial Council meets, in Armagh, for first time since suspension in 2002, with Ian Paisley in attendance as first minister.

Tony Blair stands down as UK prime minister and is replaced by Gordon Brown. Shaun Woodward is appointed Northern Ireland secretary.

The UDA announces that the Ulster Freedom Fighters have been stood down.

The British army's deployment of 'Operation Banner' comes to an end after thirty-eight years. 'Counter-terrorism' powers specific to Northern Ireland are repealed.

Jim McAllister, a former leading DUP member, announces the formation of a new political movement to oppose the DUP's sharing of power with Sinn Féin. It later reveals itself as Traditional Unionist Voice (TUV).

2008   The Rev. Ron Johnstone replaces Ian Paisley as moderator of the Free Presbyterian Church.

New District Policing Partnership Boards are formed with Sinn Féin comprising 10 per cent of the membership.

Bertie Ahern resigns as taoiseach after eleven years in office.

The UUP defeat the DUP in a local council by-election in Dromore, County Down, following the transfer of votes from TUV to the UUP candidate.

Ian Paisley stands down as first minister and leader of the DUP.

Peter Robinson is elected as leader of the DUP with Nigel Dodds as his deputy. Robinson replaces Ian Paisley as first minister. Martin McGuinness remains in his post as deputy first minister.

An Independent Monitoring Commission report concludes that the IRA campaign 'is well and truly over' and 'the army council, by deliberate choice is no longer operational or functional'.

The DUP and Sinn Féin agree a programme for the transfer of police and justice powers from Westminster.

The Assembly Executive meets on 18 November, following a five-month 'stand-off' surrounding the devolution of police and justice powers.

2009   The Consultative Group on the Past presents its report to the secretary of state for Northern Ireland. Included is the recommendation that the nearest relative of each person who died in the conflict (including non-state combatants) should receive a £12,000 'recognition payment'. The recommendation is met with widespread condemnation from victims groups and unionist politicians.

The Real IRA mounts an attack on a British army base in County Antrim, killing two soldiers and seriously wounding four others including two civilians. Less than forty-eight hours later the Continuity IRA kill a PSNI officer in Craigavon. Loyalist paramilitary groups confirm that they will not make a military response.

The European election poll is headed by Sinn Féin's sitting MEP Bairbre de Brún with 126,184 votes. In a three-way Unionist contest, Jim Nicholson of the Ulster Conservatives and Unionists – New Force takes 82,893 votes. Jim Allister of TUV polls 66,197 first preference votes, making direct inroads into DUP support, where the tally for Diane Dodds (88,346) marks a decline of almost 14 per cent on the previous European contest.

Loyalist paramilitaries announce that they have begun to decommission their weapons.

Sources: BBC News Online;[1] *Belfast Telegraph*; CAIN;[2] *Fortnight*

Tables

Acknowledgements

As always the list of people deserving acknowledgement is long. In no particular order, my sincere thanks go to Sue Bernhauser, Greg Millington, Davey Major, Pat Nixon, Gary Hare, Gerry Rice, Orla Muldoon, Dawn Purvis, Clifford Stevenson, Keith McCollum, Neil Ferguson, Andy Mycock, Alan McCully, Colin Jackson, Gordon Carr, Graham Spencer, Lyndsay Harris, Claire Guyer, Chris Gifford, Catherine McGlynn, Pete Woodcock, Aaron Edwards, Dave Robinson, Harry Maguire, Pete Shirlow, Stephen James, Peter Walker and Susan Hogan. All, and in very different ways, have provided much food for thought, help, friendship, excuses for excess, guidance and good times during the time spent writing this book.

Jon Tonge has been a true friend, and although I doubt if our singing careers shall ever replace our academic ones, he has provided me with much encouragement. His understanding and value of the true meaning of colleague displays a quality that is becoming all too rare in higher education. At home Charlotte and Rowan are growing into the people that I always hoped they would be, and continue to provide glorious distractions, some of which are even welcome. Stephanie remains at the heart of almost all that we do.

I have lost two good friends in recent times and continue to think of Noel Gilzean and Clare Cassidy often. I will always miss their conversation, humour but most of all their humanity and caring ways. I still miss David Ervine's always invigorating and sometimes challenging company. For over twenty years he provided me with invaluable help in seeking to understand loyalism and unionism more fully. The thoughts and views of many of the contacts he initiated on my behalf helped structure the contents of this book.

My thanks are also due to those many people who would readily describe themselves as unionists and loyalists and who have freely given of their time or provided other material for the book. I hope that they will feel that their views have been represented honestly. Lisa Hyde of Irish Academic Press has provided all the support necessary to bring this book into being – thank you. I am yet again indebted to Yvonne Murphy and the staff of the Political Collection at the Linenhall Library in Belfast for consistently indulging my 'kiddie in a sweetshop syndrome' in their stacks.

Preface and Overview

Defences of the union need not rely on the kind of romantic patriotism so commonly found among Irish nationalists. Indeed it is the asymmetry rather than the symmetry which is striking when one pays serious consideration to unionism and nationalism in modern Ireland. Unionism does not represent an alternative ethnic or religious nationalism, but argues for the reasonableness (indeed, the necessity) of maintaining Northern Ireland's place within a multi-national, multi-faith, multi-ethnic United Kingdom state.

Richard English.[3]

Each generation learns the past anew to contemporary purpose, edits, adjusts, and discards. History is of course not lived but written and in Ireland often not read but assumed. History is malleable, and perceptions are not for ever – even those held yesterday may not do for tomorrow. Still, past may be prologue. In Ireland this has often meant tragedy, not farce. Yet there is always something new. And so history more often serves as rationale than as determinant.

J. Bowyer Bell.[4]

This book considers the political positioning and reorganisation of the Protestant unionist loyalist population in Northern Ireland throughout the contemporary period, and especially during and following the peace process and the movement of Northern Ireland towards a post-conflict society. After almost thirty years of political violence the most obvious manifestation of the new political consonance occurred in 1998 with the signing of an historic formal accord, the Belfast Agreement (popularly known as the Good Friday Agreement, and throughout this book as the Agreement). This was widely hailed as the basis for a political settlement between the clashing political titans of unionism and nationalism. It included an agreed framework of governance based on a commitment to ensure parity of esteem between the major political and social traditions in Ireland (and since has been increasingly upheld as a model for peace processes elsewhere).[5]

Since the accord, the effects on Northern Irish society have been profound. For most, day-to-day life has changed positively to a point where it is almost unrecognisable to those who lived through the depths, and at times seeming hopelessness, of the Troubles. Although it took almost a decade of torturously slow political negotiation, and a partial reworking of the Agreement at an all-party meeting in Scotland, the accord eventually came to realisation in March 2007. As a somewhat incredulous world media looked on, Ian Paisley and Gerry Adams held a first public meeting to announce an agreed structure under which Northern Ireland would be governed by a devolved administration.

This set in place all that was necessary for the opening of the Northern Ireland Assembly on 8 May 2007, and the subsequent election of Ian Paisley as first, and Martin McGuinness as deputy first ministers to head a new working devolved government. Just over one year later, his long-time deputy Peter Robinson replaced Ian Paisley as both leader of the Democratic Unionist Party (DUP) and first minister of the Northern Ireland Assembly, to head a settled, working – if far from dynamic – government.

At the core of political change has been the vast reduction of political violence, demilitarisation and the slow transition of social relationships brought about through processes of conflict transformation. Although neither the peace process nor the ceasefires in 1994 heralded an immediate end to paramilitarism, those organisations most deeply involved in structural violence have steadily accepted the primacy of politics over violence.

Notably, the Provisional Irish Republican Army (IRA) has given up its arsenal and the major dynamic of republicanism has turned towards winning political representation and electoral mandate. Loyalist paramilitaries have also travelled that road, albeit at a much slower rate. Of the major loyalist groups involved,[6] the Ulster Volunteer Force (UVF) first renounced violence, dissolved its military structures and put its weaponry beyond use,[7] declaring that the organisation was 'leaving the stage'[8] and setting itself on a road of 'transformation from a military to a civilian organisation'.[9]

The Ulster Defence Association (UDA), always the largest paramilitary grouping within loyalism, and for long the most disengaged, has agreed that the war was over and 'stood down' the Ulster Freedom Fighters (UFF),[10] its overtly military wing. The hesitancy to participate in the broader political agenda, once common among the UDA, has eventually given way to involvement in processes of conflict transformation,[11] while its leadership has openly encouraged its membership 'to participate at all levels of regeneration and social development'.[12]For loyalism, the culmination of these dynamics came in June 2009 with the announcement that the UDA, UVF and Red Hand Commando (RHC) had begun the process of decommissioning its weapons, under the guidance of observers from the Independent International Commission on Decommissioning (IICD).[13]

None of this is to deny the still deeply divisive and conflictual aspects of Northern Irish society. Dominant social relations continue to be constructed around competing social identities and contested political identification between and within the major political blocs of Irish nationalism and Ulster unionism. Ethno-sectarian identities and divisions remain deeply entrenched.[14] Social relations within everyday life remain problematic, particularly those involving sectarian differences and conflicts, which continue periodically to threaten destabilisation of the post-Agreement political agenda. Most importantly, strong constructions of the 'other' (those stigmatised as having real or imagined differences)[15] remain prevalent, manifesting in continuing social and physical separation and in the divided symbolism and public presentation of oppositional identities in Northern Ireland.[16]

Throughout the contemporary period, unionism has remained multi-layered in its responses to key political events, sometimes reacting in complex and fractured ways that make it difficult for those outside that world to comprehend. This is nothing new of course; over a quarter of a century ago the historian, Tony Stewart felt it necessary to enquire: 'Has Protestant Ulster got a mind?'[17] He offered the question not to offend, but to enable him the opportunity of highlighting the diversity of opinions held within that section of Irish society. He went on to pose a further set of questions, which remain as relevant today as they were then, including whether the political actions of unionists are

> ... directed by rational political motives and strategy, or are they simply a set of instinctive tribal responses to threats real or imagined, a clinging to outworn attitudes and totems which have no relevance to their present circumstances?[18]

So what provides the social and political dynamics of unionism? One aspect that continues to unite unionists of all hues is their belief in the obviousness of two distinct peoples and political identities in Ireland.

This underpins unionism's core claim that those in the northeast of Ireland form a community[19] which differs in decisive ways – culturally, politically, and socially – from the rest of the island. Unionists highlight what they see as the transparent differences between the objective reality of living on the geographical entity of the island, and the subjective sense of identity held by around four-fifths of Protestants in Northern Ireland who proclaim themselves as British, and who express the desire to uphold what they see as a 'British way of life'. Hence, this part of the unionist case at least can be simply stated, it rests directly in the belief that there is no singularity between geography and politics.

However, while such differences may be an agreed starting point within unionism, it cannot begin to explain the complexities of the interlocking nature of unionist identity. Nor can it explicate the range of the political responses from within unionism, where in recent times serious divisions have manifested between those supporting and those in opposition to the Agreement. For those holding this worldview opposition to the political will of Westminster is far from irrational and resistance to government deemed justifiable. Such perspectives and actions must be placed within the broad collective social and political identity of unionism.

In outlining these, the book points to many key events upon which unionists and loyalists draw to frame their senses of history and to construct understandings of contemporary politics. What follows, however, is not an attempt to trace in detail the peace process or events that led to the Agreement and eventually to the formation of a working devolved administration in Northern Ireland. Several such excellent accounts are already in existence.[20] Nor is this book a political history of unionism or the Ulster Unionist Party (UUP); while the number of such works remains limited, recent writings have added considerably to our knowledge in this area.[21]

Most of these accounts are, however, somewhat restricted in the parameters through which they seek to frame unionism. In his otherwise extremely insightful writings on contemporary unionism, for example, Chris Farrington[22] comes late to any meaningful discussion concerning the interactions or overlaps between loyalism and unionism. Likewise, Henry Patterson and Eric Kaufman,[23] in what elsewhere is an excellent presentation of Unionist politics, offer only a restricted exploration of such concerns, concentrating most of their comments concerning the interaction between unionism and loyalism to events of the early 1970s, which even for unionist politics was an extremely urbulent period, dominated by the breakup of hegemony and the emergence of the loyalist paramilitaries.

This book considers the broader politics and social structures of unionism and loyalism, the overlaps and interfaces between them and how these have manifested in the contemporary period. One of the central question it addresses is how, if at all, unionism has changed in the periods during and following the peace process and the establishment of devolved government? In particular, the book analyses how the constructions of identity and the understanding of political processes within unionism are framed and how unionists and loyalists interpret this frame and use this as a basis for political action. It highlights how unionists and loyalists have responded to contemporary political issues, and analyses the emergence of new political discourses that have developed, especially through those political groupings which became known as 'new loyalism' and 'new unionism'.

The book further investigates the dynamics behind the social and political fractures within unionism. It identifies various factions within contemporary unionism and loyalism and suggests reasons for the flux within unionist politics. Throughout the book the ways in which unionists and loyalists interpret their social world and the parameters within which future unionist and loyalist politics and identity are likely to be expressed are also highlighted and discussed.

This forms the basis for an investigation of the extent to which the political settlement has been grounded within unionism, and to explore how unionist hegemony has reconstructed itself around the leadership and interpretative frame of the DUP. Immediately following the signing of the Agreement the overtly oppositional politics of the DUP was seen to be marginal to the unionist response. From that point, however, the DUP set about harnessing the growing belief, expressed especially at an everyday level, that post-Agreement politics had only brought about a political and social weakening of unionism.

Such views have been reflected at various times since by a lack of political confidence within unionism and a deepening understanding that the political process may not assure the future they desire. More recently, the newly found position as the political leaders of unionism has enabled the DUP to claim that it is they (and only they) that have been able to identify the major threats to the Union, and to successfully organise resistance against these threats. The DUP argue that such a strategy has finally brought Irish republicanism to account. It was this reasoning that justified their entry into a coalition government with Sinn Féin. This in turn has, however, again brought to the fore the cry of 'sell-out' from other unionists, this time aimed directly at the DUP leadership.

In seeking to understand these political currents and changes the book engages directly with the views of unionists and loyalists, and tries where possible to allow them to speak for themselves, whether in the form of published material or interviews, or by reference to speeches or other cultural artefacts. Anyone taking this approach to writing seriously about conflict situations faces a wide range of contested and contradictory explanations. Those writing about Northern Ireland face the additional problematic identified by Dennis Pringle: 'Those who have the greatest depth of understanding based upon personal experience find it difficult to remain impartial, whereas those whom one might expect to retain some semblance of impartiality often fail to develop any depth of understanding.'[24]

As a Belfast man, born and bred, no doubt part of the task I face in writing this book is to negotiate this troublesome paradox. It is for readers to judge the success of that, but it is important to reject the suggestion put forward by David Miller that almost all those who research unionism end up losing objective vision and are 'unable to distinguish between understanding a social phenomenon and identifying with it'.[25] Such a view is far from helpful to those of us seeking to develop a serious analysis of the complex weave of social and political factors that go to make up unionism.[26]

STRUCTURE OF THE BOOK

The introductory section considers the broad political and social parameters of unionism. This is developed in Chapter 2 to further outline and discuss the broad building blocks of unionist politics and identity. Chapter 3 discusses the reaction of mainstream unionism to contemporary political events and in particular the attempt to align with new ideological dynamics of civic and liberal unionisms. Finally, the chapter outlines and suggests reasons for the failure of new unionism to take hold and the decline of the UUP from its position of dominance within unionist politics.

The mantle of unionist leadership has been grasped by the DUP, which has consistently claimed to be best positioned, ideologically, politically and pragmatically, to defend the Union. Their claim to be legitimate heirs to the unionist tradition is examined in Chapter 4, which explores the role of the DUP in providing an important outlet for expressions of Protestant unionist ethno-cultural identity and in so doing considers how the DUP has forged a position of electoral and ideological dominance across unionism.

The next part of the book (Chapters 5 and 6) considers loyalist responses. Despite what some would argue (both within and without unionism) it is impossible to detach loyalism entirely from unionism and vice-versa, or to understand loyalism simply as representing the 'bully-boy' physical force end of unionism. Loyalism draws on its own reference points and understandings, most clearly understood as an expression of unionism tempered and made robust through Protestant working-class life and experiences.[27] This has given rise not just to para-militarism but to a whole series of political initiatives from within working-class loyalist communities. In particular this section traces the growth and then faltering progress of what was dubbed 'new loyalism' and analyses how loyalism has sought to reposition itself following the end of widespread overt conflict.

Finally, Chapters 7 and 8 discuss the ideological realignments and political reorganisations within contemporary unionism and loyalism. As a broad social movement unionism has experienced no small sense of tur-moil, and the reorganisation of unionist politics following the Agreement has emphasised many of the incompatibilities within unionism. The coa-lescing of unionism, both ideologically and electorally, around the DUP rests in a large part on their ability to frame a worldview that makes sense of complex social and political realities to many unionists.

The DUP position has not gone unchallenged from within union-ism. Following the formation of a power-sharing government the grouping calling itself Traditional Unionist Voice (TUV) has been overt-ly hostile to the role played by the DUP in finding an accommodation with Sinn Féin, claiming that the 'intended trajectory of the Belfast Agreement was, and is, eventual Irish unification'.[28] Nonetheless, the DUP has continued to convince large numbers of unionist voters that they are the party that can best protect their interests and the political future of the Union.

NOTES

1. BBC News Online 2007 'Timeline: Northern Ireland's road to peace'. Archived at: http://newsvote.bbc.co.uk/1/hi/northern_ireland/4072261.stm
2. CAIN, 'A chronology of the conflict – 1968 to the present'. Archived at: http://cain.ulst.ac.uk/othelem/chron.htm
3. English, R., 'Unionism and nationalism: the notion of symmetry', in J.W. Foster (ed.), *The Idea of the Union: Statements and Critiques in Support of the Union of Great Britain and Northern Ireland* (Vancouver: Belcouver Press, 1995), p.135.
4. Bowyer Bell, J., *Back to the Future: The Protestants and a United Ireland* (Dublin: Poolbeg Press, 1996), pp.378–9.
5. See, for example, Breen-Smyth, M., 'Frameworks for peace in Northern Ireland: analysis of the 1998 Belfast Agreement', *Strategic Analysis*, 32, 6 (2008), pp.1131–53; O'Kane, E., 'The impact of third-party intervention on peace processes: Northern Ireland and Sri Lanka', in A. Edwards and S. Bloomer (eds), *Transforming the Peace Process in Northern Ireland: From Terrorism to Democratic Politics* (Dublin: Irish Academic Press, 2008), pp.229–43.
6. It is estimated that during the Troubles the UVF was responsible for 542 deaths and the UDA/UFF for 415. In total, all loyalist groups killed 1,071 people. See *News Letter*, 29 January 2009; McKittrick, D., Kelters, S., Feeney, B. and Thornton, C., *Lost Lives* (Edinburgh: Mainstream Publishing, 1999).
7. BBC News Online, 'UVF calls end to terror campaign'. Archived at: http://newsvote.bbc.co.uk/1/hi/northern_ireland/6618371.stm

8. *Sunday Times*, 22 April 2007.
9. 'UVF Statement in Full'. Archived at: http://news.bbc.co.uk/1/hi/northern_ireland/6618365.stm
10. Hayes, M., 'Loyalist road to politics will be long and winding', *Irish Independent*, 12 November 2007.
11. BBC News Online, 'UFF given the order to stand down', Archived at: http://newsvote.bbc.co.uk/1/hi/northern_ireland/7089310.stm; Rowan, B., *The Armed Peace: Life and Death After the Ceasefires* (Edinburgh: Mainstream Publishing, 2008), p.223.
12. Ulster Defence Association, 'Remembrance Day statement – 11 November 2007'. Archived at: http://cain.ulst.ac.uk/othelem/organ/uda/uda111107.htm
13. McDonald, H., 'Northern Ireland's loyalist paramilitaries destroy weapons', *Guardian*, 19 June 2009.
14. Higson, R., 'Anti-consociationalism and the Good Friday Agreement: a rejoiner', *Journal of Peace, Conflict and Development*, no. 12 (2008). Archived at: www.peacestudiesjournal. org.uk
15. See Jervis, J., *Transgressing the Modern: Explorations in the Western Experience of Otherness* (London: Blackwell, 1999); Said, E., *Orientalism* (London: Routledge and Kegan Paul, 1978).
16. See for example, Hewstone, M., Cairns, E., Voci, A., Paolini, S., McLernon, F., Crisp, R. and Niens, U., 'Intergroup contact in a divided society: challenging segregation in Northern Ireland', in D. Abrams, J.M. Marques and M.A. Hogg (eds), *The Social Psychology of Inclusion and Exclusion* (Philadelphia, PA: Psychology Press, 2005), pp. 265–92.
17. Stewart, A.T.Q., 'The mind of Protestant Ulster', in D. Watt (ed.), *The Constitution of Northern Ireland: Problems and Prospects* (London: Heinemann, 1981), pp.31–45.
18. Stewart, 'The mind of Protestant Ulster', p.31.
19. Community is one of those key terms within social science literature that is so contested as to immediately require clarification. Throughout the book I use it in two main ways: first as a common sense of feeling or place, a spatial 'belonging'; second as a sense of identity, a collective that shares common characteristics or interests beyond place. In *The Symbolic Construction of Community* (London: Tavistock, 1985), p.12, A.P. Cohen importantly suggests that community always involves a social relationship of opposition against those who don't belong, defining at the same time both similarity within one's own community and difference from others. Within unionism and loyalism 'community' is used in both these senses to mobilise support.
20. See, for example, Bew, P., *The Making and Remaking of the Good Friday Agreement* (Dublin: Liffey Press, 2008); Peatling, G., *The Failure of the Northern Ireland Peace Process* (Dublin: Irish Academic Press, 2004); Ruane J. and Todd, J. (eds), *After the Belfast Agreement: Analysing Political Change in Northern Ireland* (Dublin: University College Dublin Press, 1999); Tonge, J., 'From Sunningdale to the Good Friday Agreement: creating devolved government in Northern Ireland', *Contemporary British History*, 14, 3 (2000), pp.39–60; Tonge, J., *The New Northern Irish Politics* (Basingstoke: Palgrave, 2005); Wilford, R. (ed.), *Aspects of the Belfast Agreement* (Oxford: Oxford University Press, 2001).
21. See Harbinson, J.F., *The Ulster Unionist Party 1882–1973* (Belfast: Blackstaff Press, 1973); Hume, D., *The Ulster Unionist Party 1972–92* (Lurgan: Ulster Society Publications, 1996); Walker, G., *A History of the Ulster Unionist Party: Protest, Pragmatism and Pessimism* (Manchester: Manchester University Press, 2004); Farrington, C., *Ulster Unionism and the Peace Process in Northern Ireland* (Basingstoke: Palgrave Macmillan, 2006); Farrington, C., 'Unionism and the peace process in Northern Ireland', *British Journal of Politics and International Relations*, no. 8 (2006), pp.277–94.
22. Farrington, C., 'Loyalists and Unionists: explaining the internal dynamics of an ethnic group', in Edwards and Bloomer (eds), *Transforming the Peace Process in Northern Ireland*, pp.28–43.
23. Patterson, H. and Kaufmann, E., *Unionism and Orangeism in Northern Ireland Since 1945: The Decline of the Loyal Family* (Manchester: Manchester University Press, 2007).
24. Pringle, D.G., 'Review article: objectivity, bias and insight – recent perspectives by outsiders on the conflict in Northern Ireland', *GeoJournal*, 43, 3 (1997), pp.287–91.
25. Miller, D., 'Colonialism and academic representations of the troubles', in D. Miller (ed.), *Rethinking Northern Ireland: Culture, Ideology and Colonialism* (London: Longman, 1998), p.9.
26. In seeking to unravel those complexities I refer to unionism as a broad social movement with a small 'u', and in its party political form with a capital 'U'.
27. McAuley, J.W., 'Constructing contemporary loyalism', in Edwards and Bloomer (eds), *Transforming the Peace Process in Northern Ireland*, p.16.
28. Allister, J., 'Then and now: 10 years on from the Belfast Agreement'. Archived at: http://www.jimallister.org/default.asp?blogID=982

Chapter 1
Understanding Contemporary Unionism

The defence of the Union was undertaken in many different ways – through the British Party system, in halls, clubs, meeting places, in gatherings of churchmen, in the Orange Order, in Parliament, on the streets of Ulster, in the drawing rooms of country houses, in the academic groves of Trinity College and threats to employ the rifle in the last resort.

D. George Boyce[1]

Unionist strategy is weak because unionists have yet to react fully to changing circumstances. Before 1994 they were at war. In the future, they hope to live in peace. For the moment, they are stuck somewhere in between. But even a partial peace needs a different strategy from a war. Typically, war tends towards an end point – victory for one side, defeat for the other. Peace is different. It isn't meant to stop, but to deepen. So what, in peace time, are you supposed to do about your adversaries? The easy answer is to say: trust them. But what if they're not trustworthy? What if they may be tempted to damage your interests by clandestine means?

Mick Fealty, Trevor Ringland and David Steven[2]

Despite its common public image as an often ossified and at times even regressive political and social movement, there is no agreed understanding or stable expression of what it is to be an Ulster unionist. Nor, indeed, is there concord on what constitutes unionism beyond its commitment to the existing constitutional position within the United Kingdom. Partly the reason is because unionism is built from, and reflects a wide orbit of, social, cultural and political relationships, many of which are fluid and under constant processes of negotiation and flux.

Beyond this, unionism as a mass social movement largely unites behind common understandings of what it is not – a politics of opprobrium and antipathy. Indeed, one of the few constants in the self-definition of unionism is an oppositional strand to those political values and goals with which it disagrees and contests, most obviously Irish nationalism. Unionism, however, remains much more fragmented when it comes to any positive projection of self, or when promoting that which involves an identifiable and coherent political strategy.

It is useful therefore to begin with some broad working definitions of unionism and loyalism; not that the two are always distinct, as some would claim or wish. Yet those writing about unionism often ignore the points of overlap and interactions with loyalism. At a minimum, during the conflict at least some DUP and UUP voters have supported various loyalist paramilitary groups and certainly many of those within the paramilitaries have voted for established Unionist parties (see Chapters 5 and 6). In one recent poll, while the vast majority (70 per cent), expressed no sympathy for the reasons why some loyalist groups have used violence, some 27 per cent of Protestants expressed 'a little sympathy' (even if they did not themselves condone it).[3] This raises not just moral questions, but also issues of political process and the construction of inter-group relationships within, between and across loyalism and unionism.

DEFINING UNIONISM: SOME BEGINNINGS

To understand this in more detail it is important to consider how the competing discourses and understandings on offer across unionism and loyalism are reproduced, and how these contribute to the formation of collective identities. This is no straightforward task. To begin we must identify where and when unionist and loyalist identities and politics overlap, and where and when they diversify.

Unionist identity, like other political identities, is constructed as individuals and groups discern and highlight particular differences, attaching prime significance to these while demoting other designations as less crucial.[4] Moreover, it is important to signal how constant or fragmented are the processes that bring about these identifications, and where these processes create overlaps and diversifications within senses of identity.

These questions will be addressed and developed throughout the book, to highlight not just what unites unionists and loyalists but also what divides them and to understand what provides the central political dynamics within unionism and loyalism. Broadly, unionism as the political expression of a sense of social and political difference from the rest of the island finds expression at an everyday commonsense level through the claim of a British identity, a strong attachment to the notion of 'Britishness', or simply an expression of being British. This is a theme that will reoccur at several points throughout the book.

That does not mean, however, that unionism finds common social or cultural expression or unified political organisation to express such feelings. Indeed, unionist reactions in the contemporary period have only confirmed Fergal Cochrane's view that people construct the Union in different ways and support it for differing reasons.[5] The political constituents of unionism are drawn from a wide range of groupings and from a variety of social backgrounds and cultural perspectives.[6] This fragmented nature of unionism, which had been apparent for many years, became even more manifest following the signing of the Anglo-Irish Agreement (AIA) in 1985. Since then the continued segmentation of unionism as a political movement has been reinforced.

So for example, while one group may regard unionism primarily as the means to protect the Protestant heritage of Ulster, others see it as the way to confirm Northern Ireland simply as another political region of the United Kingdom (UK), albeit one separated by geography.[7] The recent emphasis by the UUP on the development of an inclusive and more meritocratic Northern Ireland where pro-Union Catholics can benefit equally from the social welfare service provision of the UK reflects this position directly.[8]

Other unionists put greater bearing on the cultural symbolism of what is perceived as common British history. The unionist political representative Robert McCartney gives a good example of how central this is to his own identity when he says:

> I was educated ... as any other citizen on the mainland would be. I was taught British constitutional history which I identify with. Now as a schoolboy my, if you like, military heroes were people like Nelson, Wellington, [Admiral] Beattie and so forth ... So my whole development, both culturally, historically and socially, gives me a very, very positive identification as being British.[9]

For most general observers, however, unionism remains a phlegmatic movement and, as Ian McBride reminds us, the standard portrayal of a unionist remains that of someone who is irrational and backward-looking.[10] Apparently it is of little consequence that unionism is seemingly incapable of countering such views or positively promoting its case to the media.[11] Moreover, the identification of being British in Northern Ireland often presents in ways unrecognisable in Britain itself (where cultural constructions and political expressions of Britishness are increasingly contested).[12]

Many within the wider British population continue to regard unionists as 'dogmatic, old-fashioned, unwilling to compromise or listen to reason, immoderate, prejudiced, hypocritical, and politically inept',[13] and who present 'as a picture of intransigent settlers who have refused to integrate'.[14] The wide currency of such views about unionism seemingly has little bearing on the ardency with which many Protestants express their sense of 'Britishness' and promote pro-Union beliefs.[15]

While many unionists are aware that the ways in which they express themselves, the icons they draw upon, and the discourses they utilise are at best misunderstood outside Northern Ireland, it does not lessen the desire to do so, even given 'the palpable fact of British retreat from unconditionally maintaining the post-1921 commitment to "loyalist" Ulster'.[16] Although Ulster unionist identity is sometimes dismissed by outsiders as a response to a terminally declining form of Britishness,[17] or seen as the insignificant politics of residuum following the fall of empire,[18] this does little to weaken the strength of expression of Britishness as the prime identity forwarded by most Protestants in Northern Ireland.

At the time of the since much-cited survey undertaken by Richard Rose[19] in the late 1960s, one in five Protestant respondents chose 'Irish' to express their prime sense of identity, with around 40 per cent seeing themselves primarily as British. A decade later the Protestant sense of identity had changed considerably, with 67 per cent self-classifying as British while those considering themselves as Irish registered only 8 per cent.[20]

Since then expressions of Irishness and Britishness have become increasingly dichotomous, and the sense of British identity deeply located within the Protestant unionist loyalist community has taken different political shapes and directions. It has found, and continues to find, expression through a range of different perspectives on what it is to be a unionist and how that perspective should find best expression in cultural, social and political forms. One clearly recognisable expression is through the politics of loyalism.

UNDERSTANDING LOYALISM: STARTING POINTS

So what are the fundamentals of loyalism and how, if at all, does it differ from unionism? There are no short or straightforward answers to these questions. To many general observers loyalism is seen simply as a form of extreme unionism.[21] While parts of loyalism may have embraced violence, this is a far from satisfactory understanding or definition. Loyalism offers a distinct ideology, bound by its own dis-courses and frames of understanding, and resting on highly selective historical reference points.

As with other ideologies, as loyalism is constructed and reconstruct-ed, invented and reinvented, it adopts and promotes a whole series of shared values and memories, which are seen to symbolise social and political difference, both within unionism and in opposition to other identities and groups. One now common starting point is to recognise loyalism as a form of political organisation that states its primary devo-tion to the British crown rather than an allegiance to its government or political representatives.[22] To pursue this line reveals strong feelings of social and cultural 'belonging' to Northern Ireland before any other political arrangement, most commonly expressed as a connection to an imagined community of Ulster.[23]

Certainly at its core, loyalism rests on its sense of cultural separate-ness and political difference, expressed through an identifiable social identity.[24] Moreover, many of those who claim to be loyalists see this as an intuitively natural and commonsense expression of the world they inhabit. The determination of some to defend this identity has become central to understanding loyalism,[25] and this construction of loyalism as the last line of defence is understood as a central component of loyalist ideology, running 'to the very grain of modern Loyalism'.[26]

The values of loyalism, however, rest upon antithetical foundations.[27] Declarations of loyalty to the monarchy have not at times inhibited loyalists from organising overt and determined resistance to the views and actions of the UK parliament or the wishes of the political repre-sentatives of that same crown.[28] In their recent history loyalists have directly confronted the legal representatives and security forces of the UK state. At an extreme, one incident in October 1972 highlights this, when after several nights of serious rioting in east Belfast, resulting in the killing of two Protestants by the British army, one local UDA com-mander openly declared: 'To hell with the British Army. The British Government and the British Army are now our enemies.'[29]Although this statement was rescinded within hours, it highlighted the complex relationships between the British state and those organisations claim-ing to represent working-class Protestants.

Underlying the politics of loyalism is that strand identified by David Miller as being an essentially contractual relationship with the state.[30] The late Billy Mitchell of the PUP expressed this directly in its contem-porary form when he said:

> The loyalist community will honour its obligations and fulfil its
> duties to Parliament so long as Parliament acknowledges and

upholds our right to equal citizenship within the United Kingdom. As citizens of the United Kingdom we expect to be given the same rights as those enjoyed by citizens in Scotland, England and Wales, and one of the most basic of those rights is the right to have our citizenship endorsed, validated and defended.[31]

Despite the key points of reference outlined above (or perhaps because of some of them), loyalist ideology remains difficult to define with precision. Although one characteristic may be an aggressive, sometimes violent expression of politics, it cannot simply be reduced to a form of 'extreme' unionism, as some would suggest. Rather loyalism is a political phenomenon that draws on its own sense of history, frames its own discourses and finds expression through distinct forms of social organisation and structures, all of which go to construct a salient sense of social identity and solidarity.[32]

Loyalism does tend to be disproportionately working class in its social composition,[33] and its relationships within unionism are most clearly defined by class.[34] Much of loyalist popular culture can be understood as unionism experienced and expressed through a working-class filter. The resulting 'political creed'[35] gives meaning to the lives of many people who live in identifiable working-class districts. Hence, for many of its working-class supporters, loyalism is seen to represent, structure and give political expression to the everyday realities of those who see themselves in an increasingly marginalised political and economic position.

But loyalism can also represent a broader political perspective. Indeed, as we shall see, the views of those proclaiming loyalism manifest across a wide range of political organisations. As Brian Graham points out, loyalism finds expression across a wide compass of perspectives, including those who promote extreme right-wing politics, religious fundamentalism, the inseparable mix of religion and politics expressed by sections of the DUP and the left of centre ideology of the leadership of the PUP.[36]

For some, loyalist ideology is used to restate old political certainties and to strongly reinforce these through the continual reproduction of past social relationships. For others, however, it offers the possibility of being a more dynamic social force marking a site of struggle in coming to terms with new political and economic realities, and sometimes as an outlet to express new progressive political voices from within working-class unionism. Thus, while some have sought to present insular and restricted understandings of what loyalism is (expressed latterly through open hostility to the political and social outcomes of the Agreement), others have been involved in processes of political realignment across unionism, seeking to rearticulate loyalism particularly to emphasise and centre class and other forms of social divisions within it.

THEORISING UNIONISM AND LOYALISM

Unionism does not emerge as any single political or social dynamic, or present a monolithic representation – far from it. Joe Ruane and Jennifer Todd provide a useful broad conceptualisation of the circumstances within which unionism emerged.[37] They suggest that political conflict in Ireland is underpinned and reinforced by three key sociocultural dimensions: the first religious (Catholic versus Protestant), the second ethnic difference between Gaelic Irish and English/Scottish, and finally, colonial dimensions, which revolve around native versus settler relationships. These social cleavages provided the basic blocks that formed structures of dominance, dependence and inequality, which although altered over time continued to define interests, actions and locations of identity.

Writers emphasising competing aspects of unionist identity have understood these interests in different ways; hence, the range of thought on what constitutes unionism is wide. For some, unionism remains merely a consequence of neo-colonial relationships in Ireland.[38] For John McGarry and Brendan O'Leary,[39] unionists constitute a residual social and political category, the legacy of relationships between settlers and natives on the island that have created an 'ethnonational' conflict between two groupings 'who want their state to be ruled by their nation, or who want what they perceive as "their" state to protect their nation'.[40]

These differences have continued to structure politics on the island. The partition of Ireland in the 1920s is thus considered by others as the direct product of an imperialist conspiracy to retain control over an 'artificial creation, arbitrarily carved out of the state of Ulster'.[41] This perspective has given rise to several classical Marxist[42] and 'anti-imperialist' writings such as those by Geoff Bell,[43] Éamonn McCann[44] and Michael Farrell.[45] Within the 'Orange state' sectarian politics were seen as having an identifiable material base to advantage Protestant workers, reinforced by overt discrimination against Catholics. Moreover, it is argued that under the Stormont state Orangeism assumed a 'virulent life of its own to become the dominant force' in Northern Irish politics.[46]

Other writers present unionism as an expression of supremacist politics,[47] as a direct reflection of Protestant ethnic identity,[48] or as the political expression of a distinct religious grouping.[49] For yet other commentators unionism is best understood as the expression of an ethno-nationalist political identity,[50] that of 'last-gasp Britons' oblivious to wider social identities and changes in other parts of the UK,[51] or even as the politics offered by an 'unloved, unwanted garrison'.[52] For Gerald Delanty unionism and loyalism are types of nationalism that express state patriotism, and a state-centred nationalism.[53] He argues that neither seeks an independent state, but rather to constantly reaffirm the existence of that which already exists.

It is worth developing some of these understandings of unionism and loyalism in rather more detail. Unionism itself remains divided in its political opinion over key issues surrounding senses of identity, visions of the political future and sometimes over tactics.[54] However, while political differences clearly exist, the parameters within which such debates take place are widely recognised and understood by unionists. In the main, three interrelated aspects set the contours: the relationship of religion to politics; constructions of unionism as identity politics; and, the political expressions and organisations that emanate from that sense of unionist identity.

UNIONISM AS PROTESTANT POLITICS

So can unionism best be understood as politicised Protestantism? One regular commentator on this aspect of unionist political identity is Steve Bruce, who in a series of works has sought to locate changes in unionism directly in a strengthening sense of Protestant ethnic identity and in increased ethnic divisions (between Catholic nationalists and Protestant unionists) in Northern Ireland. He contends that within unionism there has been a distinct move from a dominant pre-Troubles identification as Ulster British, to a growing tendency for loyalists to define themselves as 'Ulster Protestants first and British second'.[55]

For Bruce these changes in identity are underpinned by his assertion that for Protestants, the Northern Ireland conflict is a religious one, that the 'basis for unionism is evangelical Protestantism', and that 'evangelicalism is at the heart of what it means to be a Protestant'.[56]Broadly, Bruce sees the unionist community as a distinct ethnic group, which depends upon evangelicalism as the sociological glue that holds it together. This is an important focus, and undoubtedly the role of 'fundamental Protestantism' remains important as part of the ways in which unionism and loyalism are constructed.[57]

Protestantism in Ireland has a clear political dimension, most obviously seen in the direct linking of the defence of the Protestant faith and the defence of the Union by the Orange Order and in the interplay between the politics of the DUP and the Free Presbyterian Church. Bruce suggests, for example, that DUP politics reveals the anti-élitist perspectives found within fundamental Protestantism. Hence:

> Religious elites are not to be trusted with the preservation of the true gospel, and political elites are not to be trusted with the defence either of the character of Northern Ireland or of its place in the United Kingdom.[58]

While Bruce's focus on the relationship between religion and Protestant identity is central, there remain questions concerning the emphasis and weight he gives to the role of religion in the construction of unionist politics. At times this is centred so strongly it suggests that fundamentalism and theological wrangles and quarrels are in themselves of core importance and influence within unionism. Although this may present a simplification of Bruce's arguments, and although he seeks to redress the balance in some later work,[59] there are tendencies toward a reductionist view of unionism.

This is challenged by others such as John Brewer,[60] who evidences how differences of doctrine are rarely presented by those involved as core to explaining the conflict or play a central place in everyday political discourses. Moreover, the centrality of religion in Bruce's position often marginalises (if not ignores) other secular, gender and class-based identities from within Protestantism, all of which at times have found political expression and organisation within the Protestant community.[61]

That is not to say that cultural expressions of Ulster Protestantism cannot be understood to have both religious and political dimensions. Within its reference frame, Protestantism provides a broad set of moral interpretations and understandings within which Ulster Protestant identity and politics find expression. Further, the political direction of unionism is often determined by the overlaps between these frames. This is made clear by Duncan Morrow when he says that, in Northern Ireland, 'politics and religion are a complicated series of interrelationships whose completeness can only be understood together with an understanding of the Protestant experience of violence or potential violence.'[62]

But the political expression and consequences of this are not straightforward or linear. Farrington, for example, argues convincingly that the Protestant evangelicalism espoused by Ian Paisley has not necessarily been an electoral asset to the DUP,[63] and as Claire Mitchell clearly identifies, Protestant fundamentalism does not necessarily find any common political outlet. She points out that, while there may be only one Agreement, several competing and contested interpretations of it have emerged from within the Protestant community. This has led to a range of responses, from an attempted purification of 'Protestant identity' to the assimilation of notions promoting a pluralist Britishness, within which the Protestant faith can be actively expressed.[64]

Despite this diversity, however, Mitchell recognises that there remain shared processes of identification, reinforced by reactions to contemporary political change. The interplay between religion, community and identity remains highly influential in reproducing stereotypes, which in turn feed into the cycles of conflict and expressions of difference in everyday life.[65] Mitchell also suggests that the Churches continue to influence unionist politics, sometimes directly so.

In some cases, as with the DUP, this is obvious, but Mitchell provides evidence that this is also true elsewhere within unionism, where political parties and Churches continue to have a mutual relationship, the latter often being included in political consultation and negotiation. Given this, Mitchell arrives at the conclusion of a socially constructed and politicised Protestant identity, reflected in struggles of some unionists to place Protestantism as central to their definition of Britishness.

UNIONISM AS BRITISHNESS

Ulster Protestant political identity is not unitary, but there are dominant forms of expression within it. Of the 46 per cent of Northern Ireland's population that identified as Protestant in the 2001 census, around three out of four categorised themselves as British. Perhaps even more crucially, less than 1 per cent claimed to be Irish. Despite the recognition by Muldoon and others of a movement towards those describing themselves as 'Northern Irish',[66] Brewer is surely correct to suggest that the strength of division between Protestant/unionist and Catholic/nationalist identities will remain with us for some time.[67] An overwhelming 85 per cent of Protestants see their political future as remaining within the UK, while only 3 per cent look to a politically unified Ireland as a desirable objective.[68]

So what gives orientation and direction to this attachment to the Union? A useful opening is the conceptualisation presented by Todd, which distinguishes between 'British Unionist' and 'Ulster Loyalist' traditions.[69] The former refers to those whose prime point of identification is with Britain, while the latter grouping of Ulster loyalists represents those who take the six counties of Northern Ireland as their primary imagined community. Mirroring some of the arguments outlined in the previous section, Todd argues that loyalist culture is conditional and constructed around that point where religion and politics are inextricably intertwined.

While Todd's focus has remained crucial as a starting point to interpret fundamental divisions within unionism, it lacks detail of how unionist identity is crosscut by other social categories.[70] As Graham Walker and Richard English note, unionism as a social movement has been 'riddled with tensions'.[71] The result of such cleavages, as Patrick Buckland reminds us, is that the 'unity of Ulster Unionism had constantly to be managed'.[72] The imagined community[73] of unionism has constantly to be reconstructed and reproduced, and framed and presented in ways that made sense of the contemporary world to its core adherents.

This continues to have salience to unionist identity and such considerations have led to a growing number of important works that seek to focus on the centrality of gender[74] or class[75] within the social relationships of unionism. Unionist identity comprises a set of interrelated ideological strands, but two elements are particularly important. First is the strength of the internal bonds that define unionism as a group identity. Second are those attributes that are seen to differentiate unionism from other collective identities, most centrally Irish nationalism. Unionism can thus be seen as a construct seeking to create and locate an inclusive sense of belonging and rapport under the broad banner of Britishness.

Attachment to British symbolism remains much stronger within Northern Ireland than among those who identify as British elsewhere in the UK. Indeed, as has been pointed out, there remains within Northern Ireland a sizeable minority who demonstrate what can be termed 'hyper loyalty' to British symbolism.[76] This is in contrast to elsewhere in the UK, where the past twenty-five years have witnessed a decline in those who share a strong sense of British identity and a downturn in the levels of 'pride in Britain'.[77]

Moreover, throughout the rest of the UK understandings of Britishness are questioned as devolution becomes embedded and issues surrounding social diversity and cohesion[78] (or the perceived lack of it) have increasingly moved higher up the contemporary political agenda.[79] This has become especially true following Gordon Brown's increasing attempts to portray New Labour as a modern patriotic party. An increasing focus on institutional racism,[80] debates about refugees or illegal workers, the future of multiculturalism and violence directed towards ethnic minority groups[81] have all moved the politics of ethnic differences and community cohesion to the centre ground of British politics.[82]

The intensity of this debate has been compounded by a series of occurrences, including the widespread street confrontations in 2001 across the north of England, the 11 September attacks in the US, the conflicts in Afghanistan and Iraq, the London bombings of July 2005 and the increased electoral profile of the British National Party (BNP). The reactions to these events have given rise to an identifiable challenge to the values of multiculturalism, established senses of citizenship[83] and notions of allegiance to Britain and Britishness.[84]

Alongside this, growing debates around devolution have brought into sharp relief questions concerning the comfortable consensus that Britishness reflects a society characterised by tolerance and respect for social diversity and sometimes the possible demise of the Union itself.[85] As Bhikhu Parekh indicates, debates around the UK as a multicultural society have too often has been set in a context of an unproblematic understanding of a perceived sense of British national homogeneity.[86]

To fully explore this involves a more acute awareness of the differences between all those groupings that claim Britishness as their prime identity, not just in Britain itself but in ex-colonial situations, across the Commonwealth, and so on. Such debates around the nature of Britishness should, but do not always, include Ulster unionists. One writer actively seeking to ensure this does occur is Arthur Aughey, who strongly contends that the Union is not only desirable, but also entirely rational in its formation.[87] Hence, much of his focus is on citizenship as a means to defend the Union and to demonstrate that unionism is a logical constitutional relationship with the British state. Aughey makes this clear in his claim that:

> It is not Britishness as some peculiar spiritual substance or ethnic identity which defines the United Kingdom. It is the acknowledgement by its citizens of the legitimacy of the constitutional relationship.[88]

In contrast, Aughey tends to regard Irish nationalist identity as formed around a crux of exclusive romantic nostalgia. In the political mainstream such views were directly reflected several years later, when David Trimble in a now infamous speech derided the Irish Republic as a 'pathetic, mono-cultural, sectarian state'.[89] As a counterpoint to the perceived romanticism of Irish nationalism, Aughey suggests that unionism is based on a straightforward political preference that 'has little to do with the idea of the nation and everything to do with the idea of the state'.[90] Taken broadly, Aughey's writings reveal a unilocular hostility to the concept of nationalism and regular criticism of any wider approach that seeks to encompass the politics of identity.[91]

Rather, unionism is defended as a form of rational Lockian contract within which loyalty is always conditional, and within which the UK government has displayed a consistent tendency to break by failing to defend its citizens and their legal rights.[92] As Cochrane[93] points out, however, projecting unionism in this way overlooks something blindingly obvious to others – that at an everyday level identification with unionism is rarely interpreted or expressed simply in terms of citizenship or formal legalised structures of the state. Rather, there is often an over-riding emotional attachment to being 'British', and feelings that are expressed in a crucial sense of belonging that is attached to Britishness.

Crowley argues that this sense of Britishness gives a fuller understanding representing a much 'thicker' concept than that of citizenship,[94] involving not just issues around the rights and duties of membership, but also the emotional feelings evoked by membership. Unionists draw upon and give emphasis to different cultural, social, legal and emotional aspects that make up their political identity. Thus, Aughey's model of relationships within unionism has been subject to criticism because it is seen as distant from the everyday reality and understandings of political life for many unionists and loyalists.

Colin Coulter recognises that while for some their sense of unionism may come from commitment to abstract notions such as citizenship, this is a minority experience. Most are likely to be driven by more 'substantive identities such as nationality and ethnicity'.[95] For Coulter the core model proposed by Aughey is unfettered by 'historical or political realities' and presents a view disengaged from the vast majority of unionists, whose everyday experiences continue to be largely fashioned by the salience of social class rather than abstract commitments.[96]

Coulter is one of several writers that reflect a precision of understanding that can also be found in the works of others such as Richard English,[97] Graham Walker,[98] Susan McKay,[99] Graham Spencer,[100] Pete Shirlow and Mark McGovern,[101] all of whom offer nuanced, if somewhat differing, interpretations of unionism. These writers, albeit in different ways, have provided more sophisticated understandings of unionism by emphasising the diversity and complexity of the mosaic that constitutes unionist identity and politics.

Another who falls within this category is John Cash, who has effectively demonstrated the central importance of ideology in the 'structuration of political life and political conflict'.[102] Focusing on the speeches of recent unionist leaders, including Terence O'Neill, Bill Craig and Ian Paisley, he emphasises how these draw heavily on exclusivist and triumphalist values. They ultimately helped contribute to the split between liberal inclusive modes of unionism, and an exclusive unionism, based on ethno-religious ideological values. Most importantly perhaps, Cash consistently demonstrates the sense of dynamic in the construction of unionism driven by conflicting ideologies within it.[103]

That said, much of the populist outpourings of unionism and loyalism seem only to emphasise a backward gaze, promoting a seeming near obsession with the past that remains difficult for many to understand. This is, however, not as straightforward as it may appear. For the vast majority who claim unionism as their core political identity key historical events are seen as having contemporary relevance, linking

past and present directly.[104] Part of this process of constantly recon-
structing the imagined community of unionism involves the framing
and presentation of views that makes sense of the contemporary world
to its core adherents. A core part of this construction is a politics where
it is always necessary to keep one eye in the rear view mirror to guide
unionism along the centre of its chosen political road.

Another aspect of this sees contemporary politics explained by
direct reference to past events. This sense of unionist identity draws on
a range of strong identifiers: Protestantism; loyalty to the monarchy
and crown; a sense of affinity and belonging with the people in Britain;
a strong perception of shared historical experience (especially in both
world wars); a British cultural heritage; or even more everyday matters
such as looking first to the British economy for living standards, having
relatives or friends living in Britain, or an attachment to what is understood to be a British way of life. This is well expressed by Jeffrey
Donaldson:

> We in Northern Ireland value our British citizenship and we
> recognise that it brings with it responsibilities as well as rights. We
> have never been afraid to put our shoulder to the wheel when the
> British people faced adversity, as in two world wars. Like the Scots
> and the Welsh we have a very distinct and unique culture, but we
> have always looked to the multi-cultural accommodation of diver-
> sity.[105]

Unionists consistently draw on what is seen as the common history
of such key events to enforce solidarity and identity. One such example
is the coming together of unionism in the campaign against home rule,
which has become a central 'creation myth' for unionism[106] through its
presentation as a time of ultimate unity and coherence under powerful
and successful leadership (of Carson and Craig) to resist the challenge
of the break with Britishness. This and other major reference points are
used to construct senses of unionist identity and expressions of
Britishness.

But unionists do not draw upon such identifiers in an even or linear
manner. It is this which makes definition and interpretation of unionism (beyond the desire to maintain the Union) so difficult. Unionism is
not a given, and its unity has been, and remains, subject to constant
processes of reconstruction, debate and contests over political direction. Further, because of such factionalisms and the competition for
political and ideological space between them, unionism remains a
much more dynamic political entity than many would suggest. The
recognition of this, and of the construction of unionist and loyalist
identities as multi-layered, is at the core of this book.

THE POLITICS OF UNIONISM

To develop a clearer understanding of this, unionism is presented as a broad social and political movement constantly subject to processes of redefinition and renegotiation and undergoing political flux and contestation. It is capable of simultaneously expressing notions of both continuity and change and of resistance and arbitration, of giving primacy to religion, citizenship, monarchy, and identity politics, or some combination of these.

Moreover, it is painfully obvious that in Northern Ireland the conflicts surrounding politics are far from restricted to the pages of scholarly journals. Rather, the situation is that identified by Riles whereby those involved position themselves and often theorise alongside academics, 'reading some of the same texts, orientating themselves towards similar political, ethical or theoretical problems'.[107] Throughout the Troubles there are many examples of community activists, formal political representatives and sometimes paramilitaries acting to express common concerns.

Unionist readings of contemporary political situations and reactions to this give different emphasis to the religious, political, ethnic and cultural dimensions outlined above. The specific mix of these factors determines the direction of unionist reaction and partly explains why unionist politics have taken such a variety of forms. Hence, for example, some factions within unionism were fully supportive of the peace process and made positive steps towards fulfilling the accord reached through the Agreement, establishing the organisation necessary to formalise the compromise reached with Irish nationalism. Others, however, remained fearful that what had been put in place were processes designed to undermine Northern Ireland's constitutional position.

That the DUP now occupy a position of leadership in contemporary unionist party politics is due in no little part to the position of discordance it initially adopted towards the UK government's support for the Agreement, supplemented by consistent opposition to Irish government and Irish republicanism involvement in the political process. The DUP's claim to represent the real voice of unionism gained credibility following the stagnation of the political process and was reinforced after the 2005 Westminster election when they became the largest political representatives of unionism, with the party increasing its representation from five to nine MPs.

At the time their leading opponents within unionism, the UUP, actively campaigned for the continued endorsement of the Agreement and supported a devolved government resting on the promotion and strengthening of centrist politics. This standpoint failed dramatically at the polls, with the UUP retaining only one parliamentary seat, losing four others directly to the DUP. The DUP's position of leadership was further emphasised in the 2007 Assembly election as unionist hegemony increasingly reasserted around the DUP promotion of what it calls the politics of 'traditional unionism'.

During the same period, support for smaller unionist and loyalist parties has continued to wane. The United Kingdom Unionist Party (UKUP), which had consistently opposed the Agreement, its offshoot the Northern Ireland Unionist Party (NIUP), and the pro-accord Ulster Democratic Party (UDP) have all disappeared from the political spectrum (for very different reasons). The PUP, which consistently promoted positive involvement in the negotiated settlement, has been left with a considerably smaller register on the political radar than was visible a decade previously. This does not mean, however, that the politics of unionism are settled, or that mainstream unionist representation is emblematic of loyalism.

In explaining the dynamic within contemporary unionism, what follows outlines not just the positions taken by differing unionist factions concerning political structures and issues, but also how the political identities of those involved are oriented and the sources upon which they draw upon to legitimise their political and social beliefs. Importantly, it will also consider the range of understandings from which unionists construct their worldview and give credence to their interpretations of political and social events.[108]

UNIONIST IDENTITY AND POLITICS

While unionism and loyalism draw on many common reference points, they can use history in different ways to construct links with the present. Most often the understandings that emerge span all of unionism, but sometimes unionists and loyalists draw on social memories in conflicting ways to justify contemporary actions and arguments.[109] One way to understand these differences within unionism is to consider the competing frames of reference, discourses and historical reference points that are used to construct interpretations of contemporary events. Fundamental to understanding this fully is the recognition of unionism and loyalism as something broader than party politics, which represents only one aspect of the political within unionism.

Unionist and loyalist political identities need to be understood as the product of specific constructed histories that draw on identifiable political memories. As Ruane and Todd remind us, conflict in Northern Ireland rests on an intricate set of social relationships resulting in radically different and often conflicting aspirations and identities not just between, but also within, the two communities.[110] To succeed in representing its core interests, unionism must in many respects take on the characteristics of what Charles Tilly identifies as social movement by constructing an inclusive identity that appeals to a broad community.[111]

In so doing, unionism effectively transmits messages that its supporters must be (and are) unified and committed. Thus, unionism must strive to encompass and corral other segmental identities, and to construct closed social and political formations, based on ethnicity, culture, religion, class, gender and even sometimes notions of 'race'. Unionism draws on senses of identity that are not fixed, but rather subject to constant processes of negotiation. As Homi Bhabha suggests in a different context:

> The question of identification is never the affirmation of a pre-given identity, never a self-fulfilled prophecy – it is always the production of an 'image' of identity and the transformation of the subject in assuming that image. Identity is never a priori, nor a finished project.[112]

Richard English[113] ably demonstrates the complex set of interrelated ideological strands upon which unionist identity is built, while Brian Walker begins to show fluidity in the social construction of unionism by tracing the use of historical myth within it.[114] Taken together, these works demonstrate that, for unionists, 'history has often meant a view of the past influenced by the needs of our late nineteenth- and twentieth-century world'[115] and that core to this is an understanding of Irish nationalism as the 'dangerous Other'. This creation was foremost during the constitutive period of Ulster unionism, remained central as unionists forged the institutions of the Northern Irish state and is today still deeply engrained within unionist political culture and identity.

This construction is of course double edged; having the capacity to define who is a member of the community also means constructing a common understanding of who is seen as excluded. It is within this context that the invention of traditions takes place and political memory is used in particular ways. It is through these processes that the continued formation of the imagined community of unionism is ensured. Unionism thus seeks to reinforce its inclusive sense of identify by openly excluding identifiable others through its major discourses and symbolism, whereby the need for security against external and internal threat is understood and accepted.

Too often, however, reactions to the public symbolism of unionism and loyalism, images of Ian Paisley in full flow at the pulpit or marching bands followed by massed ranks of Orangemen, sideline any attempt to understand the politics of unionism. Expressions of intolerance, exclusion and an attachment to religious fundamentalism are still taken as the be all and end all of unionism. Beyond their sometime atavistic image, however, unionism and loyalism represent the complex intersection of social, economic, cultural and political forces on the island of Ireland.

While sectarianism and political immobility are no doubt part of unionist political culture, they are only part of the weave in a range of social alliances, political identities, divisions, allegiances and collective actions, which find political expression through unionism. To consider unionism otherwise is to present it in an extremely reductionist form. People born into social circumstances most likely have initial identities imposed upon them by others, those who are more powerful and who carry greater authority. For the most part initial identities are drawn from micro experiences, they reflect the local, and are generated by the structures and relationships of the everyday.

It is only later that socialisation processes begin to induct other identities. Some of these may admittedly simply reinforce initial identities, or run in parallel with them; but others may challenge or contradict these. Unionist identity (like all other political identities) brings into relief crucial issues of self, but it also promotes the examination of broader social circumstances and relationships; drawing to the fore questions such as who are the people and groups around me, and what are my relationships to them? Together these go to compose fields of identity upon which people draw to understand and explain the world around them.

Unionism must seek to grapple with, and ultimately answer, these questions of identity. Indeed, unionism exists as a cultural and political force because for many it can answer such questions. Identifiable social and political events and challenges (real or perceived) push the social and political identities of Britishness and unionism to the fore as the key social constructs. This is especially so if those involved constructed their central identity as under attack, because as Kobena Mercer points out: 'Identity only becomes an issue when it is in crisis, when something assumed to be fixed, coherent and stable is displaced by the experiences of doubt and uncertainty.'[116]

CONCLUSION

The kernel of any serious analysis of unionist ideologies and worldview rests on an understanding of unionist identity as something that does not negate, but rather forms inter-relationships with other locations of social identity. It does so in different ways, at different times and with different outcomes. To identify as a unionist or loyalist does not mean that people lose their bearings to all other points of reference on the social compass, or that they fail to develop from other social experiences, such as economic marginalisation, or to be a woman, or heterosexual and so on.

All these and more must be organised and framed within a collective politic that addresses what is meaningful to those who proclaim to be loyalist and/or unionist at any particular point. Some aspects of unionist ideology become sedimented to form part of the stock of everyday commonsense understandings and interpretations of political life, such as the belief for many that unionism is the only 'natural' political state for Protestants in Northern Ireland.

Other aspects of unionist identity are more fluid and its formation can often be defined and redefined as contingencies demand; framed in one way when core identities are felt to be safe, but reframed when disrupted by crisis or seen to be in danger and under threat. It is commonplace for oppositional groups in a conflict situation to construct frames of reference, narratives and discourses that seek to claim legitimacy for 'the cause', that the arguments presented by their group hold moral superiority over those of other groups.[117] Hence, the study of unionist identity requires analysis of how people interpret their political location within both specific circumstances and the broader contexts outlined throughout this book.

NOTES

1. Boyce, D.G., 'Weary patriots: Ireland and the making of unionism', in D.G. Boyce and A. O'Day (eds), *Defenders of the Union: A Survey of British and Irish Unionism since 1801* (London: Routledge, 2001), p.10.
2. Fealty, M., Ringland, T. and Steven, D., *A Long Peace? The Future of Unionism in Northern Ireland* (Wimborne: Slugger O'Toole, 2003), p.15.
3. *Northern Ireland Life and Times Survey 2007*. Archived at: http://www.ark.ac.uk/nilt/2007/Political_Attitudes/LOYVIOL.html
4. Penrose, J. and Jackson, P., 'Conclusion: identity and the politics of difference', in J. Penrose and P. Jackson (eds), *Constructions of Race, Place and Nation* (London: UCL Press, 1993), p.207.
5. Cochrane, F., *Unionist Politics and the Politics of Unionism since the Anglo-Irish Agreement* (Cork: Cork University Press, 1997).
6. Hall, M., *Beyond the Fife and Drum* (Belfast: Island Pamphlets, 1995).
7. See Hanna, R. (ed.), *The Union: Essays on Ireland and the British Connection* (Newtownards: Colourpoint Books, 2001).
8. Andrews, J., 'We can safeguard the union', *Belfast Telegraph*, 29 September 2006.
9. Cited in Democratic Dialogue, *Report Number 7: With all due respect – Pluralism and parity of esteem* (Belfast: Democratic Dialogue, 2004), p.3.
10. McBride, I., *The Siege of Derry in Ulster Protestant Mythology* (Dublin: Four Courts Press, 1996), p.1.
11. Parkinson, A.F., *Ulster Unionism and the British Media* (Dublin: Four Courts Press, 1998), pp.160–4.
12. See Brown, G. and Alexander, D., *Stronger Together: The 21st Century Case for Scotland and Britain* (London: Fabian Society, 2007); Fabian Review, *Who do we want to be?: The Britishness Issue*, 17, 4 (2006); Gilroy, P., *After Empire: Melancholia or Convivial Culture?*

(London: Taylor and Francis, 2004); Lewis, P., *Young, British and Muslim* (London: Continuum, 2007); Modood, T., *Multicultural Politics: Racism, Ethnicity and Muslims in Britain* (Edinburgh: Edinburgh University Press, 2005).

13. Clayton, P., *Enemies and Passing Friends* (London: Pluto, 1996), p.228.
14. Neill, W.J.V., '"Return to Titanic and lost in the Maze": the search for representation of "post-conflict" Belfast', *Space and Polity*, 10, 2 (2006), p.111.
15. See, for example, material in Shirlow, P. and McGovern, M. (eds), *Who are 'The People'? Unionism, Protestantism and Loyalism in Northern Ireland* (London: Pluto, 1997).
16. O'Neill, M., 'Britishness and politics: towards a federal future?', in M. O'Neill (ed.), *Devolution and British Politics* (Harlow: Pearson, 2004), p.362.
17. Howe, S. 'Mad dogs and Ulstermen: the crisis of loyalism parts one and two'. Archived at: http://www.opendemocracy.net/articles; Howe, S. 'Loyalism's rage against the fading light of Britishness', *Guardian*, 10 October 2005.
18. Bartlett, T., 'Ulster 1600–2000: posing the question?', *Bullán*, 4, 1 (1988), p.10.
19. Rose, R., *Governing Without Consensus; An Irish Perspective* (Boston: Beacon Press, 1971).
20. Moxon-Browne, E.P., *Nation, Class and Creed in Northern Ireland* (Aldershot: Gower, 1983).
21. McAllister, R.J., 'Religious identity and the future of Northern Ireland', *Policy Studies Journal*, 28, 4 (2000), pp.843–57.
22. See Coulter, C., *Contemporary Northern Irish Society: An Introduction* (London: Pluto, 1999); Graham, B., 'Contested images of place among Protestants in Northern Ireland', *Political Geography*, 17, 2 (1998), pp.129–44.
23 See Graham, B., 'The past in the present: the shaping of identity in loyalist Ulster', *Terrorism and Political Violence*, 16, 3 (2004), pp.483–500; Todd, J., 'Two traditions in unionist political culture', *Irish Political Studies*, no. 2 (1987), pp.1–26.
24. See Finlay, A., 'Defeatism and Northern Protestant "identity"', *The Global Review of Ethnopolitics*, 1, 2 (2001), pp.3–20; Hall, M., *Ulster's Protestant Working Class: A Community Exploration* (Belfast: Island Pamphlet, 1994); McAuley, J.W. and McCormack, P.J., 'The Protestant working class and the state in Northern Ireland since 1930: a problematic relationship', in S. Hutton and P. Stewart (eds), *Ireland's Histories* (London: Routledge, 1991), pp.114–28; McAuley, J.W., *The Politics of Identity: A Loyalist Community in Belfast* (Aldershot: Avebury Press, 1994); Spencer, G., *The State of Loyalism in Northern Ireland* (Houndmills: Palgrave Macmillan, 2008); Taylor, P., *Loyalists* (London: Bloomsbury, 2000).
25. Cairns, D., 'Moving the immovable: discursive challenge and discursive change in Ulster loyalism', *European Journal of Cultural Studies*, 4, 1 (2001), pp.85–104; Parkinson, A.F., *Ulster Loyalism and the British Media* (Dublin: Four Courts Press, 1998); Ruane J. and Todd, J., *The Dynamics of Conflict in Northern Ireland: Power, Conflict and Emancipation* (Cambridge: Cambridge University Press, 1996).
26. Ervine, D., 'No surrender', *Corrymeela Connections*, 2, 1 (2000), p.8.
27. See Bruce, S., *The Edge of the Union: The Ulster Loyalist Political Vision* (Oxford: Oxford University Press, 1994); McAuley, J.W., 'Still "no surrender"? New loyalism and the peace process in Ireland', in J.P. Harrington and E.J. Mitchell (eds), *Politics and Performance in Contemporary Northern Ireland* (Amherest: University of Massachusetts Press, 1999); Todd, 'Two traditions in unionist political culture'.
28. See Shirlow, P. and McGovern, M., 'Introduction: Who are "The People"? Unionism, Protestantism and loyalism in Northern Ireland', in Shirlow and McGovern (eds), *Who are 'The People'?*; Presbyterian Church in Ireland, *The Aims, Ideals and Methods of Irish Loyalism and the Attitude of Irish Presbyterians to it* (Belfast: BCC/ICC Church Leaders Conference, no date).
29. Cited in Hall, M., *Twenty Years: A Concise Chronology of Events in Northern Ireland, 1968–1988* (Belfast: Island Publications, 1988), p.40.
30. See Miller, D., *Queen's Rebels: Ulster Loyalism in Historical Perspective* (Dublin: Gill and Macmillan, 1978); Miller, D., *Queen's Rebels: Ulster Loyalism in Historical Perspective*, reprinted with a new introduction by John Bew (Dublin: University College Dublin Press, 2007).
31. Mitchell, B., *Progressive Unionist Party – Principles of Loyalism: An Internal Discussion Paper* (Belfast: PUP, 2002), p.16.
32. See, for example, Cairns, E., Lewis, C.A., Mumcu, O. and Waddell, N., 'Memories of recent ethnic conflict and their relationship to social identity', *Peace and Conflict: The Journal of Peace Psychology*, 4, 1 (1998), pp.13–22; Cairns, E. and Lewis, C.A., 'Collective memories, political violence and mental health in Northern Ireland', *British Journal of Psychology*, 90, 1 (1999), pp.25–33.

33. Dixon, P., *Northern Ireland – the Politics of War and Peace* (Basingstoke: Palgrave, 2001), p.6.
34. Farrington, C., 'Loyalists and unionists: explaining the internal dynamics of an ethnic group', in A. Edwards and S. Bloomer, *Transforming the Peace Process in Northern Ireland: From Terrorism to Democratic Politics* (Dublin: Irish Academic Press, 2008), p.30.
35. Edwards, A. and Bloomer, S., *A Watching Brief? The Political Strategy of Progressive Loyalism Since 1994*, Conflict Transformation Papers, vol. 8 (Belfast: LINC Resource Centre, 2004).
36. Graham, 'The past in the present', p.484.
37. Ruane and Todd, *The Dynamics of Conflict in Northern Ireland*.
38. See Clayton, *Enemies and Passing Friends*; MacDonald, M., *Children of Wrath: Political Violence in Northern Ireland* (Cambridge: Polity, 1986).
39. McGarry, J. and O'Leary, B., *Explaining Northern Ireland* (Oxford: Blackwell, 1995), pp.351–3.
40. Ibid., p.354.
41. De Paor, L., *Divided Ulster* (Harmondsworth: Penguin, 1970), p.xv.
42. See Munck, R., 'Marxism and Northern Ireland', *Review of Radical Political Economics*, no. 13 (1981), pp.58–62.
43. Bell, G., *The Protestants of Ulster* (London: Pluto Press, 1976).
44. McCann, E., *War and an Irish Town* (London: Pluto, 1972).
45. Farrell, M., *The Orange State* (London: Pluto, 1976).
46. Ibid., p.331.
47. See McVeigh, R. and Rolston, B. 'From Good Friday to good relations: sectarianism, racism and the Northern Ireland state', *Race and Class*, 48, 4 (2007), pp.1–23.
48. See Bruce, S., *The Edge of the Union*; Bruce, S., *God Save Ulster: The Religion and Politics of Paisleyism* (Oxford: Oxford University Press, 1986); Bruce, S., *Paisley: Religion and Politics in Northern Ireland* (Oxford: Oxford University Press, 2007).
49. See Crawford, R.G., *Loyal to King Billy: A Portrait of the Ulster Protestants* (Dublin: Gill and Macmillan, 1987); Hickey, J., *Religion and the Northern Ireland Problem* (Dublin: Gill and Macmillan, 1984).
50. See McGarry and O'Leary, *Explaining Northern Ireland*; O'Leary, B. and McGarry, J., *The Politics of Antagonism: Understanding Northern Ireland* (London: Athlone Press, 1993).
51. Nairn, T., *Pariah: Misfortunes of the British Kingdom* (London: Verso, 2002).
52. Alcock, A., *Understanding Ulster* (Armagh: Ulster Society, 1994).
53. Delanty, G., 'Negotiating the peace in Northern Ireland', *Journal of Peace Research*, 32, 3 (1995), pp.257–64.
54. See Cochrane, *Unionist Politics*; Farrington, *Ulster Unionism and the Peace Process in Northern Ireland*; Farrington, 'Unionism and the peace process in Northern Ireland'.
55. Bruce, *The Edge of the Union*, p.1.
56. Bruce, *God Save Ulster*, p.647.
57. See Jordan, G., *Not of This World?: Evangelical Protestants in Northern Ireland* (Belfast: Blackstaff Press, 2001); Mitchell, C., *Religion, Identity and Politics in Northern Ireland: Boundaries of Belonging and Belief* (Aldershot: Ashgate, 2006); Mitchell, C. and Tilley, J., 'The moral majority: Evangelical Protestants in Northern Ireland and their political behaviour', *Political Studies*, 52, 3 (2004), pp.585–602; Mitchel, P., *Evangelicalism and National Identity in Ulster 1921–1998* (Oxford: Oxford University Press, 2003); Morrow, D., 'Suffering for righteousness sake? Fundamentalist Protestantism and Ulster politics', in Shirlow and McGovern (eds), *Who are 'The People'?*, pp.55–71; Morrow, D., 'Nothing to fear but …? Unionists and the Northern Ireland peace process', in D. Murray (ed.), *Protestant Perceptions of the Peace Process in Northern Ireland* (Coleraine: University of Ulster, 2000), pp.11–42.
58. Bruce, *Paisley*, p.174.
59. See Bruce, *Paisley*.
60. Brewer, J., *Anti-Catholicism in Northern Ireland 1600–1998: The Mote and the Beam* (Basingstoke: Macmillan Press, 1998); Brewer, J., 'Continuity and change in contemporary Ulster Protestantism', *The Sociological Review*, 52, 2 (2004), pp.265–83.
61. See Finlay, 'Defeatism and Northern Protestant "identity"'; Hyndman, M., *Further Afield: Journeys from a Protestant Past* (Belfast: Beyond the Pale Publications, 1996).
62. Morrow, 'Suffering for righteousness sake?', p.70.
63. Farrington, *Ulster Unionism and the Peace Process in Northern Ireland*.
64. Mitchell, *Religion, Identity and Politics in Northern Ireland*, p.32.
65. Mitchell, *Religion, Identity and Politics in Northern Ireland*, p.138.
66. Muldoon, O., McNamara, N., Devine, P. and Trew, K., 'Beyond gross divisions: national

and religious identity combinations', *NI Social and Political Archive*, no. 58 (December 2008).

67. Brewer, J., 'Continuity and change in contemporary Ulster Protestantism'.

68. NILT survey, reproduced in C. Farrington and J. Weeks (eds), *Irish Political Studies Yearbook* (Dublin: PSAI, 2007), p.254.

69. Todd, J., 'Two traditions in Unionist political culture'.

70. McAuley, J.W., 'Two traditions in Unionist political culture: a commentary', in C. McGrath and E. O'Malley (eds), *Irish Political Studies Reader: Key Contributions* (London: Routledge, 2008), pp.105–35.

71. Walker, G. and English, R., 'Introduction', in Walker and English (eds), *Unionism in Modern Ireland* (Basingstoke: Macmillan, 1996), p.ix.

72. Buckland, P., 'A protestant state: unionists in government, 1921–39', in Boyce and O'Day (eds), *Defenders of the Union*, p.218.

73. Anderson, B., *Imagined Communities: Reflections on the Origin and Spread of Nationalism* (London: Verso, 1991).

74. See Racioppi, L. and O'Sullivan, K., 'Ulstermen and loyalist ladies on parade: gendering unionism in Northern Ireland', *International Feminist Journal of Politics*, 2, 1 (2000), pp.1–29; Racioppi, L. and O'Sullivan, K., '"This we will maintain": gender, ethno-nationalism and the politics of unionism in Northern Ireland', *Nations and Nationalism*, 7, 1 (2001), pp.93–112; Ward, R., 'Invisible women: the political roles of unionist and loyalist women in contemporary Northern Ireland', *Parliamentary Affairs*, no. 55 (2002), pp.167–78; Ward, R., '"It's not just tea and buns": women and pro-union politics in Northern Ireland', *British Journal of Politics and International Relations*, 6, 4 (2004), pp.494–506; Ward, R., *Women, Unionism and Loyalism in Northern Ireland: From Tea-Makers to Political Actors* (Dublin: Irish Academic Press, 2006).

75. See Coulter, C., 'Class, ethnicity and political identity in Northern Ireland', *Irish Journal of Sociology*, no. 4 (1994); Coulter, C., 'Direct rule and the unionist middle classes', in English and Walker (eds), *Unionism in Modern Ireland*; Coulter, C., 'The culture of contentment: the political beliefs and practice of the unionist middle classes', in Shirlow and McGovern (eds), *Who Are 'The People'*, pp.114–39.

76. Heath, A., Rothon, C. and Andersen, R., 'Who feels British?', Working Paper No. 5, Department of Sociology, University of Oxford, 2005.

77. O'Neill, M., 'Britishness and politics: towards a federal future?', in M. O'Neill (ed.), *Devolution and British Politics* (Harlow: Pearson, 2004).

78. Parekh, B., 'Common belonging', in *Cohesion, Community and Citizenship*, Proceedings from Runnymede Conference (London: Runnymede Trust, 2002), pp.1–9.

79. See Home Office, *Community Cohesion: A Report of the Independent Review Team*, chaired by Ted Cantle (London: HMSO, 2001); Home Office, *Building Cohesive Communities: A Report of the Ministerial Group on Public Order and Community Cohesion*, chaired by John Denham (London: HMSO, 2001); Home Office, *Building a Picture of Community Cohesion* (London: HMSO, 2003).

80. MacPherson, Sir W., *The Stephen Lawrence Inquiry: Report of an Inquiry by Sir William MacPherson of Cluny, advised by Tom Cook, The Right Reverend Dr. John Sentamu, Dr. Richard Stone, Cm 4262–I* (London: HMSO, 1999).

81. See, for example, reports from the Runnymede Trust available at: http://www.runny medetrust.org/publications/27/74.html.

82. For a flavour of such debates, see Bradley, I., *Believing in Britain: The Spiritual Identity of Britishness* (Oxford: Lion Hudson, 2008); Caunce, S., Mazierska, E., Sydney-Smith, S. and Walton, J.K. (eds), *Relocating Britishness* (Manchester: Manchester University Press, 2004); Griffith, P. and Leonard, M. (eds), *Reclaiming Britishness: Living Together after 11 September and the Rise of the Right* (London: Foreign Policy Centre, 2002); Ware, V., *Who Cares About Britishness? A Global View of the National Identity Debate* (London, Arcadia Books, 2007).

83. See Mycock, A. and Tonge, J., 'The future of citizenship', in Political Studies Association, *Failing Politics: A Response to the Governance of Britain Green Paper* (Newcastle Upon Tyne: PSA, 2007).

84. See Blunkett, D., 'Integration with diversity: globalisation and the renewal of democracy and civil society', *Rethinking Britishness*, Foreign Policy Centre, reproduced in *The Observer*, 15 September 2002; Rattansi. A., 'Who's British? prospect and the new assimilationism', in R. Berkeley (ed.), *Cohesion, Community and Citizenship* (London: Runnymede Trust, 2002).

85. Nairn, T., *Gordon Brown: Bard of Britishness* (Cardiff: Institute of Welsh Affairs, 2006).
86. Parekh, B., *Rethinking Multiculturalism: Cultural Diversity and Political Theory* (Basingstoke: Palgrave, 2000).
87. Aughey, A., *Under Siege: Ulster Unionism and the Anglo-Irish Agreement* (Belfast: Blackstaff Press, 1989), p.1.
88. Aughey, A., 'Britishness: an explanation and a defence', in G. Lucy and E. McClure (eds), *Cool Britannia? What Britishness Means to Me* (Lurgan: Ulster Society, 1999), p.3.
89. D. Trimble, 'Leadership address to the annual conference of the Ulster Unionist Party' (Belfast: UUP, 2002).
90. Aughey, *Under Siege*, p.18.
91. Ibid., p.16.
92. Aughey, A., 'The end of history, the end of the union', in, *Selling Unionism Home and Away* (Belfast: Ulster Young Unionist Council, 1995); Aughey, A., 'The idea of the union', in Foster (ed.), *The Idea of the Union*.
93. Cochrane, *Unionist Politics*, p.77.
94. Crowley, J., 'The politics of belonging: some theoretical considerations', in A. Geddes and A. Favell (eds), *The Politics of Belonging: Migrants and Minorities in Contemporary Europe* (Aldershot: Ashgate, 1999), p.22.
95. Coulter, C., 'The character of unionism', *Irish Political Studies*, no. 9 (1994), p.16.
96. Ibid., p.19.
97. See material in Walker and English (eds), *Unionism in Modern Ireland*.
98. Walker, *A History of the Ulster Unionist Party*.
99. McKay, S., *Northern Protestants: An Unsettled People* (Belfast: Blackstaff Press, 2005).
100. See Spencer, G., 'Constructing loyalism: politics, communications and peace in Northern Ireland', *Contemporary Politics*, 10, 1 (2004), pp.37–52; Spencer, G., *The State of Loyalism in Northern Ireland* (Houndmills: Palgrave Macmillan, 2008).
101. Shirlow, P. and McGovern, M., 'Introduction: who are "the People"? unionism, Protestantism and loyalism in Northern Ireland', in Shirlow and McGovern, *Who are 'The People'?*, pp.1–15.
102. Cash, *Identity, Ideology and Conflict*.
103. Cash, J.D., 'Ideology and affect: the case of Northern Ireland', *Political Psychology*, 10, 4 (1989), pp.703–24.
104. The role of memory in constructing contemporary political and social identities is coming under ever-greater scrutiny. See, from a variety of perspectives, Barsalou, J. and Baxter, V., *The Urge to Remember: The Role of Memorials in Social Reconstruction and Transitional Justice*, Stabilization and Reconstruction Series, no 5 (Washington, DC: United States Institute for Peace, 2007), pp.1–25; Maier, C.S., 'A surfeit of memory? reflections on history, melancholy and denial', *History and Memory*, no. 5 (1993), pp.136–51; Misztal, B.A., *Theories of Social Remembering* (Maidenhead: Open University Press, 2003); Nora, P., 'Between memory and history: les lieux de mémoire [1984]', *Representations*, no. 26 (1989), pp.7–25; Nora, P. and Kritzman, L.D. (eds), *Realms of Memory: Rethinking the French Past. Vol. 1: Conflicts and Divisions* (New York and Chichester: Columbia University Press, 1996); Tota, A.L., 'Terrorism and collective memories: comparing Bologna, Naples and Madrid, 11 March', *International Journal of Comparative Sociology*, no. 46 (2005), pp.55–78.
105. Donaldson, J., 'We're Brits and we're proud of it', *Guardian*, 22 August 2001.
106. Jackson, A., 'Unionist myths 1912–1985', *Past and Present*, no. 136 (1992), p.164.
107. Riles, A., 'Ethnography in the realm of the pragmatic: studying pragmatism in law and politics', *PoLAR* 26, 2 (2003), pp.1–7, cited in R. Whitaker, 'Questions of national identity', *Identities: Global Studies in Culture and Power*, 12, 589 (2005).
108. McAuley, J.W., 'Fantasy politics? Restructuring unionism after the Good Friday Agreeement', *Eire–Ireland*, 39, 1/2 (2004), pp.189–214.
109. See Cash, *Identity, Ideology and Conflict*; Fealty, Ringland and Steven, *A Long Peace?*
110. Ruane and Todd, *The Dynamics of Conflict in Northern Ireland*.
111. Tilly, C., *Stories, Identities and Political Change* (Oxford: Rowman and Littlefield, 2002), p.88.
112. Bhabha, H., 'The managed identity – Foreword: remembering Fanon', in F. Fanon, *Black Skins, White Masks*, translated by C.L. Markham (London: Pluto Press, 1986), p.xi.
113. English, R., 'The growth of new unionism', in J. Coakley (ed.), *Changing Shades of Orange and Green: Redefining the Union and the Nation in Contemporary Ireland* (Dublin: University College Dublin Press, 2002), pp.95–105.

114. Walker, B., *Past and Present: History, Identity and Politics in Ireland* (Belfast: Queen's University of Belfast, 2000).
115. Walker, B., *Dancing to History's Tune: History, Myth and Politics in Ireland* (Belfast: Queen's University of Belfast, 1996), p.14.
116. Mercer, K., 'Welcome to the jungle: identity and diversity in postmodern politics', in J. Rutherford (ed.), *Identity: Community, Culture, Difference* (London: Lawrence & Wishart, 1990), p.45.
117. Bar-Tal, D., 'Sociopsychological foundations of intractable conflicts', *American Behavioural Scientist*, 50, 11 (2007), pp.1430–53.

Chapter 2

Framing Ulster Unionism

Unionist ideology contains diverse interest groups with little in common other than a commitment to the link with Britain. While this position remains relatively cohesive during periods of constitutional crisis when they can articulate what they do not want (namely a weakening of the link with Britain), the coherence of the ideology begins to disintegrate when unionists are forced to establish a consensus for political progress.

Feargal Cochrane[1]

Our Province, democracy, decency, the rule of law and indeed unionism have reached a defining moment ... The question for unionism is whether having been so betrayed, we can yet destroy the plan devised to bind us and deliver us as slaves into a united Ireland.

Peter Robinson[2]

This chapter explores the broad frames of understanding within which unionist political identities have been constructed and reconstructed, up to and including the contemporary period. It touches upon unionist historiography, although the chapter is far from a history of unionism or the UUP.[3] It does, however, select certain key events within 'unionist history', such as the creation of the Northern Irish state after partition, the outbreak of the most recent phase of conflict, the fall of the Stormont government, and the Anglo-Irish and Belfast Agreements to highlight how these are understood and presented by unionists and as core 'turning points' in the construction of the political world in which they live.

The chapter also begins to address some of the major political rivalries within unionism, which in turn is used to consider conflicting unionist reactions to key contemporary events and how different unionist groupings seek to frame competing understandings of such events. The peace process has revealed many of the contradictions within unionism and exposed the different political forces seeking to reshape and reframe unionism.[4]

FRAMING UNIONISM AND LOYALISM

To fully begin to understand the different varieties of unionism and loyalism the book draws, sometimes specifically, sometimes more broadly, on the notion of framing as developed by social movement theorists.[5] It was Erving Goffman who first demonstrated how individuals use a 'schemata of interpretation' to make sense of their social world.[6] This is constructed from both prior experience and existing knowledge to make up the template by which new information is processed and interpreted. Building on the works of Goffman, the concept has been developed to seek to understand how individuals understand happenings within their own life and relate to the wider political world.

Importantly, such templates provide a standardised definition of the world, a frame of understanding which guides people's perceptions and beliefs about everyday events and broader social and political issues. These interpretations form the bedrock from which are built understandings of everyday reality. Importantly, they also help construct expectations about what is likely to happen in everyday political and social worlds.[7] More broadly, frame analysis:

> ... allows us to capture the process of the attribution of meaning, which lies behind the explosion of any conflict. In fact, symbolic production enables us to attribute to events and behaviours, of individuals or groups, a meaning which facilitates the activation of mobilization.[8]

Such frames recognise that language has the power to define problems and to determine political and social actions.[9] In seeking to deepen our understanding of the relationships between political understanding and political action, framing explains not only how problems are defined, but also why particular solutions to such problems are seen as acceptable and possible.[10] Here it is important to understand how issues presented to an audience in a particular way provide clear guidelines for any response by indicating the frame of reference upon which an individual should draw to interpret events through a particular worldview.

Thus, within unionism the dominant interpretative frame has successfully inhibited the generation and reproduction of strong segmental identities, while at the same time framing a forthright definition of the subjective identity of unionism. Framing thus guides people to an identifiable understanding of situations, as well as implying the range of actions necessary to respond.[11] Unionist interpretations manifest around an expression of the claim for a distinct cultural identity on the island of Ireland, and the construction of Britishness as an exclusive ideology and political identity.

This position is capable of mobilising across a wide range of social groupings and categories. Hence, for example, throughout the period of Stormont government the Unionist bloc was able to draw directly on this frame to structure Northern Irish society and to shape its politics into a particular form. This process itself was underpinned by a specific alliance of social forces, through which identifiable political groupings dominated core areas of political discourse and identity.[12] All those outside of this dominant frame, whether Irish nationalists, Protestant liberals or those promoting class or gendered perspectives, were deemed untrustworthy, seen as threatening to undermine the very existence of the state. In mobilising around these ideas unionism set about organising and reinforcing its core discourses and aligning its central values and ideas.

This has important applications within the history of unionism. As George Boyce points out, such sets of ideas are 'an abridgement, a necessary simplification of history'.[13] That does not mean that they are used in an uncomplicated way. Importantly, at times of political anxiety, crisis or trauma, political leaders often draw on such simplifications to openly articulate a more sophisticated ideology. This draws its audience to forms of action through a series of common understandings and reinforces responses to what is being presented within a preordained and rehearsed frame.

A further key task for unionism as a broad social movement was (and remains) the linkage of past and present in an understandable and convincing way. This is achieved through particular patterns of socialisation that rely heavily on distinctive social histories and collective remembering.[14] As we shall see, central to this framing are processes of social remembering, best understood here as expressions of a perceived collective experience which not only bind and reinforce the group by 'giving it a sense of its past'[15] but which, equally importantly, also define aspirations for the future.

Such social remembering gives clear indications of the best and most feasible ways to fulfil such future desires. It is not just that key groups can frame issues in certain ways; the source for that frame must

also be seen to have authority and the analysis offered to be meaningful. Those who identify as unionists do not follow such frames blindly.
Rather because the origin of the frame is seen as so credible, it is used
to structure lives by determining how individuals interpret and
respond to their social world.[16]

Much of the success of the DUP in the contemporary period must be
understood in this context. This will be discussed much more fully in later
sections of the book, but broadly, frames shape political understandings
and interpretations by fronting some aspects of reality while downplay-
ing or marginalising others.[17] This does not involve the imposition of an
identity or some coerced sense of belonging. Rather, framing provides fil-
ters through which everyday politics and events are understood.

The DUP frame of understanding has proved increasingly meaningful to many unionists. The process of framing does not directly tell
those bound within it what to think, but it does (sometimes very sub-
tly) provide the tools through which people perceive and interpret
their social world. The understanding of politics that arises from such
processes forms a central focus for the book and we shall return to it at
several points. Broadly, however, such frames offer unionists the tools
to evaluate events in the world around them and then to prescribe
actions. As several writers suggest, a frame is a 'central organizing
idea'.[18] So what forms do these take within unionism?

CLASSICAL UNIONISM

Irish unionism in its classical form refers to the commitment to maintain the Act of Union of 1801 establishing a unitary state between
Ireland and Britain. Ruane and Todd correctly identify the two main
strands within Irish unionism at that time as a defence of Protestant
interests, and the belief that the Union would benefit the whole of
Ireland, the British Isles and the empire.[19] From its outset, key organisational and ideological tenets of unionism centred on resistance to the
political desires of Irish nationalism.

The origins of Ulster unionism in the late 1800s were based directly
in a political response of opposition to the home rule movement of
Parnell. For many unionists home rule posed the clear threat of
Catholicism becoming the dominant power in the land. Most
Protestants saw Catholics as illiberal in both theological and social doc-
trines. This gave rise to the openly articulated fear that under home
rule, 'Rome rule' would become a reality. As the Rev. Samuel Prentice,
the then Presbyterian moderator, suggested: 'The contention of the
Irish Protestants is that neither their will nor their religious would be
safe in the custody of Rome.'[20]

But there were other fears that united Protestant denominations to give unionism a political direction. Many unionists presented another fundamental argument – that Ireland's economic and political welfare would be greatly diminished by leaving the British empire. In this sense, unionists in Ulster saw themselves merely as part of a greater social and political movement embracing Ireland and Britain, and both Ulster Protestants and the Tory party vehemently opposed any policy of self-government for Ireland.

The developing frame of ideological detachment and increasing coherence of the organisation of Protestant Ulster from the rest of the island was given momentum by the Ulster Unionist Convention of 1892 as the Protestant bourgeoisie and business class increasingly recognised that there was a distinct 'northern cause'.[21] In 1905 this sense of political identity manifested in the formation of the Ulster Unionist Council (UUC), linking the Orange Order and Unionist associations in a bond that was to last for the next century, through structures that were to form the very foundations of modern unionism.

On 28 September 1912, Sir Edward Carson, MP for Dublin University and the new leader of Irish Unionism, was one of nearly half a million people (218,206 men and 228,991 women in Ulster and a further 19,612 in Britain) to sign a 'Solemn League and Covenant'. This acknowledged the pledge to use 'all means which may be found necessary to defeat the present conspiracy to set up a home rule parliament in Ireland'.[22]

As political agitation intensified, the British state again considered granting home rule to Ireland, albeit in some limited form. For vastly different reasons, large numbers within both the Catholic and Protestant populations openly rejected any such ideas. At the core of the position taken by Protestant unionists was an increasing fear of dominance by a Catholic majority across all aspects of political, social and cultural life.[23] Sections of unionism threatened secession of the northern part of Ireland, if the British government did not back down from its plans for Irish home rule.[24]

When the Liberal government in 1914 eventually enacted a home rule law, its implementation was delayed until the end of the First World War, but the early twentieth century saw an increasingly radical transformation of politics in Ireland. The Easter Rising and the attempt to impose conscription during the First World War combined to introduce a new focus, which saw the balance within nationalism shift from the Irish Parliamentary Party towards Sinn Féin. As a result, the 1918 general election witnessed the election of only six constitutional nationalists and seventy-three MPs from Sinn Féin.

Unionism too responded militarily. By 1912, the campaign against home rule intensified; ad hoc military drilling began among many Orange lodges, which became more organised and structured as the UVF increasingly appeared on the streets. It quickly recruited some 90,000 volunteers, albeit largely poorly equipped and supplied.[25] Under the command of Sir George Richardson, however, the UVF became a meaningful military entity, especially following April 1914 when they acquired over 20,000 weapons and several million rounds of ammunition. The landing of arms and munitions at Larne, and its subsequent distribution, has become central to loyalist popular culture.

The consequences of a well organised and heavily armed UVF were both immediate and far-reaching, not least because, as Jon Tonge suggests, it was the continuing threat from this quarter that 'made redundant the 1918 all-Ireland election result [and] overrode the expressed will of the British parliament'.[26] Moreover, as David McKittrick and David McVea point out, the willingness of many Ulster Protestants to take up arms against the state (and the fear that they might do so again) influenced the approach of leading politicians in Britain for many decades afterwards.[27]

The outbreak of the First World War saw the UVF join the British army en masse, its members largely forming the 36th (Ulster) division. The horrendous casualties they subsequently suffered, particularly in attacks on heavily fortified German positions on 1 July 1916, have become deeply located in loyalist political memory[28] and unionist folklore.[29] This continues to be drawn upon directly as the UVF, in particular, claim the ownership of such memories.[30] Indeed, the modern UVF has often claimed the formation of the original grouping, and its willingness to engage in militant and sometimes violent forms of political opposition, marked the beginning of organised loyalist resistance that they seek to trace directly through to the contemporary paramilitarism.[31]

The claim to such a lineage finds overt expression in some of the set pieces organised by the contemporary UVF such as band parades, where replica uniforms and artefacts of the original UVF are commonly displayed. The significance of this symbolism in the construction of loyalist identity was demonstrated directly by the 'Love Ulster' campaign, which, in 2005, distributed thousands of copies of its magazine from the same spot in Larne harbour as the UVF had distributed weapons almost a century before (see Chapter 6).

It would be wrong, of course, to suggest that at the time of the UVF's formation, unionist opposition was entirely based on the threat of physical force. Around the same period, for example, a powerful group of unionists published a book entitled *Against Home Rule*.[32] Its contributors included Arthur J. Balfour, Austen Chamberlain, Thomas

Sinclair and Lord Charles Beresford, as well as an introduction by Sir Edward Carson. The preface by Bonar Law is clearly intended to construct a sense of difference and a discourse of the Other, claiming that: 'Ireland is not a nation; it is two nations; separated from each other by lines of cleavage which cut far deeper than those which separate Great Britain from Ireland as a whole.'[33] Later Carson argued that those who wished 'should not be deprived against their will of the protection of British law and of the rights of British citizenship'.[34]

Such precepts are still recognisable to many unionists today. In the early twentieth century, however, it was becoming increasingly plain that the Union could not be preserved in its existing form. The events leading up to, and immediately following, the political division of Ireland are well documented.[35] Subsequently, unionists set about defending those northern counties in which they had a majority. The core dynamic of unionism as a social movement, to preserve the political union with Great Britain, found itself directly challenged during the political settlement of the1920s.

From the late 1880s to 1920, Irish Protestantism had largely been united in its commitment to a political future of kingdom and empire and in its opposition to a home rule parliament. All was now changed. The Irish unionist project became the Ulster unionist project and its focus and direction was changed fundamentally to marshal forces to maintain as much of Ireland within the UK as it possibly could. This meant that northern unionists had to direct their efforts and support towards the new six-county Northern Ireland, while southern unionists (including those in Cavan, Donegal and Monaghan) were cast aside into a political vacuum.

Since then unionism has engaged in processes of invention and reinvention of unionist identity. This in part involves a reappraisal by unionists of their own history and traditions (which often involves the exclusion of others histories) and the construction of a separate mythology, iconography and frames of understanding.[36] Importantly, despite much overlap, unionism and loyalism draw on somewhat different origins and traditions. Delanty clarifies this when he says:

> While unionism is a product of secular politics, with its roots in 19th century liberalism, loyalism is closer to a revived and anachronistic monarchism. Loyalists are loyal to the British crown and a royalist version of the Whig myth of the Glorious Revolution of 1688, while unionism, which historically had strong Presbyterian roots, is rooted in the social contract of 1801 and expressed a patriotic attitude to Westminster and not the crown.[37]

One result of these competing understandings has been that the resulting symbolism and emblems from these traditions have been used in differing ways by various factions of unionism and loyalism to explain and support their current political positions. This is something to which we shall return throughout the book. To begin with, however, I shall consider the construction of unionist identity and politics within the state of Northern Ireland, following the partition of Ireland.

ULSTER UNIONISM 1921–72

The legislation for a new Northern Ireland parliament was provided under the Government of Ireland Act (1920). Support for such a body was far from universal, however, and strong reservations were expressed even within unionist circles. Much acrimonious debate took place within the Ulster Unionist Party, but eventually on 10 March 1920, the UUC accepted the bill as the best they could hope for in the broad political situation.[38] In 1922 the new Belfast government excluded Northern Ireland from the Irish Free State. As Paul Ward suggests, while 'Ulster Unionists had not wanted this parliament [they] were determined to make use of it in order to defend their British identity.'[39]

As has been pointed out: 'The viability of a separate NI state in 1920/21 rested on the concentration of Protestant (and Unionist) industrial capital in the Belfast area, which in turn was integrated into the Glasgow–Liverpool complex, at a time when British imperialism was a major world force.'[40] The defence of this took several forms. Aughey suggests that a major priority for the new Unionist leadership lay in establishing economic and social parity with Britain,[41] to demonstrate, not only the inherent Britishness of Northern Ireland, but also to mark out how clearly it differed from the South in terms of living standards and economic life.

This put in place the creation of a politics constructed through a series of discourses that discouraged class politics (and any other voices of dissent), and sought to marginalise many of the Catholic population through an attempt to create an identity based on 'Ulster' rather than 'Ireland'.[42] Unionist concerns in government revolved around the perceived need to protect the very existence of the state and the constant fear of the 'enemy within'; those Catholics and unionist liberals within the boundaries of Northern Ireland who were seen as untrusting and untrustworthy by the unionist administration.

Thus, much of the focus for the organisation of the new state was in response to the sense of physical threat that many unionists believed themselves – and the Northern state – to be under. The tone for this was set early and, as Buckland identifies, three measures became central to the construction of a political culture that saw Catholics as disloyal.[43] First, in

April 1922 the new administration introduced the Civil Authorities (Special Powers) Act, and transferred powers around 'law and order' from the judiciary to the Executive (in the shape of the minister for home affairs).

Second, the Northern Ireland government took direct control of the new police force, the Royal Ulster Constabulary (RUC), supplemented by a large part-time and exclusively Protestant reserve security force, the Ulster Special Constabulary (USC). Finally, the Local Government Act (Northern Ireland) of September 1922 reorganised local political representation. Crucially, this meant abolishing the system of proportional representation, which had been introduced in 1919, and in its place were implemented structures under which unionist hegemony was ensured and gerrymandering made possible.

As partition institutionalised sectarian, political, social and economic relations across Ireland, it set in place what Thomas Hennessey refers to as a state of 'cold war' between the two states that lasted from around 1928 until 1962.[44] In the new state of Northern Ireland unionists structured the state apparatus and held power over domestic security forces, maintaining control until the late 1960s. Policy and politics were dominated and structured by a triumvirate of the UUP, the Orange Order and the RUC, including its part-time paramilitary wing, the USC, which was seen essentially as a internal security force and a defence against the IRA,[45] hence its entirely Protestant composition.

Such relationships helped foster the belief within the Protestant working class that their very livelihood rested upon unquestioning allegiance to the state and the Stormont government. This manifested in support for the UUP and the Orange Order as the central organisations giving structure to the broad political direction taken by the Northern Irish state.[46] This was reinforced by the decision of the Unionist government to support the integration of Northern Ireland into the UK welfare state, in part at least to 'placate the party's working class supporters'.[47] Social relations rested upon an essentially paternalistic relationship between the unionist bourgeoisie and Protestant working class.[48]

Colin Reid reflects on the nature of the cross-class alliance upon which these political developments were built, suggesting that: 'The imperative of containing internal divisions shaped the dynamics of Ulster unionism as much as that of facing the external threats of Irish nationalism and Catholicism.'[49] Moreover, many unionists pointed to the success of their project. As Kenneth Bloomfield expressed it:

> ... successive Unionist governments had managed to establish an efficient machinery of government and civil service, modernised

many aspects of life and – perhaps most important of all – so modernised the financial relationship originally envisaged between Northern Ireland and Britain as to make possible the policy of 'parity' in social services ... By 1963 [when Terence O'Neill became prime minister] Northern Ireland enjoyed in many important fields standards fully comparable with those in Britain, and in almost every respect far in advance of those in the Irish Republic at that time.[50]

The drive to reinforce Unionist hegemony was especially apparent at election time. The scenes recalled by one loyalist paramilitary of coal lorries bedecked with union flags and carrying flute bands, upon which unionist parliamentary candidates would appeal to the working-class electorate with impassioned pleas, were typical. He further remembers how they 'always resurrected the border issue along with the Orange card, and our people would turn up on polling day voting en masse for an Orangeman'. But he reminds us that the same candidates 'would then disappear for another four years, leaving us in the belief that Catholics were second class citizens and we had more going for us as Protestants'.[51]

That is not to say that some within unionism did not seek to challenge this, often through the expression of some form of Labourite or class-based politics.[52] Increased levels of unemployment in the early 1960s and a heightened awareness within the Protestant working class of the desirability of an advanced welfare state found its clearest expression through the Northern Ireland Labour Party (NILP).

The 1962 election saw the NILP polling 60,170 votes in Belfast, coming remarkably close to the total unionist vote of 67,450. Although it was often marginalised, an awareness of class differences could never be totally submerged. As the party of Northern Ireland's trade union movement, the NILP sought to project non-sectarianism into the political arena, and to highlight major socio-economic issues brought into relief by the modernisation of Northern Irish society. In response, the NILP did try to formulate programmes and policies to engage with issues beyond the immediate constitutional question.

That, however, was enough to raise fears within the broader sections of unionism. Unionist reaction to the growth of the NILP electorate was typified by the views of Harry West, who suggested that:

> ... many people in Belfast had got their minds filled with the economic position of the country and seemed to forget the great and important issue of the election – their constitutional position.[53]

Similar arguments could be found from at least the late 1800s when a move towards Labourist and trade union politics within the Protestant working class was countered by a re-emphasis of Orange and unionist ideology, one MP arguing that at times it was necessary to be 'manfully asserting your beliefs and acting upon them in order to counter ... liberal tendencies'.[54]

Even at the height of the social democratic project in other regions of the UK the inescapable nature of the constitutional question meant the NILP enjoyed only limited success (and then only in Belfast constituencies). In tracing the history of the NILP, Frank Wright suggests that embedded in its politics was a tacit assumption that the interests of Protestant and Catholic workers were the same, especially regarding economic and unemployment issues,[55] and that 'normal' politics could be extended to Northern Ireland.[56]

In outlining its limitations and eventual demise, however, Wright also highlights how in response to the increasing support for Labour within the Protestant working class, Ian Paisley's Protestant Unionist Party dwelt on the alleged preferential treatment the Catholic working class were receiving in relation to their Protestant counterparts, while Edwards outlines how Labourism was forced to retreat in the face of the growing social and political forces of sectarianism.[57]

Unionism was thus deeply imbued by a struggle to ensure the coherence of unionism as a political and ideological force; a position strongly articulated by the UUP's best-known leader, Sir Edward Carson (1910–21) and clearly reflected in the stances taken by his successors, such as Sir James Craig (1921–40), John Andrews (1940–3) and Sir Basil Brooke (1943–63). For half a century the political leaders of unionism did little to alter the dynamic or consciousness of unionism, and even less to change the political direction or form of the UUP. Only with the passing of the premiership of Northern Ireland from Lord Brookeborough to Terence O'Neill in 1963 did the spectre of change arise within unionism.

What O'Neill proposed was hardly revolutionary, but he did seek to move unionism away from an overtly discriminatory state towards modernity, reflecting a more progressive ethos (at least with unionist terms). He and his supporters began to at least counter the possibility of developing civil relationships between the two parts of the island.

Such changes brought shockwaves across unionism, manifesting in growing divisions between those backing O'Neill's leadership and those who saw his liberal and conciliatory actions as undermining their traditional position. In 1964, Belfast saw its worst riots and street confrontations for over thirty years. Unionist opposition to political change brought to centre stage a reasonably obscure Protestant cleric, the Rev. Ian Paisley, who along with many of his followers reacted with hostility to events. That year Paisley also formed the Protestant Unionist Party

(PrUP) to contest a handful of local government seats; by 1971 its trans-formation to the DUP was complete.

The expanding Catholic middle class largely welcomed the albeit rather limited plans for reform offered by the Unionist government of the mid-1960s, but the period also saw the growth of more radical demands from some sections of Northern Irish society calling for the dismantling of the more overt Unionist institutions. Major tensions sur-faced in 1965 when Terence O'Neill held a summit meeting with the Irish taoiseach Seán Lemass, the first such meeting between the two prime ministers on the island for forty years.

Further discontentment arose during 1966, as the fiftieth anniver-sary of the Battle of the Somme and the Easter Rising were commemo-rated by respective communities. Tensions escalated still further when the first political murder for many years occurred in Belfast. This brought to the stage what appeared to be an increasingly organised loyalist resistance movement fronted by an underground group calling itself the UVF.[58]

As the situation in Northern Ireland increasingly drew attention from both national and international media, the momentum for politi-cal and social change gathered pace. Discrimination against national-ists was widespread across civil society, but it was particularly evident in some areas of employment.[59] Although its extent[60] and the degree of government policy involvement are still contested,[61] even many union-ists now recognise the level of day-to-day discrimination. Esmond Birnie makes this clear when he argues that there is:

> … clear evidence that systematic and orchestrated discrimination against the minority community was a fact of everyday life. It would be going too far to describe the discrimination as govern-ment policy; but it is true that successive unionist administrations did very little to hold out the hand of friendship, or to become an inclusive rather than an exclusive doctrine.[62]

When a progressive reform movement grew in the mid-1960s to mirror others emerging across the world, it found support from the political left, some students and liberal unionists as well as large sec-tions of nationalism. This precipitated the development of a more for-mal organisation, the Northern Ireland Civil Rights Association (NICRA), which by 1967 had increasingly begun to articulate griev-ances around a range of issues, including unfair housing allocation and bias in the system of voting rights at local government level.[63] The bon-fire had been sparked. But as Coakley points out, few could have imag-ined that what had been set in motion was a sequence of events that pushed Northern Ireland to the fore of the international stage resulting in more than 3,500 deaths, with 'thousands more physically injured or psychologically scarred'.[64]

More immediately, the Northern Irish state reacted strongly to suppress NICRA activity on the streets, mobilising militarily through the police and USC in the form of the 'B' Specials.[65] As the Unionist government refused to implement reforms, public protests soon degenerated into street confrontations and violence, fuelled by those who saw a communist/republican conspiracy unfolding before them.[66] Unionist politics were in turmoil. Terence O'Neill was called to London, where under mounting political pressure he agreed to implement reforms, including a more transparent allocation of public housing, the replacement of Londonderry Corporation, reform of local government and amendments to the Special Powers Act.[67] He failed to agree, however, to introduce 'one man one vote' or to repeal the Special Powers Act.

As the situation failed to calm, O'Neill sought endorsement for his leadership. In what he termed as the 'crossroads' election O'Neill sought to secure a general mandate for the political changes he proposed. In reality the attempt by O'Neill to isolate and his opposition within unionism proved futile.[68] Following the poor election results for himself and his supporters, O'Neill resigned.[69] By August 1969, following widespread street violence in Derry and Belfast and the inability of the RUC to police the situation, the British army was called in by the new Northern Irish prime minister, James Chichester-Clark.[70] Violence only escalated, however, as following a brief honeymoon period, the British army became increasingly involved, firstly in policing roles and then in an engagement with organised violence.

The IRA, which had stood down in 1962 after an abandoned border campaign, had moved towards political organisation and agitation and away from its military base. Initially it was ill placed to respond directly to the anger and fear within Catholic communities.[71] It began to recruit, reorganise and rearm. The Provisional IRA was quickly conceived and born[72] following a public split at the Sinn Féin árd-fheis in January 1970, leaving behind what became known as the Official movement. During the first months of 1970 the Provisionals 'began to gather weapons, and to train volunteers'.[73] As the organisation took on an overtly offensive military role,[74] even moderate unionists began to perceive a growing challenge to the existence of the state.

The early 1970s saw an escalation in the physical conflict; violent act followed upon violent act, driven on the streets by Provisional IRA bombing and the assassination campaign of loyalist paramilitaries. During that spring Brian Faulkner (who had resigned from the O'Neill government) replaced James Chichester-Clark as prime minister, whose short-lived premiership was, at best, characterised by a series of somewhat contradictory and confused political initiatives.[75] Faulkner, who was generally perceived as much more hardline than O'Neill, actually introduced some key reforms, promoting legislation against religious discrimination in employment and appointing the long-time Labour leader David Bleakley to a new ministry of community relations.

However, faced with growing dissent within and across unionism, Faulkner brought forth the view that loyalist paramilitarism had emerged in the context of a general collapse of confidence among unionism (particularly regarding the intentions of the government in Westminster) and that any mounting Protestant 'backlash' could only be subdued by swift and decisive action.[76] Under pressure from the right within unionism, Faulkner persuaded the Westminster government to allow the introduction of internment without trial as a final throw of the dice by the unionist state. Internment had been used by Unionist administrations with some limited success in previous times of crisis, such as 1921–4, during the Second World War, and during the IRA campaign of 1956–62.

This time, its implementation on 9 August 1971 proved an abject failure. The SDLP withdrew from Stormont, promising never to return while internment was in place. Largely reliant on outdated intelligence, it alienated most Catholics and did little to arrest the organisation of the new generation drawn to militant republicanism; it precipitated widespread disenchantment and street confrontations in many nationalist areas and, if anything, only served to stimulate recruitment to the IRA.[77]

Violence grew apace. In the seven months of 1971 before internment was introduced, twenty-eight people had died on the streets of Northern Ireland; between 9 August and the end of the year, however, 144 lost their lives. Events came to a head on 30 January 1972, when in Derry the British army killed thirteen Catholic civilians following a civil rights march. The repercussions of what became known as 'Bloody Sunday' and the international response it raised proved critical to the future structure of politics in Northern Ireland.

As the reaction and response reverberated across the globe, the Irish government withdrew its ambassador from London and demanded that the United Nations take on a peacekeeping role in Northern Ireland. Heated exchanges took place between Ted Heath and Jack Lynch and the British embassy in Dublin was petrol bombed following a huge demonstration. In response to the growing outrage expressed from across the globe, the UK government demanded it take responsibility for security in the province, introducing direct political rule from Westminster in March 1972.

Unsurprisingly, the decision was deemed to be totally unacceptable by the Unionist government, and Faulkner and his entire cabinet resigned amid widespread claims that direct rule marked a victory for republicanism and those seeking to undermine the Northern Irish state.[78] John Taylor, the former minister for home affairs, typified the mood within unionism: 'There should be no doubt in the minds of any loyalists that the people of Ulster have witnessed the surrender of the British government to the threats of the IRA.'[79] The anguish among unionists and loyalists was laid bare. Workers in Belfast's heavy industries protested on the streets, while the Ulster Vanguard movement, led by Bill Craig, organised a two-day 'strike' on 27 and 28 March, displaying the full strength of its support at a massive rally in the grounds of Stormont attended by up to 200,000 people.[80]

UNIONISM AFTER STORMONT

Following Bloody Sunday, however, the British state had few remaining political options other than to impose direct rule on what many saw as a 'quasi-state' now 'in an advanced state of collapse',[81] and the Stormont administration was suspended (it last met on 28 March 1972). The paramilitary war escalated. A total of 145 members of the security forces were killed throughout 1972 (compared to fifty-nine in 1971), while the number of reported shooting incidents rose to 10,628 (from 1,765 in 1971). By the end of 1972 a total of 496 had lost their lives (the highest annual total throughout the entire Troubles).

Political pressure built from within unionism for a co-ordinated reaction; it became intense as the relationship between the British administration and loyalists deteriorated rapidly. On the streets such concerns were directly reflected in the increased presence of the many local vigilante associations that had formed in Protestant districts. These mobilised around an open concern that the state was incapable or unwilling to deal with the situation and the fear that all they perceived as solid under Stormont was at best vulnerable, at worst crumbling around them.

The security of the state, both physical and political, became paramount for unionists; the feared backlash to the dismantling of the Protestant state[82] was beginning to take form.[83] As various Protestant defence groupings amalgamated, the resulting organisation, the UDA, rapidly mobilised, quickly boasting 25,000 dues-paying members[84] and anything up to double that in fringe membership and associates. Many of these could be, and at times were, rallied on the streets in reaction to political events.[85] The UDA increasingly found expression through illegal marches, industrial stoppages, parades and eventually the setting up of loyalist 'no-go' areas for security forces (which they claimed were in direct response to those in existence in some nationalist districts).

One incident on 1 July 1972 is illustrative of the politics of the time. Following an attempt to establish a no-go area around Ainsworth Avenue in Belfast, something approaching 10,000 UDA members found themselves in a direct stand-off with the British army, a pitched battle only being avoided following lengthy discussions between General Robert Ford and senior UDA officials.[86] As the significance of formal party politics receded from day to day life, some within loyalist para-militarism, most notably sections of the UVF, engaged in a murderous campaign aimed largely at Catholic civilians.[87]

The split in the republican movement further compounded the move towards everyday political violence. While the Official IRA declared a ceasefire in May 1972, the Provisional IRA war against the British increasingly took shape. Sectarian violence and killings became commonplace as daily news reports recorded the growing brutality across Northern Ireland. During a brief period of ceasefire, talks between the Provisional IRA leadership and representatives of the UK government ended in acrimony in July 1972; this was followed by a resumption of violence, amid escalating IRA claims that they 'were on the verge of defeating the British'[88] and mounting fears of a widescale loyalist backlash.

A new power-sharing Assembly elected in 1973, supported by the UUP, Alliance Party and including SDLP members in its Executive, offered some glimmer of hope for a political solution. When the eleven-minister power-sharing Assembly met, however, it faced widespread resistance, both from republicans and many unionists, opposed to the 'Irish dimension' it sought to institutionalise through a Council of Ireland (commonly known as the Sunningdale Agreement). The diffi-culties were clearly represented at the first meeting of the Assembly, when unionists, led by Ian Paisley and William Craig, filibustered the official proceedings and then refused to accept its adjournment, con-tinuing for some time with an unofficial meeting of their own in the absence of other members.[89]

In the Westminster election of February 1974, anti-Sunningdale and anti-power sharing unionists took eleven of the twelve seats in Northern Ireland. Widespread unionist opposition to political change came to a head in May 1974 when the UWC, an ad hoc organisation based largely in the industrial heartlands of the shipyards and power stations, organised a 'general strike'.[90] Backed by the muscle of loyalist paramilitary groups, it brought life throughout large parts of Northern Ireland to an almost complete standstill. During the strike UVF car bombs[91] in Dublin and Monaghan killed thirty-three people.[92] After

fourteen days, as the infrastructure of Northern Ireland faced near collapse, the power-sharing Assembly Executive resigned, precipitating
widespread celebrations in loyalist districts and causing many to proclaim it as their finest hour.[93]

The result was the re-establishment of direct rule from Westminster.
In the absence of new Assembly elections the period that followed is
best characterised by an almost total lack of political initiative or design.
Violence from both republican and loyalist paramilitary groupings continued at an unrelenting pace. In 1975, the Constitutional Convention
was set up with a majority of unionist members. When it reported it
demanded a return to the former system at Stormont. Elsewhere, an
attempt to express coherent opposition to the continuing violence saw
the Peace People come to international prominence.[94] The movement
quickly faded, however, its leadership unable to agree future policy or
to reconcile the conflicting demands emanating from the different
communities.

Political stalemate continued, reflected in the failed attempts to
implement devolved institutions in 1977 and 1980, which were
opposed at different times by the SDLP and then by the UUP. In 1977
the United Unionist Action Council (UUAC) organised another strike
(modelled directly on the UWC) to protest against continuing direct
rule and what they regarded as the weakness of government security
policy. This time, however, the security forces intervened directly to
keep roads open and allow people to journey to work. The strike
petered out as a pale imitation of the events of 1974.

Between 1982 and 1984 the new secretary of state for Northern
Ireland, Jim Prior, introduced a process of 'rolling devolution'. In an
attempt to move the momentum away from paramilitarism and back
towards local political parties, a new seventy-eight member Assembly
was to be elected, initially with only a consultative role to play. The
plan, however, involved a gradual movement towards fully devolved
government in the seemingly unlikely circumstances that their representatives could confirm a process and method for agreed government
and develop a 'cross-community' base. This format (and the Assembly)
also collapsed, boycotted by the SDLP, who contested the election but
refused to take their seats because power sharing was not guaranteed
within its constitution. The Assembly ran its course and was finally
abandoned in 1986, having failed to win any realistic level of cross-
community support or to produce any hint of political compromise.

Unionism was pulled in conflicting and often contradictory directions. The UUP increasingly divided over competing claims around
strategy and tactics, not least between those who believed that complete integration with the rest of the UK marked the best way forward

for unionism and others who saw the future resting in the restoration of a devolved administration. This set the template for years to come, as the party struggled to contain tensions between 'devolutionist' and 'integrationist' wings (strains that were also present within the DUP). Faulkner's successors as UUP leader, Harry West (1974–9) and James Molyneaux (1979–96), achieved little success in implementing the party's aims of a devolved government without enforced power sharing, and working relationships with the Irish Republic without any institutionalised dimensions.

Elsewhere, the DUP offered itself as the legitimate political voice of unionism, while others aligned with the UDA abandoned the idea of the Union altogether by producing coherent plans to promote an independent Ulster. The two decades following 1972 saw unionism severely fragment ideologically, socially and in its political representation. From that time, within unionism, 'lost hegemony' was 'paralleled by lost harmony'.[95] Walker and English summarise the entire period well when they explain that unionism and loyalism:

> ... collapsed into a cacophony of angry voices. Self-confidence and intellectual argument were at a premium. The Protestant middle class to a great extent opted out of politics. The Protestant working class became more 'alienated' and tended either to be comprehensively dismissed by commentators as bigoted, or naively celebrated as proto-Republicans by those who misinterpreted their frustrations and resentments.[96]

UNIONISM'S IRISH DIMENSION

Throughout the above, one of the few things unionists agreed upon was that they operated within a political frame of reference bounded by the UK state. Throughout the contemporary period some of the greatest ideological shifts for unionists have involved the changing relationships with the southern Irish state.

Dennis Kennedy suggests that in the period following partition a quite understandable anxiety in Northern Ireland was exaggerated into an obsession with differences between the two states.[97] The mould had been quickly and firmly set. Following partition both northern and southern jurisdictions set about constructing narratives of mutual exclusion reinforced through the production of conflicting historiographies that framed the dominant state values.[98] The situation was clear:

> Partition ensured the relative isolation of both states, each founded on opposing religious cultures, from each other. Partition thus created conditions for isolation and homogeneity. The protectionist-economic nationalism practised in the South and the devolution

granted by Westminster in the North allowed the two states to pursue repressive politics aimed at isolating liberal-secular and left-wing currents.[99]

Within the southern state, scholarship interpreted the development of Irish society through a frame confined to the existing state. In Northern Ireland reference points were distinctly British and political aspirations and the norms of public debate were seen to take place within these boundaries.[100] Further, these relationships developed in the context of an arena with its own parliament, largely ignored by the rest of the UK polity.

If unionists did air any clear feelings about the South, they usually concerned expressions of fear regarding the political intentions of the Republic. Such views were fed by the strengthening unionist stereotype of the rest of the island as socially inhibited, economically backward, and where the organisation of the state was driven by the moral values of the Catholic Church.

By the early 1970s, however, unionists were no longer in control of their own state. One of the most important consequences following Stormont's demise was the introduction of a series of secretaries of state, directly responsible for political and security matters, and who administered without the necessary consent of local political representatives. Although originally seen only as a temporary measure until some working consensus was found, as the search for a solution lengthened it became a long-term semi-colonial form of government,[101] as the period between 1972 and 1993 witnessed no fewer than seven failed attempts to broker peace and introduce some agreed form of government.[102]

The focus shifted, and the beginning of the 1980s witnessed a series of meetings between the Irish and British prime ministers, following which, in late 1981, the decision was made to form the Anglo-Irish Intergovernmental Council to discuss matters of 'common concern'. This was to involve regular ministerial-level meetings between the British and Irish governments, but immediately following its design the outbreak of the Falklands/Malvinas conflict in 1982 put Anglo-Irish governmental relations under intense diplomatic pressure, not eased when the Irish government failed to follow the rest of the EEC in embargoing trade with Argentina.[103]

It was 1983 before the summit next met, by which time the political face of Northern Ireland had altered. Not least, Irish republicanism had repositioned through its 'Armalite and ballot box' strategy[104] and Gerry Adams had been elected both as Sinn Féin president and MP for West Belfast, a result of successfully mobilising mass electoral support following the hunger strikes. Both the UK and Irish governments reacted to these developments with alarm, sharing common concern around Sinn Féin's newfound political expression and its growing electoral challenge to the SDLP.

At the same time John Hume, as leader of the SDLP, appealed directly to the Irish government for support, resulting in the creation of the New Ireland Forum to discuss the political future of Ireland. The body held its inaugural meeting in the summer of 1983, without any input from Sinn Féin, unionists, or indeed the UK government, all of which boycotted the event. Framing the Forum, however, was a broad ethos of bringing about Irish unity by consent, albeit underpinned by overt assurances to northern Protestants that there would be irrevocable guarantees to protect their identity and interests in any New Ireland state.

When the Forum reported in May 1984 it suggested three possible future political scenarios for the island: a united Ireland; a confederation of Northern Ireland and the Republic; and joint political authority over Northern Ireland.[105] The leadership of both main unionist political parties reacted strongly as 'outrage at the agreement quickly took on near rebellious proportions'.[106] Harold McCusker, MP, in a Westminster debate, gave perhaps the most eloquent statement of opposition when he spoke at length of the desolation, ignominy and humiliation felt by unionists.[107] The UUP published its own counter-proposals in a paper entitled *The Way Forward*, while the DUP rejoinder was *The Unionist Case: The Forum Report Answered*.

Two further papers, *Opportunity Lost* by the UUP and *Ulster: the Future Assured* by the DUP, quickly followed. Both were highly critical of the Forum, indicating that they regarded the proposal of joint authority as a first step to a united Ireland (highlighted by the constant references to joint authority as joint sovereignty). For the DUP this meant only one conclusion was possible:

> Joint Sovereignty unalterably reverses Northern Ireland's constitutional affiliation as part of the United Kingdom and delivers it out of the United Kingdom irretrievably halfway to an all-Ireland republic; and this without the least consent of the people of Northern Ireland.[108]

Unionist opposition to any 'Irish dimension', and their fears surrounding any form of closer relationship between the two states, seemed largely to be dispelled, however, when the British and Irish governments next held a summit meeting in November 1984. Margaret Thatcher also reacted strongly and in a forthright statement denounced the conclusions of the Forum Report, declaring: 'A unified

Ireland was one solution. That is out. A second solution was confederation of the two states. That is out. A third solution was joint authority.
That is out. That is a derogation from sovereignty.'[109]

The political consequences of Thatcher's riposte seemed clear, and
most unionists seemed in agreement with the editorial of the *Belfast
Newsletter* on 8 June 1985, which suggested that: 'Dublin's influence is
likely to be almost totally excluded from the affairs of Northern
Ireland.' Unionists reacted with barely controllable glee, the mood typified by Peter Robinson, who claimed that Thatcher's statement had
reinforced the reality of 'Ulster as an entity within the United
Kingdom'.[110]

But the issue was far from resolved. In November 1984 an independent think-tank chaired by Lord Kilbrandon published a document
entitled *Northern Ireland: Report of an Independent Inquiry*, which promoted a much greater role for the Republic in Northern Ireland's political affairs. The Haagerup Report (written by a Danish European member of parliament) strongly suggested that the provision of greater economic and social resources by the European Parliament could help promote peace in Northern Ireland. Arguments that the problems of
Northern Ireland could be solved by an amalgamation of political
forces from beyond the UK were gathering momentum, bringing to the
fore some unionist unease at any sustained input beyond the control of
the Westminster administration.

UNIONISM AND THE ANGLO-IRISH AGREEMENT

Despite these broader developments the gaze of unionist leadership
quickly readjusted to the internal politics of Northern Ireland. The
main concerns of unionism were directly toward the May 1985 local
government elections. Bolstered by the stance of Thatcher and the
Conservative administration, the major concern for all of unionism's
political representatives was the expanding political mobilisation of the
republican movement, and the predicted growth in electoral support
for Sinn Féin in forthcoming elections.

Hence, manifestos for both the UUP and DUP all but ignored any
wider Irish dimension, and gave primary place to organising resistance
to the political development of Sinn Féin. By later that year, however, it
was clear that unionism had badly miscalculated, and the faith they put
in Thatcher's utterances was misplaced. Although overtly opposed by
all shades of unionism, an institutionalised Irish dimension was becoming more and more of a reality.

The common purpose agreed in secret negotiations between the UK
and Irish governments was made public on 15 November 1985 when

Mrs Thatcher and Dr Fitzgerald met at the third of a series of meetings of heads of government, in the Anglo-Irish Intergovernmental Council. The two premiers signed the Anglo-Irish Agreement as a binding accord, aimed at furthering the reconciliation of Ireland's two major political traditions by creating new modes of cooperation between the people of the two countries and their governments.[111] As part of the accord the Irish government confirmed that a united Ireland was an aspiration, best regarded as a long-term objective, to be brought about only through majority consent in both parts of the island.

The pact, however, also allowed the Dublin government some consultative role regarding Northern Ireland, especially in relation to 'security and political issues'. Unionists objected to this with fury, dismayed at what many regarded as only the most thinly disguised form of joint rule between the Dublin and London governments.[112] They further argued that this meant that Northern Ireland was 'no longer a part of the United Kingdom on the same basis as Great Britain'.[113] Peter Smith expressed such sentiments directly, claiming that the AIA had created something:

> ... so terrible that the British government was letting it be known that Mrs Thatcher, the 'Iron Lady', had determined to face down majority Unionist opposition in the Province just as she had already faced down the Argentineans and striking miners.[114]

WALKING WITH LUNDY'S GHOST

The Agreement was a benchmark for unionist politics against which all subsequent political formations must be assessed. Opposition was widespread, with only one in ten Protestants supporting a role for the Irish government in Northern Ireland's affairs.[115] The deep sense of unionist foreboding was neatly encapsulated in the *News Letter* editorial of 16 November 1985, the day after the AIA was signed, which suggested that now 'the ghosts of Cromwell and Lundy walked hand in hand'. James Molyneaux, the UUP leader, even went so far as to claim it was 'the beginning of the end for the Union'.[116]

At best for unionists, these were 'confusing and unhappy times'[117] marked by underlying and mounting feelings of betrayal, anger, humiliation and shock, expressions that have remained core constructs within unionism until today. The unionist political response focused on three specific areas of protest: the extent to which the Republic had an input into the governance of Northern Ireland; the process by which the Agreement had been arrived at; and finally, the undemocratic nature of the Agreement, foisted upon the 'Unionist people'.[118]

Underlying this was, as Dominic Murray once put it, the belief held by many unionists that the Irish Republic was a '"sleeping lion" waiting to pounce on the north if defences are even marginally lowered', and that this perception continued 'to engender the "not an inch" response'[119] from unionists. But not an inch it was. The starkest demonstration of outright unionist hostility was seen in a huge rally at Belfast City Hall on 23 November 1985 attended by around 200,000 people. Addressed by both Ian Paisley and James Molyneaux, it marked perhaps the last mass expression of hegemonic unionism.

Following the protest the unionist MPs (who were already boycotting Westminster) called for a referendum to be held, arguing that any proposed change to the constitutional position should be validated on the same basis as the devolution referendums held in Scotland and Wales in 1978. When the UK government quickly rejected the demand all fifteen Unionist Westminster MPs resigned, forcing what unionists claimed was a 'mini-general election' on the legitimacy of the AIA. In the resulting by-elections, held on 23 January 1986, the UUP and DUP stood agreed candidates on a joint manifesto and issued a *Joint Unionist Election Bulletin*, part of which stated: 'This election is not about sending a representative to the House of Commons, our MPs got the endorsement in June 1983. This election is about one issue – the Anglo-Irish Agreement.'[120]

The overall unionist vote totalled 418,230, around 44 per cent of the electorate, which was claimed as an overwhelming mandate to oppose the AIA. Even if we accept the unionist position, however, the results were not straightforward. Only fifteen out of the seventeen seats in Northern Ireland were contested, and in several cases those supporting the AIA were only given the opportunity to vote for 'Peter Barry', a fictitious candidate put forward by unionists to make the by-election possible.

Driven by the election results and growing levels of populist resistance, the campaign against the AIA intensified as unionist-controlled councils across Northern Ireland refused to carry on normal business. The affairs of the Northern Ireland Assembly also became concentrated solely on opposition to the AIA and it was eventually dissolved on Monday 23 June 1986 amid continuing unionist protests. Meantime, the Maryfield Secretariat that convened on 11 December 1985 to consider cross-border matters of mutual interest became the main focus for unionist demonstrations.

For unionism the AIA represented not just a formal accord between the Westminster and Dublin governments, but the imposition, in all but name, of joint authority. It was simply beyond the comprehension of many of the unionist population that the government of the UK could impose the AIA on them without consultation or the opportunity to give their consent, undermining what many claimed to be their birthright and paying scant attention to the strength of allegiance they felt towards the Union.

Perhaps most importantly, unionist reaction highlighted a frame of understanding that has continued to develop within sections of unionism ever since. This involved the increasing prominence of ideas that British identity was being 'hollowed out', that the Union was being weakened by the actions of the Westminster government. Increasingly unionists felt they had been betrayed by the British state, giving credence to Enoch Powell's view at the time that, for the previous two decades, 'British governments have been consistently bent on getting a united Ireland.'[121] It was becoming apparent to many that it was up to unionists alone to seek to negotiate the best terms for their own political destiny.

BEYOND THE ANGLO-IRISH AGREEMENT

The first anniversary of the signing of the AIA was marked by another huge unionist protest under the banner of 'Ulster Says No'. Unionist resistance, however, increasingly proved to be ineffectual. More centrally perhaps, the coherence of unionist protests and strategy began to unravel. The period marked the end of a unified political response from unionism, the death throes for any lingering feeling of unionist hegemony, which dissolved as the struggle for the political leadership of unionism between the DUP and the UUP took shape.[122] The contest between those parties for the soul of unionism has of course dominated unionist politics ever since.

More broadly, the AIA proved critical to political events that followed, because it meant that:

> ... neither community within Northern Ireland could use the London or Dublin government against the other, because while the Governments might still disagree, they recognised that what they had in common was greater than their divisions.[123]

If they didn't already believe so, many unionists were forced to recognise that they could no longer regard the British state as straightforward guardians of the Union; or that the UK government would uphold the direct interests of unionism to the exclusion of others.

The AIA precipitated an overt political stalemate in Northern Ireland that was to last for the next five years with disaffected unionists refusing to consider any form of negotiation with nationalists.

Within a reasonably short time, however, direct action by unionists to remove the AIA began to subside. As unionism began to further assess its position, a cross-party grouping headed by Paisley and Molyneaux was formed. From within the group Harold McCusker, Peter Robinson and Frank Millar produced *An End to Drift* in June 1987. It was a robust denial of the British government position, but a close reading revealed a subtle if noteworthy change in the construction of the unionist position, including the willingness to abandon majority rule in return for devolution.[124]

Dermott Nesbitt goes so far as to suggest that the response saw the beginning of a new mode of thinking within unionism which recognised that unionists needed to be more prepared to adapt to changing circumstances, including abandoning majority rule in Northern Ireland.[125] By May 1988 the UUP declared in public its willingness to exchange position papers with the Dublin government, and the possibility of inching towards a political settlement was at least ruminated. The seeds of a new unionism had been planted and the signs of flexibility from sections of unionism added, at least tentatively, to the climate of change that suggested the possible development of new relationships across the political spectrum.[126]

Elsewhere, although the IRA military campaign continued and the British state responded directly, both sides were increasingly coming to realise that they were locked in a near military stalemate. Some within the republican leadership and in the prisons increasingly began to question and quietly articulate whether military action could ever force the UK government to withdraw from Northern Ireland and if their goals could not better be achieved by other means.[127] Moreover, there was a recognition that the 'long war' strategy upon which militant republicanism had embarked had drawn a heavy toll from the Catholic community and had led to 'exclusion, demonization and lack of legitimacy'.[128]

Likewise, similar realisations by key factions of the British establishment that it could not defeat the IRA were being aired. Behind the scenes negotiations began to take place to persuade the IRA to end their campaign and to declare a ceasefire in order to engage militant republicanism and allow Sinn Féin to come to the negotiating table. The search had begun for a settlement revolving around the notion of integrating political representatives from the constitutional parties and both loyalist and republican paramilitaries into a new political process.[129]

The period following the AIA changed the political landscape dramatically. In retrospect, it paved the way for the development of an embryonic peace process. More immediately it delivered a clarion call to unionists that their relationship with the British state was subject to negotiation and that support was not automatic or without demands. This did not make for easy relationships between unionists and government. Before the AIA, unionists had frequently expressed concern about the details of government strategy; now many claimed that they could never fully trust their sovereign government again.

THE PEACE PROCESS EMERGES

Mitchell suggests that in its subsequent readjustments UUP supporters sought to reposition the party not only in direct opposition to Irish nationalist aspirations, but also to provide a direct counterweight to both loyalist paramilitarism and what was seen as the outdated and hardline Protestant unionism of the DUP.[130] As the seeds of new unionism started to take root, some within the UUP began to project a more 'rational, modern, and secular apologetic for the Union'.[131] Many of the recent alternations within unionism are in no small part due to responses to its repositioning, both internally and externally, in relation to the subsequent political accord which manifested in the Agreement. Although impossible to date the beginning of the peace process precisely, the major political dynamics contributing to its origins can be identified.[132] That is not to say that new unionism marked a clear break with existing forms of unionism, but it did begin to stretch the existing parameters of unionist ideology and its understandings.

This was part of a wider dynamic, which emerged from the mid-1980s onwards and saw the main protagonists in the conflict beginning to re-evaluate approaches to achieving long-term political goals. It is now clear, for example, that even while the IRA campaign was at its height, Sinn Féin was involved in making contacts across Church and state, seeking to engage in talks.[133] Following the failure of the Sunningdale Agreement to win local support, the British and Irish governments increasingly began to develop a joint analysis of the situation and a common approach to its resolution. Jeremy Smith summarises the period as follows:

> The period 1984 to 1988 witnessed some profound shifts and reassessments. Little of this was done in public, but it is clear that behind the scenes pockets of leaders were beginning to scrutinize their tactics, revisit 'first' principles and re-examine fixed positions to see whether a changing world had not rendered them obsolete ... Both [republican and unionist] movements edged away from their marginalized status into positions where some involvement in political discussions and negotiation was possible.[134]

Both governments openly agreed to the desirability of a devolved power-sharing government in Northern Ireland and that Northern Ireland could only be removed from the UK when a majority of its citizens chose to do so.[135] Alongside this, the politics of republicanism had undergone significant changes, particularly following internal questioning of the military strategy as a means to erode British resolve in Northern Ireland.[136] There were even suggestions from within republicanism that continued violence was proving counterproductive. As a consequence, an initiative promoting political change emerged from within the republican movement. The secret talks revealed a sense of an approaching turning point from all quarters, a feeling that the 'long war' might be drawing to a close and a widening recognition that all sides had fought themselves to what William Zartman has described as a position of mutually hurting stalemate.[137]

This altered political dynamic was seen at several levels, but most notably in the dialogue that emerged in early 1993 between John Hume, the leader of the SDLP, and Gerry Adams, the Sinn Féin president. The discussions encouraged the republican leadership at least to conceive of a more politically orientated strategy to achieve its ends, reflected in the calls from *An Phoblacht/Republican News* for 'immediate inclusive dialogue'.[138] As Bowyer Bell suggests, while this did not bring us immediately to an endgame, it did mark changed perceptions and priorities within republicanism:

> That made the British gestures relevant to Republicans and the Republicans open to discussion – if most of such discussion was secret. An unarmed strategy offered – might offer – a way forward while, the IRA recognised, a military strategy simply guaranteed no defeat.[139]

Many unionists were unconvinced, simply fearing the construction of a new 'pan-nationalist' front. Aside from any political reservations, however, the project was put under immense pressure when on Saturday 23 October 1993 the IRA exploded a device in a shop on the Shankill Road, killing ten, including four women, two young girls and one of the bombers. The embryonic peace process almost evaporated as the inevitable reprisals from loyalist paramilitaries followed, including the killing by the UFF of eight people in a pub in the mainly Catholic village of Greysteel on Halloween night.

The immediate future direction of loyalist paramilitarism and its level of engagement with the peace process were unclear. There were several reasons for this beyond the perceived need to retaliate for the Shankill Road bombing. Not least were the internal dynamics of loyalism. A new and much more politically sophisticated leadership had been forged through the political experiences of paramilitary prisoners in the jails.[140] While this grouping was becoming more prominent and were to gain increasing relevance as loyalist paramilitaries began to recognise the centrality of projecting a coherent political position, they were certainly not in a position of command or dominance over the paramilitaries.

Moreover, belligerents within loyalist organisations had acquired a much greater military capacity and weaponry.[141] Indeed, in the years immediately preceding its ceasefires in 1994 loyalist paramilitaries were much more active than their republican counterparts.[142] Much of the increase in violence, according to loyalists, was directly attributable to the Hume–Adams talks, a supposed signal that, despite the peace plan communicated to Dublin, there must be no Irish government dimension to any political settlement. Some saw conciliatory messages from republicans merely as a sign of weakness, arguing that loyalists should actually intensify their campaign and 'finish the job off'. There was clearly still much up for debate within loyalist paramilitarism.

Meanwhile, the broader unionist population remained less than convinced that the opportunity existed for the development of any political movement, let alone progress. Still affronted by the manner in which the AIA had been implemented, and still suffering from a sense of psychological and political retreat, the level of unionist disaffection from politics remained high. While the development of the peace process was never a given, it had become apparent by the late 1980s that the broader political environment was becoming more conducive to political change than for many years. As a result, Northern Ireland's main political parties, excluding Sinn Féin, began 'talks about talks' (which lasted from January 1990 to November 1992).

Feedback from informal discussions between Sinn Féin and the UK government indicated that republicans were at least considering some notion of change in tactics that might achieve their goals by means other than overt violence. Part of this reflected recognition from within sections of the Sinn Féin leadership that its electoral campaign was being inhibited by IRA violence, and that there was a need 'to sell the idea of a political alternative'.[143]

The developing process was revealed through a round of discussions involving representatives from all of Northern Ireland's main political parties and the UK and Irish governments. On 15 December 1993, after considerable debate, the two governments released a joint statement, the 'Downing Street Declaration'.[144] In a crucial section, clearly designed to attract support from the nationalist community, it stated that the UK government agreed that it is 'for the people of the island of Ireland alone ... to exercise their right of self-determination'.[145]

Despite the perception of its 'Green tinge' by many unionists (a far deeper shade was perceived by the DUP), the Declaration was also designed to reach out to that community. The Irish government restated its commitment that constitutional change to Northern Ireland could only be brought about with the consent of the majority. It also promised to embed this principle in the Constitution of the Republic of Ireland, marking a major change in the legislation, which claimed that Northern Ireland was politically subordinate to the whole island. Articles 2 and 3 of the Irish Constitution, for so long seen as provocative to unionists, were to be abandoned.

Meanwhile, discussion within the republican movement gathered momentum as they sought to clarify the likely political response to an end to violence. When in reply both governments made clear they would be magnanimous in the event of paramilitary ceasefires, it seemed progress might be made. Many unionists, however, remained intensely suspicious that a backdoor deal was being done to reward the IRA if it ended its military campaign. Such fears were not eased when news broke in the media that, despite many public assurances that the UK government did not 'talk to or negotiate with terrorists', there had for many years been a secret back channel between them and the republican movement.[146]

When the UK government was seen as willing to meet the request from Sinn Féin for 'clarification' around issues in the Declaration it created some room for political manoeuvre and encouragement to those most keen on developing the process. By early 1994 John Major's Conservative administration seemed increasingly convinced that a new political initiative in Northern Ireland could win populist support.[147]

Following a brief ceasefire that Easter, the IRA declared a cessation of military activities from midnight on 31 August 1994, issuing a statement claiming: 'We believe that an opportunity to secure a just and lasting settlement has been created.'[148] While there was no immediate response by way of an invitation to formal talks with government, it was clear that relationships were being built. Contacts continued to take place between Sinn Féin and British government representatives, while Albert Reynolds met openly with Gerry Adams and John Hume in Dublin.[149]

The public and media gaze turned towards loyalist paramilitarism. Their response was neither as positive nor as rapid as many had hoped. Indeed loyalist paramilitaries remained active, the UDA killing a Catholic civilian less than a day into the IRA cessation, while three days later a UVF car bomb exploded outside a Sinn Féin advice centre in Belfast. After a wait of some six weeks, however, and following much internal discussion, the Combined Loyalist Military Command (CLMC), representing the UDA, UVF and Red Hand Commando (RHC) also called a ceasefire, declaring: 'We are on the threshold of a new and exciting beginning with our battles in future being political battles fought on the side of honest decency and democracy.'[150]

Events continued apace, driven by what Paul Dixon has identified as a series of highly orchestrated and planned engagements,[151] and protracted negotiations eventually precipitated a general agreement on 22 February 1995. When this was drawn up as *Frameworks for the Future* (commonly known as the Frameworks Documents) it contained proposals to create more formal relations between the two governments and for a devolved political administration in Northern Ireland. Despite being described as 'the nadir of political development for Unionists',[152] its main proposals formed the core of the Agreement, eventually signed some three years later, although by then the Irish dimension had been lessened somewhat.

Negotiations began in Stormont Castle between all the major political parties except Sinn Féin,[153] excluded following the planting of an IRA bomb in London's Docklands on 9 February 1996 that killed two and caused immense economic damage. The broad parameters of the talks on 10 June 1996 reflected the key aspiration of manufacturing agreed political space, which would allow civil society to develop and challenge the existing ethno-political blocs. The strategy designed to bring this about was the development of a pluralistic polity that openly recognised the equal worth of the opposing traditions of unionism and nationalism and creating a parity of esteem between them.[154]

The implementation of the strategy was not made easier, however, when less than a week after the talks broke up the IRA unleashed another massive explosion in the busiest shopping district of central Manchester. There followed an extremely politically turbulent twenty-two months before the process produced a multi-party accord, the Belfast Agreement, which on 10 April 1998 was supported by representatives of all of Northern Ireland's major political parties, and the British and Irish governments.[155]

Central was the development of an agreed devolved administration with legislative and executive powers.[156] The idea of a devolved government was overwhelmingly approved in dual referenda held in both jurisdictions on the island. In Northern Ireland over 70 per cent of voters supported the accord, receiving almost unanimous backing among Catholics voters, while among Protestants the votes were almost evenly split.[157]

Following this result, an election was called on 25 June 1998 to choose 108 Members of the new Legislative Assembly (MLAs). The election saw the UUP emerge as overall winners with twenty-eight seats, followed by the SDLP with twenty-four. The DUP were elected in twenty constituencies, while Sinn Féin gained eighteen seats, and the Alliance Party and the UKUP five each. The PUP and the Women's Coalition[158] each had two representatives elected, with the overall total made up by three Independent Unionists.

The workings of the devolved Assembly proved to be far from straightforward, however. Although there was some evidence of cooperation between the main political blocs outside executive level,[159] it took almost a decade for a meaningful devolved Executive to come to fruition as originally planned. In the meantime, the Assembly and its interlinked institutions suffered from a whole series of disruptions and suspensions – beginning in February 2000, followed by those in August and September 2001 and then again in October 2002. Moreover, throughout this time, even when the Assembly was operational it was often embroiled in arguments over highly divisive issues such as the future of policing, the display of the union flag on public buildings, the future of paramilitary prisoners released as part of the settlement, and the decommissioning of paramilitary weapons.

The issues clearly reflected much wider schisms in the political culture of Northern Ireland. While Sinn Féin believed they had a place as of right in any future government, expressed through a mandate from its voters, many unionists still regarded republicans as untrustworthy. For many unionists, demands from Sinn Féin to be treated as a 'normal' political party could not be met without a long transition period during which they could demonstrate their transformation from political violence to electoral politics.

The gulf between the political visions and desires of the DUP and Sinn Féin remained ever apparent. Even following an IRA announcement that its armed campaign was over and that its units had been ordered to 'dump arms', there were voices of concern from within unionism regarding the transparency of such actions, that evidence should be made available and further demands that unionists should be able to appoint witnesses to oversee such events.

REORGANISING UNIONISM

Throughout the above, unionist political ideology was consistently challenged and contested from within, bringing about new forms of political expression. It is important to identify and categorise the shape of these. A useful starting point is to consider McGarry and O'Leary's claim that British ideology has both civic and ethnic components.[160] These strands can usefully be separated out within unionism. Cash, for example, expresses the difference between what he terms exclusive and inclusive constructs of unionism, the latter representing a more liberal form and political direction.[161]

Similar distinctions are drawn by Aughey, who suggests that divisions within unionism can be understood as resting on tensions between 'fearful' and 'confident' groupings.[162] Building on such ideas, Porter importantly identifies the development of differing forms of unionism, which he terms cultural, liberal, and civic.[163] Here I will briefly outline these core constructs along with what I term 'intellectual unionism'.

CULTURAL UNIONISM

The politics of cultural unionism will be considered in much more detail later in the book, especially when we look at the politics of the DUP. Briefly, however, cultural unionism celebrates the values of Protestantism and the Union within a distinct ethnic identity. It frames a self-perception based upon common religious and cultural practices; a self-definition that it represents a Protestant British way of life as its core; and promotes an identity based upon a culture that is seen as distinct on the island.

Thus, central to the ideology of cultural unionism is the notion that Northern Ireland has and should be shaped within the boundaries of a Protestant British frame. This is often given its shape by reference to 'Protestant history' as cultural unionism draws upon and incorporates identifiable social memories – ranging from the massacre of Protestants in 1641 to the UWC strike in 1974,[164] and from the formation of the state to mass protests against the AIA – to construct a particular understanding of its political world.

Porter argues that the power of such symbolism to mobilise is often underestimated. Further, he points out how difficult it is for unionists to break the bonds of cultural unionism, and how the institutions upon which civic unionists seek to draw are still often perceived as biased towards cultural unionism.[165] Always running counter to the development of a civic unionism is the active promotion of cultural and ethnic unionism drawing on established frames of meaning and appealing to established understandings of myths, culture and religion within unionism.

Cultural unionism gives primacy to Ulster above Britain (as in Todd's Ulster loyalist tradition) and attempts to identify and give emphasis to the cultural distinctiveness and historical separation of Northern Ireland.[166] This form of cultural unionism, which finds its clearest expression within the DUP but is also deeply located in other groupings such as large sections of the Orange Order, will be considered in much more detail in Chapter 4.

CIVIC UNIONISM

Much of the new thinking within unionism manifested through expressions of civic unionism. At its nucleus are strategies to build pluralist institutions to which all political traditions, including nationalism and unionism, can give allegiance. This also involves constructing a positive new symbolism that breaks from traditional communal loyalties and which can gain cross-community support. Aughey once described this as the 'positive voice' for which unionism had long waited,[167] something that could be embraced by all of Northern Ireland's citizens.

Civic unionism thus seeks to turn away from traditional unionist values to construct a politics that embraces both communities within Northern Ireland. This was clearly seen, for example, in recent efforts of the UUP to use civic unionism in an attempt to attract more Catholics to the party. Also central to civic unionism is the creation of institutions that are deemed to be widely acceptable to both communities in Northern Ireland.

As Porter, perhaps the strongest proponent of the civic unionist model, argues, to survive unionism must adopt a more flexible form. As he puts it, this would involve developing a situation where people:

> ... as citizens identify with particular institutions and practices that define crucial elements of their polity's way of life and are regarded as the common possession of all rather than the exclusive preserve of one group, tribe or tradition.[168]

For Porter, Northern Ireland is a place where Britishness and Irishness collide and mutate into different forms. In promoting civic unionism Porter recognises the 'shameless maintenance of discriminatory practices against Catholics under the Stormont government'[169] and suggests that because of the structure of social relationships within Northern Ireland, even liberal unionism developed a conception of politics that was too narrow.[170] In its place he advocates the deeper engagement of unionism in civil society, to promote a form of social and political organisation where unionism and nationalism can discover common ground to transcend communal divisions.[171]

Porter provides much of the conceptual basis for new unionism by arguing that in order to bring about a pluralist Northern Ireland the state must adopt new political and legal practices and develop new socio-economic institutions to encourage the emergence of a more active (and differently organised) civil society. It is only as 'nationalists as well as unionists are persuaded fully to invest in political life ... that an identity based on concerted actions become conceivable'[172] and primacy will be given not to the union itself but rather 'the quality of social and political life' it brings about.[173]

It can now readily be seen how heavily Trimble drew upon some of these strands of thinking in creating the parameters of new unionism and his formulation of a 'pluralist parliament for a pluralist people'[174] in Northern Ireland. The notion of a new inclusive unionism, for example, was central to the 2001 UUP election manifesto. Again drawing on this, the basis of the UUP's vision as projected during that campaign was a sense of inclusive Britishness defined as resting upon a desire to engage directly in the affairs of the British nation.[175] As we shall see in the next chapter, however, Trimble was unable to develop a coherent political programme to make civic unionism the dominant political force within unionism.

Essentially, new unionism sought to make Porter's plan a reality by creating a sense of accommodation and political unity through overtly recognising difference. The political strategy of new unionism, however, highlighted just how problematic the task was to locate the notion of civic unionism within strategies that made it politically viable and appealing to the wider unionist electorate. Porter himself was aware of this problem and the difficulty in implanting the civic model as a core understanding within unionism because it 'does not share the priorities of cultural and liberal unionists'.[176]

LIBERAL UNIONISM

Another set of ideas has emerged that can best be categorised as liberal unionism. Porter's conceptualisation of liberal unionism lies close to Todd's 'Ulster–British' tradition, and what Chris Farrington argues is best understood as 'the secular element to Unionism'.[177] This frames its point of reference as the entire UK, actively promoting the notion that Northern Ireland should be treated as just another part of a multi-national, multi-ethnic state with a polity based on equal citizenship and a non-sectarian form of political contract. Such views have largely developed within an identifiable socio-economic context and an expanded unionist middle class, which has:

> ... attracted the titans of the British high street – Tesco, Sainsbury, Debenhams, Halfords, Currys. They read *The Times* or the *Mail*, not the *News Letter*. They prefer their news read by Huw Edwards, not Rose O'Neill. They no longer look on Ireland as hostile territory but a nice location for a holiday break.[178]

While fully accepting Coulter's analysis of the paradoxical position of the unionist middle classes throughout the conflict as on the one hand marginalised by the British state while largely remaining employed in the state-led public sector, and his further assertion that the majority response of middle-class unionists has been to absent themselves from politics,[179] that section of Northern Irish society has not been completely devoid of political expression. The driving logic of their position is a belief that Northern Ireland should be indistinct in its political governance and economic position from any other area within the UK.

One manifestation of liberal unionism has been found in the political interventions of Robert McCartney, who over several decades has consistently criticised what he terms 'traditional unionism' and in particular the UUP for its failure to develop meaningful political policy. In its place McCartney claims the UUP relied on an inbuilt unionist majority and a cultivated paranoia about the constitutional question to maintain control under Stormont.[180] One result of this constructed constitutional anxiety was the development of extremism and sectarian loyalism.

It is this which McCartney has sought to challenge, arguing that if the Union is to be preserved then its benefits to all must be made transparent, and unionism must move itself away from its sectarian past to present a more moderate, non-sectarian liberal face. In so doing unionists must resist the pressure to express themselves through cultural unionism.[181] This has strong appeal to sections of the unionist middle class, especially those whose sense of Britishness rests in what they recognise as the reality of a civic UK state rather than an expression of overt attachment to cultural icons of Britishness which have long since ceased to be meaningful to them. Hence, for example, McCartney's advocacy of the Campaign for Equal Citizenship (CEC) in the mid-1980s and its support for the organisation of other British political parties in Northern Ireland.

That said, McCartney has in recent years taken a distinct stance in consistently aligning with those groupings opposing the Agreement and the politics emerging from it, arguing that its main political dynamic lay in a resolution of the conflict between Sinn Féin/IRA and the British state, in order to protect the British mainland.[182] Hence, for him the peace process and the subsequent political arrangements have been little other than 'a disguise for marketing a political settlement ... regardless of how unpalatable it may be to the pro-Union majority'.[183]

Thus, McCartney argues that one consequence of the political process was to raise Irish nationalist expectations to unrealistic heights, in turn deepening unionists' resentment 'by an increasing awareness that their culture, their education, their tradition, the future values of their children, and the symbols of their British identity are being sys-tematically eroded'.[184] This is seen as part of a grand strategy in which the British and Irish governments, the United States administration and the SDLP (and latterly the DUP) were all seen as complicit in an attempt to provide a blueprint for a united Ireland, which, if successful, would render ultimate consent to a transfer of *de jure* sovereignty inevitable.

From this perspective the UK government sought to persuade the pro-Union majority that the sacrifice of their British identity was a fair exchange for the IRA ceasefire.[185] For McCartney, armed republicanism has negotiated a ceasefire bargain with the British state, part of which involved persuading unionists to mutate their political identity 'into that of the State to whom sovereignty over their territory is intended to be passed'.[186] McCartney suggests that the foundations for this process were laid with the AIA through a transfer of executive power to the Republic, was heightened with the Joint Declaration and then taken to its high point with the Agreement.[187] All of these initiatives were designed to protect 'Great Britain's economic interests rather than ... to secure a democratic and permanent peace'.[188]

At the crux of such views is McCartney's desire to project unionism as a rational political choice that benefits the vast majority, if not all of Northern Ireland's citizens, through the rights that such citizenship brings.[189] McCartney consistently challenged the politics of the peace process as something designed to dupe unionists,[190] through a process that merely heightened the imbalance between unequivocal conces-sions made to Sinn Féin and the vague commitments offered to union-ists. Such views eventually resulted in McCartney's direct opposition to the DUP in the contest for the 2007 Assembly elections.

INTELLECTUAL UNIONISM

Another reasonably recent manifestation within unionism has been the active defence and promotion of the Union by an identifiable grouping of academics and writers.[191] While in no sense marking a coherent or structured output, this intellectual thrust was brought into focus by the Cadogan Group, the core members of which has included the political scientists Arthur Aughey and Paul Bew, economists Graham Gudgin and Patrick Roche, journalist David Kennedy, and Arthur Green, a retired civil servant who suggests that 'Irishness' is a false social con-struct upon which the rationale of cultural difference, and ultimately the Irish state, depends.[192]

Drawing on such ideas, a key task for such writers is to counter the main arguments forwarded by Irish republicans and their 'dogma' that the Union is merely a negotiable political arrangement.[193] The position has found strong support among populist writers such as the polemicist Ruth Dudley Edwards and journalist Eoghan Harris (later elected as an Irish senator), both of whom have added their intellectual weight to the unionist cause. Harris has recently proposed that the UUP and DUP should merge to maximise the unionist vote,[194] while underpinning the views of both is the idea that unionists are extremely poor ambassadors for their own cause and are constantly put on the back foot by more wily and worldly republican propaganda.

These arguments reach crescendo in the projection of unionists as 'a wonderful, warm-hearted community'[195] that has lost out to the slick propaganda machine of Irish republicanism.[196] The intellectual defence of unionism can be further identified in the writings of Patrick Roche and Esmond Birnie, who suggest that the 'professional mendacity of government ministers' and the media's 'mawkish rhetoric of the so-called peace process'[197] have obscured the reality of Ulster's betrayal. For Roche and Birnie this has come about because unionists have failed to successfully challenge the intellectual creditability and political foundations of Irish nationalism. Hence, they openly set about amassing arguments to counter this failing within unionism and to highlight what they see as the fundamental flaws in the Irish nationalist position.

For Roche and Birnie, arguments supporting Irish nationalism can be reduced to a form of geographical determinism to produce a national identity, and they directly challenge the idea that unification would bring about any real economic benefit to the people of Ireland. Roche and Birnie further suggest that Irish unity 'would for decades – if not indeed permanently – deprive the inhabitants of the island of an acceptable level of economic well-being'.[198] They state the case as follows:

> The vague expectations of constitutional nationalists on the issue of economic viability and the patent absurdity of Sinn Féin economic policy represent a refusal to face economic reality ... there is nothing in either the present situation ... or the history of the Irish economy since 1920 to suggest that a unified Irish state could survive at an acceptable level of economic welfare without massive and open-ended external subventions from the British exchequer.[199]

Wilson suggests that no set of arguments – cultural, geographical or historical – can justify the alleged unity of the 'Irish nation'.[200] Thus, the Irish nationalist position merely represents 'the politics of the absurd', and part of unionism's weakness lies in its failure to 'undermine the intellectual creditability of Irish nationalism'.[201] Indeed, as Roche and

Birnie put it, there are 'no criteria of national identity which can be used to sustain the core Nationalist claim that there is a single nation on the island if Ireland'.[202] Such views even caused Arthur Green to propose that Ireland is a 'false construct' within which unionists continue to be regarded as 'colonists' at best.[203]

In support, Denis Kennedy argues that the definition of Irish nationalism and identity has been constructed in ways to bond together nation and state.[204] This makes the construction of 'Irishness' as meaning anything other than direct allegiance to a thirty-two-county Irish Republic almost impossible. Kennedy's analysis reinforces the core unionist belief that those in the northeast of Ireland remain a distinct community, who differ from the people of the rest of the island in core matters such as religion, place of origin, cultural, social and national identity.

Taken together, these works represent an inherent belief of the superiority of the Union in political, cultural, social, economic, structural and even moral terms. As Foster puts it, they seek to:

> ... repudiate a notion that has been a dogma with Irish Republicans since 1920 and that, worrisomely, has lately threatened to take hold among British political parties and media – namely, that the union of Northern Ireland with Great Britain is merely a political arrangement (and an inconvenient and even somewhat bogus one) and therefore rightly vulnerable to manipulation, diminishment and, in the end, extinction. The idea of the Union rests on the proposition that the Union is a social, cultural and economic fabric, with reality and history as its warp and weft.[205]

These discourses developed by the intellectual defenders of the Union are increasingly reflected in broadening unionist readings and specific political projects such as 'liberal' or 'civic' unionisms. Liam O'Dowd[206] lists a wide range of writers including Paul Bew, Brian Barton, Dennis Kennedy, Richard English and Graham Walker, alongside the politician Robert McCartney as representative of new unionist voices.

Although the above commentators have produced a plentiful defence for the Union, certainly more so than previously existed, and while at times they present extremely articulate arguments, at their core remains a simple mirror image of that which they oppose. Moreover, in their belief that 'policies which encourage minority aspirations for and expectations of constitutional change are destabilising',[207] they suggest that they see clear boundaries to the limits of political change with the existing constitutional arrangements.

CONCLUSION

The political culture of unionism remains complex and multi-layered, reflected in the range of political reactions across unionism to current events. Aughey suggests that the signing of the Agreement drew three broad types of responses from unionists.[208] The first was apathy and resignation to being ignored by UK governments; second, a stubborn resistance to change; and, third a pragmatic response that sought to ensure that they could get the best out of the situation. In this context, some have projected a fluid vision of unionism and sought to locate its composition in a more rational and intellectually based set of arguments than have previously existed.

The resulting new unionism was not homogeneous, having different locations in the notions of UK citizenship, economic interpretations, senses of Britishness and cultural and political identities. This led some to argue strongly for the political modernisation of unionism, while for others cultural unionism marked a more meaningful response to fears that unionist and British identity were being eroded. The next chapter considers how these ideas manifested in political arguments around the emergence of new unionism.

NOTES

1. Cochrane, *Unionist Politics*, p.35.
2. Robinson, P., 'Speech at the Young Democrat conference, 29 January 2000'. Archived at: http://www.dup.org.uk.
3. For a useful review of the debates here, see Farrington, C., 'Ulster unionism and the Irish historiography debate', *Irish Studies Review*, 11, 3 (2003), pp.251–61.
4. See Finlayson, 'Loyalist political identity after the peace'; McAuley, J.W., 'Surrender?: Loyalist perceptions of conflict settlement', in J. Anderson and J. Goodman (eds), *(Dis)Agreeing Ireland* (London: Pluto Press, 1998), pp.193–210.
5. See Entman, R.M., 'Framing: toward clarification of a fractured paradigm', *Journal of Communication*, 43, 4 (1993), pp.51–8; Gamson, W., 'The social psychology of collective action', in A. Morris and C. McClurg (eds), *Frontiers in Social Movement Theory* (New Haven: Yale University Press, 1992), pp.53–76; Garner, R. *Contemporary Movements and Ideologies* (New York: McGraw-Hill, 1996), pp.16–17, 56–61; Johnston, H. 'A methodology for frame analysis: from discourse to cognitive schemata', in H. Johnston and B. Klandermas (eds), *Social Movements and Culture* (London: UCL Press, 1995), pp.217–46; McAdam, D. and Rucht, D., 'The cross-national diffusion of movement ideas', *Annals of the American Academy of Political and Social Sciences*, no. 528 (1993), pp.56–74; Snow, D.A. and Benford, R.D., 'Master frames and cycles of protest', in A. Morris and C. McClurg Mueller (eds), *Frontiers In Social Movement Theory* (New Haven: Yale University Press, 1992), pp.133–55; Snow, D.A., Rochford, B.E., Worden, S. and Benford, R.D., 'Frame alignment processes, micromobilization, and movement participation', *American Sociological Review*, no. 45 (1992), pp.787–801; Tarrow, S. *Power in Movement: Social Movements, Collective Action and Politics* (Cambridge: Cambridge University Press, 1994), pp.118–34.
6. Goffman, E., *Frame Analysis: An Essay on the Organization of Experience* (London: Harper and Row, 1974).
7. Donati, P.R., 'Political discourse analysis', in M. Diani and R. Eyerman (eds), *Studying Collective Action* (London: Sage, 1992), pp.141–2.
8. Della Porta, D. and Diani, M., *Social Movements: An Introduction* (Oxford: Blackwell, 1999), p.69.

9. Snow, D. and Benford, R., 'Ideology, frame resonance, and participant mobilization', *International Social Movement Research*, no. 1 (1988), pp.197–217; Swidler, A., 'Culture in action: symbols and strategies', *American Sociological Review*, 51, 2 (1986), pp.273–86.
10. Entman, 'Framing: toward clarification of a fractured paradigm', p.52.
11. Hartman, T.K., 'Talking the gun out of Irish politics: framing the peace process', *paper presented at the 44th Annual International Studies Association Convention*, Oregon, USA, 2003.
12. Bew, P., Gibbon, P. and Patterson, H. *Northern Ireland 1921–1996: Political Forces and Social Classes* (London: Serif, 1995).
13. Boyce, D.G., 'Weary patriots: Ireland and the making of unionism', in Boyce and O'Day, *Defenders of the Union*, p.34.
14. See Gillespie, N., Lovett T. and Garner, W., *Youth Work and Working Class Youth Culture: Rules and Resistance in West Belfast* (Buckingham: Open University Press, 1992), pp.135–68; Jarman, N., *Material Conflicts: Parades and Visual Displays in Northern Ireland* (Oxford: Berg, 1997).
15. Fentress, J. and Wickham, C., *Social Memory* (Oxford: Blackwell, 1992), p.25.
16. See Druckman, J.N., 'On the limits of framing effects: who can frame?', *The Journal of Politics*, no. 63 (2001), pp.1041–66.
17. Entman, 'Framing: toward clarification of a fractured paradigm', p.55.
18. Segvic, I., 'The framing of politics: a content analysis of three Croatian newspapers', *Gazette: The International Journal for Communication Studies*, 67, 5 (2005), pp.469–88.
19. Ruane and Todd, *The Dynamics of Conflict in Northern Ireland*, pp.88–9.
20. Cited in Hennessey, T., *Dividing Ireland, World War One and Partition* (London: Routledge, 1998), p.18.
21. Gibbon, P., *The Origins of Ulster Unionism: The Formation of Popular Protestant Politics and Ideology in Nineteenth-Century Ireland* (Manchester: Manchester University Press, 1975), p.130.
22. Reproduced in Carlton, C. (ed.), *Bigotry and Blood: Documents on the Ulster Troubles* (Chicago: Nelson-Hall, 1977), p.65.
23. Liechty, J., *Roots of Sectarianism in Ireland: Chronology and Reflections* (Belfast: Irish Inter-Church Meeting, 1993), p.40.
24. To give a flavour of the mood, on 11 May 1912 the *News Letter* reported a speech by Sir Edward Carson at a banquet in London as follows: 'Among those who also attended the banquet the most notable were the Duke of Somerset, Lord Londonderry and the Earls of Ancaster, Halsbury and Malmesbury, as well as some 30 MPs and representatives of "the United Liberal Unionist, United Empire, Junior Constitutional and Patriots Clubs". Sir Edward told those at the banquet that the question of Home Rule was one on which the Unionists of Ulster would not be swayed; only by refusing to accept Home Rule, said Carson, could "the gravest disasters" to the country be averted. He also warned the Government that any threat of coercion would turn Ulster even more against the administration and that they would make Ulster "a hostile part" of the empire. He denied that Unionists did not have an alternative. They did, said Carson, and that alternative was the Union.' (reproduced in Armitage, D., 'Through the Archives', *News Letter*, 11 May 2009).
25. For a detailed review of events during this period see, Stewart, A.T.Q., *The Ulster Crisis: Resistance to Home Rule 1912–1914* (Belfast: Blackstaff Press, 1997).
26. Tonge, J., *The New Northern Irish Politics*, p.147.
27. McKittrick, D. and McVea, D., *Making Sense of the Troubles* (London: Penguin Books, 2003), p.236.
28. See Brearton, F., 'Dancing unto death: perceptions of the Somme, the Titanic and Ulster Protestantism', *Irish Review*, no. 20 (1997), pp.89–103; Officer, D. and Walker, G., 'Protestant Ulster: ethno-history, memory and contemporary prospects, *National Identities*, 2, 3 (2000), pp.293–307.
29. The battle is, for example, commemorated annually in a major Orange Order parade organised in east Belfast and in wreath-laying ceremonies at Belfast City Hall Cenotaph.
30. Brown, K., '"Our father organization": the cult of the Somme and the unionist "golden age"' in modern Ulster loyalist commemoration', *The Round Table – The Commonwealth Journal of International Affairs*, 96, 393 (2007), pp.707–23; Graham, 'The past in the present'.
31. See, for example, DVD recording produced by Great Wars Historical and Culture Society, 'The Ulster Volunteer Force, 1912–2002'.
32. Rosenbaum, S., *Against Home Rule: The Case for the Union* (London: Frederick Warne and Co., 1912).

33. Ibid., p.13.
34. Cited in ibid., p.14.
35. From a vast range of historical accounts see, for example, Bardon, J., *A History of Ulster* (Belfast: Blackstaff Press, 2001); Foster, R.F., *Modern Ireland 1600–1972* (London: Penguin Books, 1990); Lee, J.J., *Ireland 1912–85: Politics and Society* (Cambridge: Cambridge University Press, 1990); Lyons, F.S.L., *Ireland Since the Famine* (London: Collins Fontana, 1982).
36. See Anderson, *Imagined Communities*; Gellner, E., *Nations and Nationalism* (Oxford: Blackwell, 1993); Hobsbawn, E. and Ranger, T. (eds), *The Invention of Tradition* (Cambridge: Cambridge University Press, 1983).
37. Delanty, G., 'Negotiating the peace in Northern Ireland', p.258.
38. Buckland, P., *Irish Unionism, 1885–1922* (London: Historical Association, 1973), p.30.
39. Ward, P., *Unionism in the United Kingdom, 1918–1974* (Basingstoke: Palgrave Macmillan, 2005), p.127.
40. O'Dowd, L., Rolston, B. and Tomlinson, M., *Northern Ireland: Between Civil Rights and Civil War* (London: CSE Books, 1980), p.30.
41. Aughey, A., 'Unionism', in A. Aughey and D. Morrow (eds), *Northern Ireland Politics* (London: Longman, 1996).
42. MacDougall, S., 'The projection of Northern Ireland to Great Britain and abroad, 1921–1939', in P. Catterall and S. MacDougall (eds), *The Northern Ireland Problem in British Politics* (Basingstoke: Macmillan, 1996), pp.29–46.
43. Buckland, *Irish Unionism*.
44. Hennessey, T., *A History of Northern Ireland, 1920–1996* (London: Macmillan, 1996).
45. Follis, B., *A State Under Siege: The Establishment of Northern Ireland, 1920–1925* (Oxford: Clarendon, 1995).
46. McAuley, J.W. and Tonge, J., '"For God and for the Crown": contemporary political and social attitudes among Orange Order members in Northern Ireland', *Political Psychology*, 28, 1 (2007), pp.33–54.
47. Farrington, C. and Walker, G., 'Ideological content and institutional frameworks: unionist identities in Northern Ireland and Scotland', *Irish Studies Review*, 17, 2 (2009), p.143.
48. Probert, B., *Beyond Orange and Green: The Political Economy of the Northern Ireland Crisis* (London: Zed Press, 1978).
49. Reid, C., 'Protestant challenges to the "Protestant state": Ulster unionism and independent unionism in Northern Ireland, 1921–1939,' *Twentieth Century British History*, 19, 4 (2008), pp.419–45.
50. Bloomfield, K., *Stormont in Crisis: A Memoir* (Belfast: Blackstaff Press, 1994), p.63.
51. Sloan, S., 'A hard youth from the Hammer', *Fortnight*, no. 185 (1978), p.18.
52. See Edwards, A., 'Democratic socialism and sectarianism: the Northern Ireland Labour Party and Progressive Unionist Party compared', *Politics*, 27, 1 (2007), pp.24–31; Finlay, 'Defeatism and Northern Protestant "identity"', pp.14–15.
53. Cited in the *News Letter*, 11 February 1962.
54. Cited in Wright, F., *Two Lands on One Soil: Ulster Politics Before Home Rule* (Dublin: Gill and Macmillan, 1996), p.215.
55. Wright, F., 'Protestant ideology and politics in Ulster', *Journal of European Sociology*, 14, 2 (1973), pp.213–80.
56. Edwards, A., *A History of the Northern Ireland Labour Party* (Manchester: Manchester University Press, 2009), p.220.
57. Ibid., pp.216–19.
58. See Boulton, D., *The UVF 1966–73: An Anatomy of Loyalist Rebellion* (Dublin: Torc Books, 1973); Cusack, J. and McDonald, H., *UVF* (Dublin: Poolbeg, 1997).
59. Teague, P., 'Discrimination and fair employment in Northern Ireland', in P. Teague (ed.), *The Economy of Northern Ireland* (London: Lawrence & Wishart, 1993).
60. Whyte, J., *Interpreting Northern Ireland* (Oxford: Clarendon Press, 1990), p.64.
61. See Kingsley, P., *Londonderry Revisited: A Loyalist Analysis of the Civil Rights Controversy* (Belfast: Belfast Publications, 1989); Wilson, T., *Ulster: Conflict and Consent* (Oxford: Basil Blackwell, 1989), pp.210–11.
62. Birnie, E., 'Speech at a debate hosted by the Literary and Historical Society of University College Dublin', Belfast: Ulster Unionist Party, 24 October 2005.
63. Purdie, B., *Politics in the Streets: The Origins of the Civil Rights Movement in Northern Ireland* (Belfast: Blackstaff Press, 1990).
64. Coakley, J., 'Nation identity in Northern Ireland: stability or change?' *Nations and*

Nationalism, 13, 4 (2007), pp.573–97.
65. See Ó'Dochartaigh, N., *From Civil Rights to Armalites: Derry and the Birth of the Irish Troubles* (Cork: Cork University Press, 1997); Purdie, B., *Politics in the Streets: The Origins of the Civil Rights Movement in Northern Ireland* (Belfast: Blackstaff Press, 1990).
66. Purdie, B., 'Was the civil rights movement a republican/communist conspiracy?' *Irish Political Studies*, no. 3 (1988), pp.33–41.
67. Boyce, D.G., *The Irish Question and British Politics, 1868–1986* (Basingstoke: Macmillan, 1988), p.106.
68. Mulholland, M., *Northern Ireland at the Crossroads: Ulster Unionism in the O'Neill Years, 1960–69* (Basingstoke: Palgrave, 2000).
69. Cochrane, F., 'Meddling at the crossroads: the decline and fall of Terence O'Neill', in English and Walker, *Unionism in Modern Ireland* (Gill and Macmillan: Dublin, 1996).
70. Hennessey, T., *Northern Ireland: The Origins of the Troubles* (Dublin: Gill and Macmillan, 2005), pp.237–85.
71. Patterson, H., *The Politics of Illusion: A Political History of the IRA* (London: Serif, 1997).
72. See Bell, J.B., *The Secret Army: The IRA 1916–1979* (Dublin: Irish Academic Press, 1979); Kelley, K., *The Longest War: Northern Ireland and the IRA* (Dingle: Brandon, 1982); Taylor, P., *Provos: The IRA and Sinn Féin* (London: Bloomsbury, 1997).
73. Downing, T., *The Troubles: The Background to the Question of Northern Ireland* (London: MacDonald Futura), p.156.
74. See Bishop, P. and Mallie, E., *The Provisional IRA* (London: Corgi, 1988); English, R., *Armed Struggle: The History of the IRA* (London: Pan, 2004); Moloney, E., *A Secret History of the IRA* (London: Penguin, 2002).
75. Bleakley, D., *Faulkner: Conflict and Consent in Irish Politics* (London: The Alden Press, 1974).
76. Faulkner, B., *Memoirs of a Statesman* (London: Weidenfeld and Nicolson, 1978), p.164.
77. Tonge, J., *Northern Ireland: Conflict and Change* (London: Prentice Hall), pp.42–3.
78. Faulkner, B., *Memoirs of a Statesman* (London, Weidenfeld and Nicolson, 1978).
79. Cited in Galligher, J.F. and DeGregory, J.L., *Violence in Northern Ireland: Understanding Protestant Perspectives* (Dublin: Gill and Macmillan, 1985), p.117.
80. *Belfast Telegraph*, 29 March 1972.
81. Wilson, R., 'Northern Ireland: what's going wrong' (Queen's University Belfast: Institute of Governance, Public Policy and Social Research, Working Paper, QU/GOV/1, 2003), p.8.
82. Boyle, K., 'Northern Ireland: Dismantling the Protestant State', *New Blackfriars*, 52, 608 (1971), pp.12–18.
83. McKeown, C., *The Passion of Peace* (Belfast: Blackstaff Press, 1984), p.44.
84. Nelson, S., *Ulster's Uncertain Defender: Loyalists and the Northern Ireland Conflict.* (Belfast: Appletree Press, 1984), p104.
85. Flackes, W.D., *Northern Ireland: A Political Directory* (London: Ariel Books, 1980), p.229.
86. Wood, I.S. *Crimes of Loyalty: A History of the UDA* (Edinburgh: Edinburgh University Press, 2006), pp.102–3.
87. Dillon, M. and Lehane, D. *Political Murder in Northern Ireland* (Harmondsworth: Penguin Books, 1973).
88. Dixon, *Northern Ireland: The Politics of War and Peace*, pp.132–3.
89. Brown, D., 'Loyalists turn Assembly into a farce', *Guardian*, 1 August 1973.
90. Anderson, D., *14 Days in May: The Inside Story of the Loyalist Strike of 1974* (Dublin: Gill and Macmillan, 1994).
91. The UVF finally admitted responsibility for the attacks in 1993.
92. Tiernan, J., *The Dublin and Monaghan Bombings and the Murder Triangle* (published by the author, 2002).
93. Fisk, R., *The Point of No Return: The Strike Which Broke the British in Ulster* (London: Andre Deutsch, 1975).
94. See Buscher, S. and Ling, B., *Mairéad Corrigan and Betty Williams: Making Peace in Northern Ireland* (New York: The Feminist Press, 1999); Deutsch, R., *Mairéad Corrigan/Betty Williams* (New York: Barron's Educational, 1977); McKeown, *The Passion of Peace.*
95. Quinn, D., *Understanding Northern Ireland* (Manchester: Baseline Books, 1993), p.62.
96. Walker and English, *Unionism in Modern Ireland*, p.xi.
97. Kennedy, D., *The Widening Gulf: Northern Attitudes to the Independent Irish State, 1919–1949* (Belfast: Blackstaff Press, 1988).
98. Letourneau, J., 'The current great narrative of Quebecois identity', in V.Y. Mudimbe (ed.), *Nations, Identities, Cultures* (Durham, NC: Duke University Press, 1997), pp.1039–53.

99. Delanty, 'Negotiating the peace in Northern Ireland', p.259.
100. Mitchel, P., *Evangelicalism and National Identity in Ulster 1921–1998* (Oxford: Oxford University Press, 2003), p.614.
101. Wichert, S., *Northern Ireland Since 1945* (London: Longman, 1991), p.179.
102. See Darby, J. and MacGinty, R., 'Northern Ireland: long cold peace', in J. Darby and R. MacGinty (eds), *The Management of the Peace Process* (Basingstoke: Macmillan, 2000), p.61; Tonge, J., 'From Sunningdale to the Good Friday Agreement: creating devolved government in Northern Ireland', *Contemporary British History*, 14, 3 (2000), pp.39–60.
103. Boyce, *The Irish Question and British Politics*, p.120.
104. McAllister, I., '"The Armalite and the ballot box": Sinn Féin's electoral strategy in Northern Ireland', *Electoral Studies*, no. 23 (2004), pp.123–42.
105. *New Ireland Forum Report* (Dublin: The Stationery Office, 1984).
106. Smith, J., *Making the Peace in Ireland* (London: Pearson Education, 2002).
107. Kenny, A., *The Road to Hillsborough: The Shaping of the Anglo-Irish Agreement* (London: Pergamon, 1986), p.103.
108. Allister, J., *The Unionist Case: The Forum Report Answered* (Belfast: DUP, 1984), p.8.
109. Cited in *Fortnight*, no. 210, p.7.
110. Robinson, P., *Ulster in Peril: An Exposure of the Dublin Summit* (Belfast: DUP, 1985), p.5.
111. See Hadden, T. and Boyle, K., *The Anglo-Irish Agreement: Commentary, Text and Official Review* (London: Maxwell and Sweet, 1985); Kenny, *The Road to Hillsborough*, pp.96–104.
112. Bew and Patterson, *The State in Northern Ireland*, p.49.
113. *Grand Committee of the Northern Ireland Assembly First Report*, cited in Hadden and Boyle, *The Anglo-Irish Agreement*, p.25.
114. Smith, P., *Opportunity Lost: A Unionist View of the Report of the Forum for a New Ireland* (Belfast: no publisher, 1984), p.6.
115. Cox, W.H., 'Public opinion and the Anglo-Irish Agreement', *Government and Opposition*, 22, 3 (1987), p.339.
116. Cited in Millar, F., *David Trimble: The Price of Peace* (Dublin: The Liffey Press, 2004), p.49.
117. Morrison, D., 'Confusing and unhappy times for loyalists', *Fortnight*, no. 225 (1985), p.7.
118. Connolly, M. and Loughlin, J., 'Reflections on the Anglo-Irish Agreement', *Government and Opposition*, 21, 2 (1986), p.55.
119. Murray, D., 'Tracking Progress', *Democratic Dialogue*, no. 11 (June 1999).
120. *Joint Unionist Election Bulletin*, January 1986, p.1.
121. Powell, E., *Unionist Voice*, February 1992, cited in Aughey, A., 'Contemporary unionist politics', in B. Barton and P.J. Roche (eds), *The Northern Ireland Question: Perspectives and Policies* (Aldershot: Avebury, 1994), p.63.
122. McAuley, J.W., '(Re) constructing Ulster loyalism: political responses to the "peace process"', *Irish Journal of Sociology*, no. 6 (1996), pp.165–82; McAuley, J.W., 'Flying the one-winged bird: Ulster unionism and the peace process', in Shirlow and McGovern (eds), *Who Are 'the People'?*, pp.158–75.
123. Lennon, B., *Peace Comes Dropping Slow: Dialogue and Conflict Management in Northern Ireland* (Belfast: Community Dialogue, 2004), p.16.
124. Purdy, A., *Molyneaux: The Long View* (Antrim: Greystone Books, 1989), pp.158–9.
125. Nesbitt, D., 'Redefining unionism', in Coakley (ed.), *Changing Shades of Orange and Green*, p.50.
126. Arthur, P., *Special Relationships: Britain, Ireland and the Northern Ireland Problem* (Belfast: Blackstaff Press, 2000); Holland, J., *Hope Against History: The Ulster Conflict* (London: Hodder and Stoughton, 1999).
127. See Bean, K., *The New Politics of Sinn Féin* (Liverpool: Liverpool University Press, 2007); O'Brien, B., *The Long War: The IRA and Sinn Féin* (New York: Syracuse University Press, 1999), pp.365–95.
128. Darby, J., *The Effects of Violence on Peace Processes* (Washington, DC: United States Institute of Peace Press, 2001), p.19.
129. Mallie, E. and McKittrick, D., *The Fight for Peace: The Secret Story Behind the Irish Peace Process* (London: Mandarin, 1997).
130. Mitchell, C., 'Protestant identification and political change in Northern Ireland', *Ethnic and Racial Studies*, 26, 4 (2003), pp.612–31.
131. Ibid., p.33.
132. O'Kane, E., 'When can conflicts be resolved? a critique of ripeness', *Civil Wars*, 8, 3/4 (2006), pp.268–84.

133. Bew, J., Frampton, M. and Gurruchaga, I., *Talking to Terrorists: Making Peace in Northern Ireland and the Basque Country* (London: Hurst & Company, 2009), pp.112–23.
134. Smith, *Making the Peace in Ireland*, pp.138–9.
135. Spencer, G., 'Containing dialogue: the British government and early talks in the Northern Ireland peace process', *The British Journal of Politics and International Relations*, 10, 3 (2008), pp.452–71.
136. For a variety of perspectives on this, see Adams, G., *A Farther Shore: Ireland's Long Road to Peace* (New York: Random House, 2005); Adams, G., *The New Ireland: A Vision for the Future* (Dingle: Brandon, 2005); Feeney, B., *Sinn Féin: A Hundred Turbulent Years* (Dublin: O'Brien Press, 2002); Frampton, M., *The Long March: The Political Strategy of Sinn Féin, 1981–2007* (Basingstoke: Palgrave Macmillan, 2009); Maillot, A., *New Sinn Féin: Irish Republicanism in the Twenty-First Century* (London: Abbingdon, 2005).
137. Zartman, I., 'The timing of peace initiatives: hurting stalemates and ripe moments', in J. Darby and R. MacGinty (eds), *Contemporary Peacemaking: Conflict, Violence and Peace Processes* (Basingstoke: Palgrave, 2003), pp.19–29.
138. Cited in Frampton, M., *The Long March*, p.95.
139. Bowyer Bell, J., *The IRA 1968–2000: Analysis of a Secret Army* (London: Frank Cass, 2000), p.311. See also Bean, K., *The New Politics of Sinn Féin*, pp.185–98.
140. Shirlow, P., Tonge, J., McAuley, J.W. and McGlynn, C., *Abandoning Historical Conflict? Former Paramilitaries in Northern Ireland* (Manchester: Manchester University Press, forthcoming).
141. The extent of this was indicated in November 1993, when a large consignment of arms bound for the UVF was intercepted at Teesport. It included 300 AKM assault rifles, pistols, thousands of rounds of ammunition, hundreds of grenades and several tons of military grade explosives. See Kirby, T., Pithers, M. and McKittrick, D., 'Loyalists defiant after huge weapons seizure', *Independent*, 25 November 1993.
142. See McKenna, P., 'Protestant groups link up in huge arms deal', *Irish Independent*, 6 February 1988; Rodwell, B. and Cooney, J., 'Protestants match IRA build up', *The Times*, 6 February 1988.
143. Moloney, *A Secret History of the IRA*, p.241.
144. Sometimes known as the Joint Declaration for Peace.
145. BBC News Online, 'The Downing Street Declaration and the IRA ceasefire'. Archived at: http://news.bbc.co.uk/1/hi/northern_ireland/69283.stm
146. *Observer*, 28 November 1993.
147. McKittrick, D., 'Major in upbeat mood over Irish peace process', *Independent*, 22 December 1995.
148. Irish Republican Army, 'Ceasefire Statement, 31 August 1994'. Archived at: http://cain.ulst.ac.uk/events/peace/docs/ira31894.htm
149. McKittrick, D., 'Sinn Féin returns to the fold', *Independent*, 7 September 1994.
150. Combined Loyalist Military Command, 'Ceasefire Statement, 13 October 1994'. Archived at: http://www.cain.ulst.ac.uk/events/peace/docs/clmc131094.htm
151. Dixon, *Northern Ireland: The Politics of War and Peace*.
152. Martin, G., 'Visions of the union', in *The Case for the Union* (Belfast: Business and Professional People for the Union, no date).
153. Adams, G., 'Transforming hope into reality: negotiating a new beginning', planned speech to be delivered at the Plenary Session of All Party Talks (from which Sinn Féin was excluded). Archived at: http://www.sinnfein.org/releases//negotiating.html
154. See material in Elliott, M. (ed.), *The Long Road to Peace in Northern Ireland* (Liverpool: Liverpool University Press, 2002).
155. The US administration also helped guide the participants towards an accord. See Beggan, D. and Indurthy, R., 'The conflict in Northern Ireland and the Clinton administration's role', *International Journal on World Peace* (December 1999); MacGinty, R., 'American influences on the Northern Ireland peace process', *Conflict Studies Journal*, 17, 2 (1997). Archived at: http://www.lib.unb.ca/Texts/JCS/bin/get.cgi?directory=FALL97/articles/&filename=MACGINTY.html
156. See Constitution Unit 2003; Wilson, R. (ed.), *Agreeing to Disagree? A Guide to the Northern Ireland Assembly* (London: Stationery Office, 2001).
157. Wolff, S., 'The peace process in Northern Ireland since 1998', in J. Neuheiser and S. Wolff (eds), *Peace at Last? The Impact of the Good Friday Agreement on Northern Ireland* (Oxford: Berghahn Books, 2002), pp.205–32.

158. See Fearon, K. (ed.), *Power, Politics, Positioning: Women in Northern Ireland* (Belfast: Democratic Dialogue, 1996); Fearon, K., *Women's Work: the Story of the Northern Ireland Women's Coalition* (Belfast: Blackstaff Press, 1999); Wilford, R., 'Women's candidacies and electability in a divided society: the Northern Ireland Women's Coalition and the Northern Ireland Forum election 1996', *Women and Politics*, 20, 1 (1998), pp.73–93.

159. McAuley, J.W. and Tonge, J., 'Over the rainbow?: relationships between loyalists and republicans in the Northern Ireland Assembly, *Études Irlandaises*, 28, 1 (2003), pp.177–98.

160. McGarry and O'Leary, *Explaining Northern Ireland*.

161. Cash, *Identity, Ideology and Conflict*.

162. Aughey, A., 'Trimble hangs on for a white-knuckle ride', *Guardian*, 26 March 2000.

163. Porter, N., *Rethinking Unionism: An Alternative Vision for Northern Ireland* (Belfast: Blackstaff Press, 1996).

164. Porter, *Rethinking Unionism*, p.87.

165. Ibid., p.166.

166. Graham, 'The past in the present', p.493.

167. Aughey, *Under Siege*, p.19.

168. Porter, *Rethinking Unionism*, p.163.

169. Ibid., p.123.

170. Ibid., p.43.

171. Ibid., p.180.

172. Ibid., p.201.

173. Ibid., p.170.

174. See 'Post-Agreement Ireland: North and South', speech given by David Trimble, MP to the annual conference of The Irish Association, 20 November 1998.

175. Godson, D., *Himself Alone: David Trimble and the Ordeal of Unionism* (London: Harper Collins), 2004.

176 . Porter, *Rethinking Unionism*, p.169.

177. Farrington, C., 'Ulster unionist political divisions in the late twentieth century', *Irish Political Studies*, no. 16 (2001), p.53.

178. Thomas, A., 'The Protestant future', originally presented at the John Hewitt Summer School, 2000.

179. Coulter's 1994a; 1994b; 1996, 1997; 1999.

180. Cited in *News Letter*, 7 March 1995.

181. *Irish Times*, 3 May 1996.

182. McCartney, R., *The McCartney Report on Consent* (Belfast: J.C. Print, no date); McCartney, R., *The McCartney Report on the Framework Documents* (Belfast: J.C. Print, no date).

183. McCartney, R., 'Sovereignty and seduction', in Foster (ed.), *The Idea of the Union*, pp.65–8.

184. *Irish Times*, 8 December 1997.

185. *News Letter*, 23 February 1995.

186. *Belfast Telegraph*, 21 February 1995.

187. *Belfast Telegraph*, 12 March 1996.

188. McCartney, R., 'This is a situation hardly calculated to produce either clarity or truth', *Belfast Telegraph*, 26 October 2006.

189. McAuley, J.W., 'Divided loyalists, divided loyalties: conflict and continuities in contemporary unionist ideology', in C. Gilligan and J. Tonge (eds), *Peace or War? Understanding the Peace Process in Northern Ireland* (Aldershot: Ashgate, 1997), pp.37–53.

190. *Irish Times*, 26 January 1998.

191. See Cadogan Group, *Northern Limits, the Boundaries of the Attainable in Northern Ireland Politics* (Belfast: Cadogan Group, 1992); Cadogan Group, *Blurred Vision, Joint Authority and the Northern Ireland Problem* (Belfast: Cadogan Group, 1994); Nesbitt, D., *Unionism Restated: An Analysis of the Ulster Unionist Party's 'Statement of Aims'* (Belfast: Ulster Unionist Information Institute, 1995); Roche, P.J. and Birnie, J.E., 'The poverty of Irish nationalism', in *People for the Union* (Belfast: no publisher, no date); Roche, P.J. and Birnie, J.E., 'Irish nationalism: politics of the absurd', *Ulster Review*, no. 20 (Summer 1996), pp.13–15.

192. Green, A., 'Ireland: A False Construct', paper presented to the Irish Association, November 1999. Archived at: http://www.Cadogan.org/articles/FALSE.htm

193. See various in Foster (ed.), *The Idea of the Union*.

194. 'Time to disappear, speaker tells UUP', *News Letter*, 29 September 2007.

195. Dudley Edwards, R., *The Faithful Tribe: An Intimate Portrait of the Loyal Institutions*

(London: Harper Collins, 1999).

196. Dudley Edwards, R., 'A dull and dreary travesty': review of *Northern Protestants: An Unsettled People*, by Susan McKay, *Independent*, 25 June 2000.
197. Roche and Birnie, 'Irish nationalism', p.14.
198. Ibid., p.15.
199. Roche, P.J. and Birnie, J.E., *An economics lesson for Irish nationalists and republicans* (Belfast: Ulster Unionist Information Institute, no date), p.43.
200. Wilson, *Ulster: Conflict and Consent*, pp.1–10.
201. Roche and Birnie, 'Irish nationalism: politics of the absurd', p.14.
202. Roche and Birnie, 'The poverty of Irish nationalism'.
203. Green, 'Ireland: a false construct', p.2.
204. *Irish Times*, 14 November 1997.
205. Foster, *The Idea of the Union*, p.5.
206. O'Dowd, L., '"New Unionism", British nationalism and the prospects for a negotiated settlement in Northern Ireland', in D. Miller (ed.), *Rethinking Northern Ireland*, pp.70–93.
207. Cadogan Group, *Square Circles, Round Tables and the Path to Peace in Northern Ireland* (Belfast: Cadogan Group, 1996), p.36.
208. Aughey, 'Trimble hangs on for a white-knuckle ride'.

Chapter 3
The Struggle for New Unionism

The people of Northern Ireland are not fools. They can see that we have achieved all that we wanted in the constitutional arena. They will not listen to those voices who cry out 'treachery' and accuse us of selling the Union.

David Trimble[1]

'What shall we do with the traitor, Trimble? What shall we do with the traitor, Trimble? What shall we do with the traitor, Trimble? Ear-lye in the morning.'

Sung to David Trimble by women on the Shankill Road[2]

The importance of the UUP within the history of unionism and the politics of Northern Ireland cannot be overstated. Even the briefest viewing of material dealing directly with the history of the party indicates its remarkable electoral record.[3] From the formation of Northern Ireland in 1921 until direct rule from Westminster was introduced in 1972, the UUP succeeded in winning every general election it fought. Indeed, it has been argued that in its dominance of a demarcated geographical polity the UUP should be considered as one of Europe's most successful and remarkable electoral phenomena.[4]

After 1929, when proportional representation was strategically abandoned by the new state, it became almost impossible for UUP electoral dominance to be broken, and although there was some internal opposition from a number of Independent Unionists, the UUP were never seriously challenged.[5] It was only following the political and social turmoil precipitated by the outbreak of the conflict in late 1969 and the end of Northern Ireland's system of devolved government under Stormont that unionist political hegemony began to disjoint.

Despite the subsequent fragmentation of unionism's political representation, and the more recent partial reconstruction of hegemony around the DUP, support for the UUP remains widespread. At the core of this chapter is an analysis of how mainstream unionism has reacted to contemporary political events. In particular it discusses the political positions and policy directions adopted by the UUP and the struggles to realign the party with the ideology of new unionism. In so doing it drew directly, if unevenly, on some of the notions of intellectual, civic and liberal unionisms outlined in the previous chapter.

In its support for the Agreement, new unionism demonstrated sophisticated skills of presentation and a level of articulation that contrasted directly with other parts of unionism.[6] Finally, however it is important to note how the UUP position was contested within unionism, and the chapter ends by outlining the demise of the UUP as the dominant party political force within unionism.

THE POLITICS OF NEW UNIONISM

Although unionism was split as to the merits of the Agreement, in the wake of its signing, the dominant expressions were of high optimism that Northern Ireland was about to enter a new post-conflict period of peace and prosperity. One of those most actively promoting and supporting the accord was David Trimble, the then UUP leader. Indeed, core to this new unionist thinking was the emergence of Trimble at the head of a section of unionism that was at least willing to contemplate entering into a working relationship with Irish republicanism. As Liam O'Dowd points out, underpinning this was the sense that for many years unionism had been in the hands of the 'wrong people' and that things were about to change.[7]

New unionism claimed it was about to redress this by abandoning 'the politics of immobility, replacing inertia with a belief that Unionism needed to venture outside and engage with the outside world'.[8] In seeking to negotiate such a position it claimed to be 'pro-active, inclusive, open, pluralist, dynamic, progressive, outward, articulate, intelligent, coherent, professional and confident'.[9]

This reorientation of unionism rested on a developing ideological shift (see previous chapter) which manifested in a growing political realism within parts of unionism that power sharing would be integral to the formation of any devolved administration acceptable to the UK government (see later chapters). In part, what Trimble and his supporters were attempting to project was another sense of what it was to be a unionist, one that moved beyond the commonly expressed imperative of simply rejecting the validity of Irish nationalism and denying its political opponents.[10]

Rather, this brand of unionism was seen as a positive and flexible force within the peace process, while still upholding what he regarded as unionism's core principles.[11] This was reflected in the broad belief across new unionism that positive support for the Agreement was a way of bringing unionism 'back to the heart of government'[12] and that unionism should be prepared to concede some political ground 'so that the overall siege of this state can be lifted'.[13]

It is worth setting this in the context of Trimble's broader vision, most especially his resolve that the Union was secured by the Agreement and his desire that its benefits should be actively promoted (and recognised) across both communities. This perspective under-pinned Trimble's belief that under his steerage the UUP could bring about an effective and working devolution and an end of the IRA. Trimble continued to reflect a confidence in the position he had nego-tiated, arguing that a devolved administration would allow 'the people of Ulster to determine their future' and that the UUP had 'copper-fas-tened partition'.[14]

The belief that the Union was in safe keeping and that a settlement inclusive of republicanism was a reasonable price to pay for the end of the armed conflict brought Trimble and his supporters into direct con-frontation with other factions of unionism (especially the DUP). Such tensions were revealed in the following speech, in which Trimble strongly criticised other parts of the unionist political leadership, and particularly the tactics of the DUP, as weakening rather than strengthen-ing the unionist cause. In direct reference to Ian Paisley, and to a lesser extent Robert McCartney, he said:

> Their actions and attitudes have been counterproductive. They have let nationalists off the hook: they have driven London into the arms of Dublin. We must warn against supporting them. Unfortunately the methods of those who denigrate us continue to do damage to the Union at home, in the rest of the United Kingdom and elsewhere. The reasonable case we present is being obscured by aggressive, loudmouth Unionists.[15]

In directly challenging such 'loudmouth Unionists', new unionism sought to consolidate and expand the support base for the Union, driven by a new brand of professional intelligent unionism, and to take political unionism in new directions. One example was an attempt to identify and corral those who may support the Union for utilitarian reasons, to broaden the electoral base and appeal of unionism and to set this in a wider political context. This is clearly demonstrated in the following statement from David Trimble to the Irish Association:

> Unionists can sometimes act defensively. We can be inclined to see

ourselves as inhabiting an embattled enclave in these islands. Certainly the experience of the last 30 years has encouraged and reinforced that attitude. But there is another more important side to unionism: the belief that all the different people of these two islands – English, Welsh, Scottish and from our own island too – share far more than divides us; a belief that there is as much value in continuous and various diversity as there is in mutual conformity; a belief that all will gain from being freely associated together within a wider union. They are inclusive beliefs not unique to our part of the island of Ireland.[16]

In contrast to the often inward looking expressions commonly found across unionism, new unionist politicians demonstrated 'sophisticated skills of presentation' and offered an 'articulate defence of their views, policies and principles'.[17] As one political commentator suggested at the time:

> New unionism really took off under David Trimble. His is a positive, assertive leadership. He realises that unionists must stop sulking like spoilt children when they don't get their own way. He knows that they must start taking the initiative, rather than constantly reacting to the agenda of others.[18]

DIVISIONS WITHIN UNIONISM

But not all unionists were so positive about the new ways of thinking that emerged from within unionism. New unionism was subject to criticism, both from within and outside the UUP. Within the party, Trimble's vision of a more inclusive politics was initially validated on 11 April 1998 when the UUP Executive supported his position on the Agreement by fifty-five to twenty-three votes. That endorsement was far from universal, however. Most of the ten UUP MPs, including some of the leading personalities in the party such as Martin Smyth, Jeffrey Donaldson, Roy Beggs, Willie Thompson and Willie Ross, all declared themselves opposed to the leadership position.

The depth of divisions within the party about its direction was further revealed when it became clear that five of the twelve-strong UUP talks team were also opposed to the Agreement. The situation was compounded when the leadership of the Grand Orange Lodge of Ireland openly set against the UUP's position on the Agreement, aligning itself with the broad anti-Agreement forces within unionism. These included the DUP and the UKUP alongside those dissident UUP members, who gathered ranks behind the United Unionist Campaign Against the Agreement (UUCA). Much of this coalesced around the platform set by Jeffrey Donaldson, who actively challenged even the use of the term 'peace process', arguing that the word 'appeasement' was a more apt description.[19]

Things came to a head in March 2000, when Martin Smyth challenged Trimble in a party leadership contest. Smyth's was a last-minute decision to stand, seemingly motivated by reports he had received during a visit to the US that Trimble had stated that it was not inconceivable that some day the UUP might enter into government with Sinn Féin. Although the declaration angered many in the UUP, there was little sense that Smyth was anything other than a stalking horse, or that he offered more than a token challenge. With no more than two days to canvass, and little or no time to organise, however, Smyth won just over 43 per cent of the vote.

The strength of support for Smyth gave a clear indication of the task that Trimble faced, and from then on Trimble's chosen path was to become more and more difficult as support for the Agreement diminished within the UUP. Mounting political tensions were further revealed in a whole series of angry meetings of the executive body of the party, the UUC. From its formation in 1905 the UUC had acted as the crucial forum that linked Unionism, through its local voters, to UUP associations, the Orange Order and the parliamentary group.[20]

While its effectiveness varied over time, and it was reasonably quiescent during the Stormont years, the UUC always remained central to the heartbeat of Unionist Party politics. Indeed, in more recent years the body has increasingly come to be seen to represent the soul of the party and adjudicated over competing claims to its political direction. Hence, these were important struggles for Trimble that he could little afford to lose, either in terms of contemporary politics or unionist symbolism. As confrontation became more pronounced, Trimble's claim to leadership was increasingly weakened.

UNIONISM AND THE ASSEMBLY

Within the Assembly Trimble's leadership was also in some turmoil. The initial deadline for the Executive to be formed passed at the end of October 1998, precipitating further multi-party talks at Hillsborough. In July 1999 another attempt at forming an Executive failed, this time when the UUP Assembly grouping declined to attend. As a consequence the proposals to form an Executive failed, unable to receive the necessary formal cross-community approval, and leading John Taylor to predict that the entire process had a less than 50:50 chance of survival.

There began an intensive round of talks, with the two governments taking the lead by publishing two joint statements, the *Hillsborough Declaration* and, later, *The Way Forward*. The response from the political parties was limited, prompting the UK government to set in place yet another initiative, a wide-ranging analysis of the situation under the chair of a former US senator George Mitchell. After ten weeks of negotiations the 'Mitchell review' reported, offering new hope of advancing the peace process and suggesting that the time was right for a devolved Executive to be put in place.[21]

Hopes of progress were enhanced when the IRA indicated a willingness to appoint a representative to the IICD, the body appointed to oversee decommissioning. Following the IRA's announcement, the focus returned to unionism.[22] At another turbulent meeting the UUC voted to support the Mitchell deal (by 480 votes to 349), a mandate that allowed Trimble to agree to the formation of a devolved government. The situation was far from stable or static, however, and it soon became clear that any UUC support was conditional on IRA decommissioning. As a consequence Trimble promised to resign as first minister if there were no clear indications that the IRA had begun to put its weaponry beyond use.

In early 2000, the IICD reported little progress had been made on IRA decommissioning and a new crisis emerged. The UUP and other unionists demanded Trimble carry out his resignation threat, thus forcing the UK government to again suspend the devolved institutions. In May 2000 the two governments set the end of June 2001 as a final deadline for the full implementation of the Agreement. In response, the IRA promised that its leadership would 'initiate a process that will completely and verifiably put IRA arms beyond use'.[23]

One again, on the back of perceived movement by the IRA, Trimble was allowed some room for manoeuvre and led the UUP back into the Executive on the promise of full IRA decommissioning. Returning to the UUC on 27 May 2000 he once more succeeded in winning endorsement for his position, albeit again by a narrower margin of 459 votes to 403. As a consequence devolution was restored, but paramilitary decommissioning continued to be a major bone of contention for all involved, the issue causing continuing conflict and inhibiting any political progress for years to come.

RE-ELECTION OF A FIRST MINISTER

Within the UUP internal disputes rumbled on for several months, eventually forcing the UUC to convene yet another special meeting on 28 October 2000.[24] In a key debate, Jeffrey Donaldson (who was proving to be the most effective point of internal opposition) called on Trimble to withdraw from the Executive. Although the party leader and his supporters were able to defeat the motion, it was obvious to all that the UUP was openly fractured around its future political direction, both outside and inside the Assembly.

Within the UUP Assembly group, eight (out of twenty-eight) MLAs openly presented themselves as hostile to the Agreement. This was especially problematic given the regulation built into the Assembly that the first and deputy first ministers were only to be elected with the support of cross-community votes, requiring 50 per cent of registered nationalists and unionists as well as a majority of all Assembly members to support any candidate.[25] Pragmatically, the UUP split meant that any pro-Agreement majority within the Unionist bloc was narrow at best.

Following the election on 1 July 2001, Trimble was indeed forced to activate the post-dated letter of resignation he had presented to the speaker of the Assembly on 7 May. His resignation provoked further trauma, initiating yet another round of political negotiations. More talks among the pro-Agreement parties began at Weston Park on 9 July 2001. Premiers Blair and Ahern reacted almost immediately, issuing an 'Implementation Plan' to the parties on an 'all or nothing' basis, with barely a week for the parties to respond. Events were given further momentum when the IICD made public that the IRA had put forward a verifiable method for taking its weapons beyond use. In what was no doubt a pre-planned move, the UK government issued a new scheme for decommissioning.

The response from the two main parties in the Assembly was diametrical. The SDLP was highly positive, but the UUP rejected both the government's plan and the proposals of the IRA. Trimble countered that the IRA had not gone far enough in its proposals and insisted that decommissioning must begin before any further political movement took place. As a consequence the Assembly underwent a further technical suspension on 10 August 2001, a device invoked to allow the parties an extra six weeks for negotiation. Outside the Assembly, however, the IRA withdrew its proposals for decommissioning, seemingly disillusioned by the limited Unionist response.

As another deadline came into focus the Assembly was again suspended for twenty-four hours. The impending sense of crisis strengthened on 8 October 2001 when the UUP proposed a motion to exclude Sinn Féin ministers, declaring that if it wasn't supported the UUP would be forced to withdraw its ministers from the Assembly. In an Assembly based on voting arrangements of parallel consent requiring cross-community support, the motion was never likely to succeed and when it failed to gather the necessary support, both DUP and UUP ministers resigned.

Faced with what would most likely be a long-term suspension of the institutions, or at best another election to the Assembly (with no guarantee it would sit), the situation was given a new dynamic on 22 October 2001. In a groundbreaking, if somewhat choreographed, speech, Gerry Adams openly urged decommissioning from the IRA because of the changing political circumstances. Within twenty-four hours the IRA issued a statement claiming that the organisation had begun to put arms beyond use, an event confirmed by the IICD.

Following direct discussions with General de Chastelain, the chair of the IICD, Trimble recommended to the party leadership that the UUP again take up their Executive seats. In endorsing Trimble's position, the UUP leadership demanded that its MLAs support the party leader in any re-election as first minister. The request was immediately rejected by two MLAs, Peter Weir and Pauline Armitage, and as a result, Trimble was unable to get the necessary level of cross-community support to be elected first minister. The issue was only resolved with the temporary redesignation by the Alliance Party of Northern Ireland (APNI) of their MLAs from 'non-aligned' to 'unionist', thus allowing Trimble to meet the Assembly regulations designed to ensure effective power sharing in the Assembly.[26]

On 1 December 2001, Trimble survived yet another challenge by the anti-Agreement elements within his own party, with 56 per cent of the overall vote at the UUC. The Assembly was again suspended, however, in October 2002, overtly because of a police raid on the Stormont offices of Sinn Féin, investigating an alleged IRA spy ring operating from within Stormont. As a result the DUP withdrew its two ministers, and the UUP threatened to quickly follow should Sinn Féin remain in the administration. Direct rule from Westminster returned as the Assembly was suspended for a fourth time (following those in February 2000 and August and September 2001).

NEW UNIONISM AT THE POLLS

Under challenge in the Assembly from his own MLAs and outside from his own party members and the DUP, Trimble was forced to look to the wider electorate for validation of his policies. In the 2001 election the core message from the UUP was that it would continue to deliver on an Agreement, which they argued offered the best protection for the Union. Moreover, the party's election material highlighted the role the UUP had already played in securing an accord, claiming credit for bringing Northern Ireland into a brave new age.

In transmitting this message, Trimble underestimated (or chose to ignore) the level of opposition to the Agreement within unionism.

Despite the contradictory evidence widely available in the opinion polls, he stood by his claim that the majority of Protestants had moved on from the conflict and remained pro-Agreement.[27] He argued fiercely that it was UUP strategy that had forced republicans into making concessions and that it was his party which was best placed to deliver greater prosperity and improve the overall quality of life for all the citizens of Northern Ireland.

In doing so the UUP set out a policy and vision within a particular definition of Britishness and it was clear that Trimble, following his new unionist instincts, was seeking to define Britishness in terms of an ideology capable of including most, if not all, sections of Northern Ireland in a more pluralist society. Central to this was the presentation of a pro-Agreement unionism willing to recognise nationalist aspirations.

In presenting his case in this way Trimble found himself under fierce criticism from both the DUP and the anti-Agreement element within his own party. Indeed, much of the energy and time of the UUP's campaign was spent seeking to counter the onslaught of derision coming from the DUP towards the UUP strategy. In reply the UUP leader accused the DUP of hypocrisy, pointing out that in the Assembly the DUP had worked with all the other parties, including Sinn Féin, on a daily basis.[28]

LOSING GRIP: THE 2001 AND 2003 ELECTIONS

On 7 June 2001, the Labour Party retained power in Westminster with its second consecutive landslide win, while in Northern Ireland the election saw Sinn Féin become the largest political representatives within nationalism for the first time. In the Unionist bloc, the DUP won five seats, losing to the UUP in South Antrim, but taking seats from them in three other constituencies. Elsewhere, the UUP captured North Down (from the UKUP), but also lost four seats, two to Sinn Féin in Fermanagh/South Tyrone and West Tyrone and two to the DUP in North Belfast and East Londonderry. David Simpson, the almost unknown DUP candidate, standing for the first time, pushed Trimble himself hard in Upper Bann.

By comparison the DUP more than doubled its representation from 1997, up from two to five seats. While the UUP remained the largest unionist party, the 2001 election marked a clear change in unionist patterns of voting. Unionist politics was now operating in a dramatically altered context, with the DUP, driven by anti-Agreement policies, snapping at the heels of the UUP for the claim to be the legitimate representatives of unionism.

The next opportunity to assess those competing claims at the ballot box should have been the Assembly elections planned for 29 May 2003. These did not eventually take place, however, until November of that year, and even then there was no prospect of a working legislative body; election was only to what Hazleton termed a 'virtual Assembly'.[29] Broad debates and arguments continued across unionism surrounding the differing interpretations of whether the political changes that had occurred had been beneficial to the Union.

For the DUP, however, the issues were clear. They presented the election as yet another defining moment in the political history of Northern Ireland. This was made clear by Maurice Morrow, the DUP candidate for Fermanagh/South Tyrone, who claimed that the election presented the unionist electorate, with:

> ... an opportunity to give their verdict on the Belfast Agreement, an agreement that could only deliver for Republicans. Gerry Adams has declared 'the Belfast Agreement is as good as it gets for unionists.' The news for Adams is that it's not going to get any better for him. Republicans may have dictated the terms and pace over the past five years, but unionism under DUP leadership will bring this to an end. The DUP enters this Election campaign determined that unionism will not be subject to four more years of deceit, broken pledges and promises with Republicans taking all. The DUP will campaign for a mandate for a new Agreement. Unionists must seize the opportunity. Pushover Unionists who have placed Sinn Féin/IRA in government, released prisoners, destroyed the RUC and established unaccountable all-Ireland bodies must never again be allowed to negotiate on behalf of unionism.[30]

In contrast, the UUP campaign again concentrated on a strongly pro-Agreement message, highlighting the substantial economic and

Table 1: Unionist Voting in the 1998 and 2003 Assembly Elections

Party	% of Vote		No of Seats	
	1998	2003	1998	2003
DUP	35.9	50.5	20	30
UUP	42.1	44.5	28	27
UKUP	8.9	1.6	5	1
PUP	5.0	2.3	2	1
UDP	2.1	0	0	0
Independent Unionists	5.6	0	3	0
Other Unionists	0.4	1.1	0	0
Totals	100	100	58	59

Sources: Adapted from ARK;[31] CAIN;[32] Electoral Commission[33]

social benefits of devolution and the need to move forward, rather than backwards into violence and instability. While there is evidence that the message did indeed mobilise a substantial Protestant middle-class vote (in constituencies such as South and East Belfast and North Down), it did not resonate with other substantial sectors of the unionist community. Many unionists, however unjustly, saw the UUP as the party that allowed Sinn Féin into government, and Bairbre de Brún and Martin McGuinness to become ministers within the Executive.

The continued disillusionment of unionists with the outcomes of the Agreement was palpable and feelings of political loss found direct expression in the unionist vote.[34] In June 2003 three leading MPs, David Burnside, Jeffrey Donaldson and Martin Smyth, all resigned the UUP whip at Westminster. Following his election to the Assembly, Donaldson resigned from the UUP in December 2003 to join the DUP. The defection marked yet more public success for the DUP.

At the 2003 Assembly election the DUP, which had trailed in all previous local and UK elections,[35] overtook the UUP for the first time with 25.7 per cent of the vote. While at 22.7 per cent of the overall vote support for the UUP did not decline dramatically (rather it was support for minor parties that was squeezed), the result meant that the DUP had increased its share of the unionist vote by almost 15 per cent between 1998 and 2003 (see Table 1). This reinforced a trend within the unionist vote that had been apparent from the mid-1990s. There was much speculation within unionism as to whether the pattern would be reinforced at future elections, and if the DUP could move to a position of electoral dominance.

THE 2005 ELECTION: THE BATTLE FOR UNIONISM

The electorate did not have long to wait for an answer. Although the inability to secure a working Assembly and the tensions raised through allegations that the IRA had organised the massive Northern Bank robbery and been involved in the murder of a Catholic man outside a Belfast pub again heralded a period of political stagnation, it did not mean that the 2005 election was not keenly contested.

One of the more predictable aspects of the election campaign was the intra-Unionist conflict, which continued unabated. The DUP again projected itself as the voice of resolute unionism drawing on traditional unionist values, while the UUP sought to identify itself as the party that had actually achieved any tangible results. The UUP argued that its active involvement in the political process had 'forced Republicans to sign up to democracy and disarmament'.[36]

The UUP campaign rested on the argument that the Agreement had brought about a more peaceful Northern Ireland, and that the UUP stance was the only viable framework within which political parties could make progress. They also argued that it was the UUP that had taken most political risks, that the party still represented the most acceptable and stable face of unionism, and that David Trimble had generated a reasonable level of cross-community trust throughout Northern Ireland.[37]

In response the DUP campaign emphasised opposition to an Agreement that, it claimed, had largely failed the unionist people, not least by rewarding the representatives of terrorism with ministerial office in the Assembly. Hence, the DUP criticised what they branded as the 'pushover unionism' presented by the UUP, arguing that the political process in which the UUP were complicit offered little beyond yet more concessions to nationalists. Central to the DUP's campaign was its stress on the need to elect a strong unionist leadership, especially given its (admittedly correct) prediction that Sinn Féin would emerge as the largest party within nationalism and that the UUP were simply incapable of providing the necessary leadership.

This emphasis can be seen clearly in the following extract from a speech made by Jeffrey Donaldson:

> The DUP has been clear in its pledges and promises to voters. Mr Trimble cannot be trusted; he has let us all down so many times in the past. He assured us that the future of the RUC was safe; he assured us that ministers were accountable to the Assembly; he assured us that he would not enter into government with Sinn Féin/IRA until the IRA had fully decommissioned and he assured us that North–South bodies could not operate in the absence of an Assembly. On each promise he let us all down.[38]

The antagonisms within unionism at the time manifested directly in what one commentator termed the 'indecent row' around the UUP's main election slogan: 'Decent people vote Ulster Unionist.'[39] It was immediately branded as 'grossly offensive' and 'insulting' by the DUP, with deputy leader Peter Robinson even suggesting that some Sinn Féin voters might be decent people, although he immediately clarified that they were no doubt very mistaken and manipulated. The UUP's tactics even came under criticism from within, David Burnside (who lost his seat) complaining that the UUP's main election slogan was 'puerile and amateurish'.[40]

THE ADVANCE OF THE DUP

The 2005 Westminster general election marked an emphatic victory for the DUP over the UUP. While, overall, the unionist and nationalist share of the votes remained almost unchanged from 2001 (at 51.4 per cent and 41.8 per cent respectively), the results within unionism saw a restructuring of the votes that reinforced the electoral ascendancy established by the DUP in 2003. In the party's best-ever performance it took 66 per cent of the combined DUP–UUP vote. The DUP returned nine MPs to Westminster, representing a net gain of four from 2001 with a 34 per cent share of the overall vote.

A breakdown by votes and seats of the 2005 contest illuminates the growing dominance of the DUP. It was only in North Down where the UUP outpolled the DUP; elsewhere, the once dominant UUP was reduced to Northern Ireland's fourth party in Westminster. The DUP vote of 241,856 marked a swing to that party of just over 11 per cent, with the UUP totalling 127,314 votes. While this varied from the dramatic in Lagan Valley, East Antrim and Strangford to more moderate shifts in voting patterns in East Belfast and North Down (which was somewhat exaggerated because the DUP contested constituencies where it previously had stood aside for the UUP), the broad pattern within unionism was stark. This is even more telling if we consider the pattern of vote transfer from the DUP to the UUP over the decade beginning 1997 (see Table 2).

Table 2: UUP and DUP: Local, Assembly and General Election Comparative Results,
1997–2007

Election	% of First Preference Votes by Party	
	UUP	DUP
1997 General	32.7	13.1
1997 Local	27.8	15.6
1998 Assembly	21.3	18.1
2001 General	26.8	22.5
2001 Local	23.0	21.5
2003 Assembly	22.7	25.7
2005 General	17.7	33.7
2005 Local	18.0	29.6
2007 Assembly	14.9	30.1

Sources: Adapted from ARK;[41] CAIN;[42] Electoral Commission[43]

ORANGEISM AND DUP POLITICS

So how can we begin to explain this pattern of votes transfer within unionism and why should unionist voters have moved in numbers to support the DUP? One grouping within unionism where the switch of support to the DUP has been apparent is the Orange Order. Historically the UUP had successfully drawn upon traditional support from the Orange Order as a keystone of unionism's hegemonic structures. At its peak around two out of every three adult male Protestants was an Orange Order member, and the organisation was core in linking the different social strata within unionism.[44]

But such direct links are very much of the past. Following the 2001 Westminster election it became clear that sizable numbers of Orange members were choosing to vote for the DUP in preference over the UUP. By 2004, this pattern had strengthened to a position where two members to one expressed a preference in favour of the DUP over the UUP.[45] While the Orange Order certainly doesn't speak for unionism as a whole, the shifts in allegiance within Orangeism have mirrored broader political realignments within unionism.[46]

Most centrally, the DUP's position directly reflected major concerns of the Orange Order leadership, which had consistently refused to endorse the Agreement and has continued to speak out against its political consequences.[47] Thus, Martin Smyth, the former grand master and ex-UUP MP, claimed in July 2007 that the make-up of the Assembly marked the 'erosion of democracy' and that the 'elevation of terrorists' marked 'a sad decline in our national and international standards'.[48]

Primary in any explanation of the changes in political allegiance across Orangeism is the sense of fear expressed by members that Protestant unionism is in cultural and political reverse. This was brought into sharp relief by the Agreement; hence the resistance expressed by around two-thirds of the Orange Order's members in the 1998 referendum marked a far higher level of dissent than across the unionist population as a whole.[49] By 2004, just over three-quarters (some 78 per cent) pledged their opposition to the Agreement and members remained hostile to what they saw as the continual process of concessions emerging from it.[50]

In recent years much of this has crystallised around the cultural demands of Orangeism, witnessed, for example, in the Order's insistence that it should be able to march its 'traditional routes'. This became most contentious, and most public, at Drumcree, where due to large-scale population changes over several decades the longstanding route now traverses a largely nationalist area. The resulting dispute became a watershed in contestations surrounding the place of Orange culture in Northern Irish society.[51]

For the Order, any limitations on parade routes are seen as a clear example of attacks on Protestant cultural identity. Hence, they argued that any concession to a prohibition on parades represented another step in a broader retreat by the Protestant community. Such a perspective reflects how deeply themes of vulnerability and insecurity have been embedded within Orangeism,[52] the effects of which are clearly traceable through editions of the *Orange Standard*, which at times has even claimed that recent events mark a deliberate attempt to 'ethnically cleanse' Northern Irish Protestants.[53]

REPOSITIONING ORANGEISM

Such concerns were further revealed in the Orange Order positioning as a grouping that has consistently rejected the Agreement.[54] This has been driven by two broad dynamics. First, the belief by the Orange leadership that unionists have been 'betrayed by their own government' and that the 'voices of traditional Protestant Ulster – churches, Unionist parties, and in particular the loyal orders – have been disregarded or tossed aside'.[55] Second, the changing patterns of political support within the membership that eventually motivated the Order to sever its century-old bonds with the UUP in March 2005.

This was of no little significance. Although Trimble had previously promoted a break in the link between the UUP and the Order as part of his modernising agenda, he never had enough support or authority to carry this through.[56] When the split did occur, and despite the attempts by some in the UUP to represent it as part of a more pluralist approach from within unionism,[57] it was clear that the uncoupling was driven by the Order.

This was not least because its leadership recognised that many, if not most, of its members now supported the DUP. Despite residual historical and emotional ties, particularly among older members of the Orange Order,[58] the political momentum within Orangeism has steadily shifted towards the DUP, whose overt positioning as defenders of the Protestant–British–Unionist ethnic bloc diffused unionism[59]and reassembled support behind the DUP.[60]

So how might these changes be explained? Broad social and political changes have meant that the scope of the Order to manage patronage has been dramatically reduced. Moreover, the socio-economic profile of Order membership has changed dramatically in recent times, with fewer than 20 per cent of the membership now seeing themselves as middle class.[61] Moreover, Orangeism is increasingly held in disdain by large sections of the Protestant middle class,[62] who largely regard 'membership as beneath them'.[63]

Another part of the explanation rests within the ideological construction of politics by the DUP. Orange ideology remains centred around a discourse of Protestant faith and Christian principles; allegiance to the crown; civil and religious liberty under the law; and the maintenance of the constitutional link.[64] It is clear that all these elements are seen as being guaranteed only by a continuance of the

Union, which in turn is seen as only being assured through support for the DUP version of unionism, a perspective that has become ever more deeply imbued in the political outlook of Orangeism.[65]

Meanwhile the Orange leadership continues to promote itself as a force for unionist unification, urging an electoral pact to maximise the unionist vote.[66] The claim that Orangeism acts as a unifying force within the Protestant community is long standing, and in recent times has been seen in demands that 'Unionists must unite for the cause'[67]and 'unite and vote'.[68] The Orange Order continues to appeal for the construction of unionist unity on all key issues.[69] This position is reflected directly in the claim that:

> It is not too late for Unionists to get their act together and to defeat this evil conspiracy which seeks to destroy their position and this Province and put it under the heel of Dublin.[70]

At one level this simply replicates similar utterances coming from Orangeism for decades; from at least 1911 onwards the Order identified one of its central roles as providing an effective framework to organise against exclusion from the UK.[71] However, the recent political motivations within the Order are different. Not least is that the older and more conservative generation, which traditionally has directed and controlled the organisation (and regarded the UUP as the 'natural' party of unionism), has largely retired or been replaced. Today, many of the previous alliances have been shattered. The political direction of the Order is guided by the leadership's response to a membership that predominantly supports the DUP.

The increasing closeness of the relationship was demonstrated in February 2007 when the Orange Order and DUP formed a joint delegation to meet with the secretary of state to 'promote and protect the Protestant and unionist cultural cause'.[72] It was again revealed in a leaflet issued in July 2008, highlighting the role of the DUP as a key protector of British identity and culture, and which was quickly supported by a pledge by Peter Robinson to work closely with the loyal Orders to 'deliver a strong, vibrant and confident unionist community'.[73]

It is clear that the DUP regard 'the Loyal Orders as a key stakeholder in the cause of maintaining ... British culture',[74] and post-Agreement political realities have forced a reappraisal by many Orange Order members, who no longer see the UUP as best expressing their interests. The cohesiveness of the DUP and Orange Order groupings, to the point where they are seen to be working to advance common cause and making joint public representation, is something inconceivable in previous times. This repositioning of the Orange Order, which continues to occupy a significant role in Northern Irish civil society, should not be underestimated.

In providing a focal point in opposition to the accord, the Order could no longer formally be seen as part of the hegemonic formation of unionism.[75] It has continued to provide a counterbalance to the engagement of unionists in the post-Agreement period, including growing resistance to the involvement of the DUP in power-sharing government (see Chapters 7 and 8). Just what that means for the level of electoral support by Orange Order members for the DUP remains to be seen.

THE END OF NEW UNIONISM?

While ideological elements of new unionism still exist, it is a depleted political force. Further, it is clear that new unionism failed to penetrate the political consciousness of unionism more widely, or achieve success at the ballot box. The attempt to establish a more inclusive form of unionism was not aided by continual UUP infighting, to the 'point of exhaustion, where they appeared to the wider unionist electorate and the world beyond to be more or less dysfunctional'.[76]

The 2005 general election saw the UUP further decline as an electoral force, an indication of 'both a crisis of identity and a failure to positively influence public perceptions in the changing political landscape'.[77] The fallout was widely felt across unionism and has been ably traced by Michael Kerr.[78] Although criticism from within the UUP had consistently undermined his position, until then Trimble had been able to resist his opponents, at least in terms of his own party organisation.

Following electoral defeat in 2005 and the loss of his seat, however, Trimble was forced to resign as leader of the party, laying the blame directly at the feet of those who had failed to force decommissioning from the IRA, and castigating the DUP as a political grouping still dominated by the values of the Free Presbyterian Church.[79] The UUP quickly elected Sir Reg Empey to the position of party leader on 24 June 2005. According to one of his supporters, Empey's politics continue to display a 'tolerant and pluralist vision'.[80] Perhaps the most public statement of this was in June 2006, when in an *Irish News* interview he claimed that both Unionist parties must recognise that over the period of the contemporary conflict, some unionist rhetoric had been negative and divisive, and that in some cases this may even have encouraged sectarian violence.

Civic unionism did seem to revive in a different form following the formal announcement by David Cameron[81] that the Conservative Party and the UUP were creating a new electoral alliance in Northern Ireland to be called the Ulster Conservatives and Unionists – New Force (UCUNF).[82] Much remains to be seen how such a concord takes shape, although Lady Sylvia Hermon, its sole surviving Westminster MP, has opposed the development.

CONCLUSION

Although the contemporary period has produced change within both the structure and ideology of traditional unionist politics, it would be incorrect to see the new unionism described above as seeking to make a clean break with what had gone before. Its emergence did, however, open up critical debates around the future political direction of unionism, and whether the Union had been strengthened or weakened because of the decisions taken in 1998.

As a consequence, the UUP was a party seemingly in some confusion concerning its political direction. The split between Orangeism and the UUP further revealed an organisational crisis within unionism and heralded the final breakup of the old unionist hegemony. Overall the UUP has witnessed decline from a position of leadership within the unionist community to one in which it threatens to be electorally marginal and politically isolated.

This resulted in further conflict concerning the direction unionism should take. Many regard the DUP as directly articulating that form of ethnic Protestant British identity that they hold most dear (although the strength of support among Orangeism and others may have weakened following the entry of the DUP into government with Sinn Féin). For many unionists the contemporary period has offered nothing but an increased sense of political insecurity and ideological fragmentation. They sought solace in those prepared to guarantee the continuance of the existing structures and cultures of unionism. The most forthright response and articulation of this came in the political discourse of the DUP.[83]

NOTES

1. Trimble, D., 'Post–Agreement Ireland: North and South', *Speech to the Annual Conference of the Irish Association*, Glenview Hotel, Co. Wicklow, 20 November 1998.
2. Cited in O'Brien, C., 'Trimble is serenaded by Shankill shoppers', *Irish Times*, 11 November 2003.
3. See Harbinson, *The Ulster Unionist Party*; Hume, D., *The Ulster Unionist Party 1972–92* (Lurgan: Ulster Society Publications); Walker, *A History of the Ulster Unionist Party*.
4. Coakley, J., 'Constitutional innovation and political change in twentieth-century Ireland', in Coakley (ed.), *Changing Shades of Orange and Green*, p.11.
5. Reid, C., 'Protestant challenges to the "Protestant state": Ulster Unionism and independent Unionism in Northern Ireland, 1921–1939', *Twentieth Century British History*, 19, 4 (2008), pp.419–45.
6. English, 'The growth of new unionism', p.97.
7. O'Dowd, 'New unionism', p.76.
8. McKittrick and McVea, *Making Sense of the Troubles*, p.236.
9. *Ulster Review*, 1995/96, p.15.

10. O'Dowd, 'New unionism', p.78.
11. Spencer, G. 'The decline of Ulster unionism: the problem of identity, image and change', *Contemporary Politics*, 12, 1 (2006), pp.45–63.
12. Trimble, D., 'An immediate assessment: Northern Ireland Forum for Political Dialogue', 17 April 1998, reproduced in *To Raise up a New Northern Ireland: Articles and Speeches, 1998–2000* (Belfast: The Belfast Press, 2001).
13. McDonald, H., *Trimble* (London: Bloomsbury, 2000), p.6.
14. Trimble, *To Raise up a New Northern Ireland*, p.8.
15. Ulster Unionist Council, Press Release, 22 March 1997.
16. Trimble, D., 'Initiatives for consensus: a unionist perspective', in C. Townshend (ed.), *Consensus in Ireland: Approaches and Recessions* (Oxford: Clarendon Press, 1998), p.4.
17. English, 'The growth of new unionism', p.97.
18. Breen, S., 'The glacier shifts', *Fortnight*, no. 344 (November 1995), p.7.
19. Donaldson, J., *The Northern Ireland Peace Process: Blurring the Lines Between Democracy and Terrorism* (London: Friends of the Union, 2000).
20. McAuley, J.W., 'The emergence of new loyalism', in Coakley (ed.), *Changing Shades of Orange and Green*, pp.106–22.
21. BBC News Online, 'The Downing Street Declaration and the IRA ceasefire'. Archived at: http://news.bbc.co.uk/1/hi/northern_ireland/69283.stm.
22. Godson, D., *Himself Alone: David Trimble and the Ordeal of Unionism* (London: HarperCollins, 2004), pp.451–5.
23. *Guardian Unlimited*, 'IRA arms decommissioned'. Archived at: http://www.guardian.co.uk/Northern_Ireland/Story/0,2763,1578667,00.html.
24. Coulter, J., 'No union among the unionists', *Sunday Business Post*, 29 October 2000.
25. McDermott, B., 'Q&A: the Northern Ireland elections', *Guardian*, 1 November. Archived at: http://www.fairvote.org/?page=54&articlemode=showspecific&showarticle=255; McEvoy, J., 'The institutional design of executive formation in Northern Ireland', *Regional and Federal Studies*, 16, 4 (2006), pp.447–64.
26. Northern Ireland Assembly, 'The work of the Assembly'. Archived at: http://www.niassembly.gov.uk
27. BBC, *Hearts and Minds*, 31 May 2001.
28. McAuley and Tonge, 'Over the rainbow?'
29. Hazleton, W.A., 'Suspended vote: the 2003 Northern Ireland Assembly election', *The Political Quarterly*, 75, 3 (2004), p.234.
30. Morrow, M., 'Election will be a defining moment', press statement from Fermanagh/South Tyrone candidate (Belfast: DUP, 2003).
31. ARK, 'Northern Ireland Election Results'. Archived at: http://www.ark.ac.uk/elections
32. CAIN, 'Results of Elections held in Northern Ireland since 1968'.
33. Electoral Commission, 'Election Results'.
34. See Constitution Unit, 'Monitoring Devolution, Quarterly Report'; Constitution Unit, 'Nations and Regions: The Dynamics of Devolution, Northern Ireland – Quarterly Report', November; Thornton, C., 'Ulster poll shock rocks Agreement: voters are disillusioned', *Belfast Telegraph*, 19 February 2003.
35. Except elections to the European Parliament, where each party stands only a single candidate.
36. Ulster Unionist Party, *Election Manifesto, 2005: A Fair Society* (Belfast: UUP, 2005), p.1.
37. University of Ulster, 'Don't write off UUP and SDLP just yet, conference told', News Release, 22 September 2004.
38. Donaldson, J., 'Vote DUP – leadership that's working: DUP are the mainstream unionist party'.
39. McAdam, N., 'Unionist row rages', *Belfast Telegraph*, 16 April 2005.
40. BBC Northern Ireland, *Spotlight*, 10 May 2005.
41. ARK, 'Northern Ireland election results'.
42. CAIN, 'Results of elections held in Northern Ireland since 1968'.
43. Electoral Commission, 'Election results 2007'.
44. Lyons, F.S.L., *Ireland Since the Famine* (London: Fontana, 1973), p.720.
45. Tonge, J. and Evans, J., 'Eating the oranges? The Democratic Unionist Party and the Orange Order vote in Northern Ireland', paper presented to the PSA Elections, Public Opinion and Parties annual conference, September 2004.
46. McAuley, J.W. and Tonge, J., '"For God and for the crown": contemporary political and

social attitudes among Orange Order members in Northern Ireland', *Political Psychology*, 28, 1 (2007), pp.33–54.

47. Grand Orange Lodge of Ireland, 'Press statement on Belfast Agreement', 12 May 1998.
48. Cited in McAdam, N., 'Terrorists in power shows sad decline in national standards; ex-Orange chief issues challenge to republicans', *Belfast Telegraph*, 12 July 2007.
49. Tonge, J. and Evans, J., 'The onward march of Paisleyism or a triumph of unionist apathy?', paper presented to the PSA Elections, Public Opinion and Parties annual conference, September 2005.
50. McAuley and Tonge, 'For God and for the crown', p.44.
51. See Bryan, D., *Orange Parades: The Politics of Religion, Tradition and Control* (London: Pluto, 2000); Jarman, N. and Bryan, D., *Parades and Protest: A Discussion of Parading Disputes in Northern Ireland* (Coleraine: University of Ulster, 1996).
52. English, 'The growth of new unionism', p.102.
53. *Orange Standard*, October 2001, p.6.
54. Ibid., May 1998, p.1.
55. Ibid., March 2002, p.1.
56. Millar, *David Trimble*, p.217.
57. Andrews, J., 'We can safeguard the union', *Belfast Telegraph*, 29 September 2006.
58. This was clearly demonstrated in the UUC vote, where those who held office in the Orange Order remained more in favour of continuing the alliance than those who did not. More generally, see Kaufmann, E. and Patterson, H., *Unionism and Orangeism in Northern Ireland Since 1945* (Basingstoke: Palgrave, 2004).
59. McAuley and Tonge, 'For God and for the crown', pp.43–8.
60. McAuley, J.W., 'Ulster unionism after the peace', in J. Neuheiser and S. Wolff (eds), *Breakthrough to Peace? The Impact of the Good Friday Agreement on Northern Irish Politics and Society* (New York and Oxford: Berghahn Books, 2002), pp.76–93.
61. McAuley and Tonge, 'For God and for the crown'; McAuley, J.W. and Tonge, J., 'The contemporary Orange Order in Northern Ireland', in M. Busteed, F. Neal and J. Tonge (eds), *Irish Protestant Identities* (Manchester: Manchester University Press, 2008), pp.289–302.
62. Kaufmann, E., *The Orange Order: A Contemporary Northern Irish History* (Oxford: Oxford University Press, 2007).
63. Pollak, A., 'Drumcree exposes depth of unionist alienation and anger.' *Irish Times*, 13 July 1996.
64. *News Letter*, 13 July 2007.
65. Tonge and McAuley, 'The contemporary Orange Order in Northern Ireland', pp.289–302.
66. Drew Nelson cited in *News Letter*, 13 July 2007.
67. *Orange Standard*, November 2004.
68. Ibid., May 2005.
69. Ibid., April 2005.
70. Ibid., April 2003.
71. Stewart, *The Ulster Crisis*, p.69.
72. Democratic Unionist Party, 'DUP and Orange Order meet with the secretary of state'.
73. Cited in Dempster, S., 'DUP issues leaflet on its achievements', *News Letter*, 14 July 2008.
74. Dempster, S., 'DUP issues a leaflet on its achievements', *News Letter*, 13 July 2008.
75. Gilligan, C., 'Northern Ireland ten years after the Agreement', *Ethnopolitics*, 7, 1 (2008), pp.1–19.
76. Millar, F., *David Trimble: The Price of Peace* (Dublin: The Liffey Press, 2004), p.217.
77. Spencer, 'The decline of Ulster unionism', p.45.
78. Kerr, M., *Transforming Unionism: David Trimble and the 2005 General Election* (Dublin: Irish Academic Press, 2005).
79. 'Focus: Trimble pays price of peace', *Sunday Times*, 8 May 2005.
80. Andrews, J., 'We can safeguard the union', *Belfast Telegraph*, 29 September 2006.
81. Porter, A., 'David Cameron launches biggest Conservative shake-up for decades', *Daily Telegraph*, 23 July 2008.
82. BBC News Online, 'UUP, Tories consider closer links'. Archived at:http://news.bbc.co.uk/2/hi/uk_news/northern_ireland/7522326.stm
83. See Democratic Unionist Party, 'The tragedy of a false peace'. Archived at: http://www.dup.org.uk; Democratic Unionist Party, 'Towards a new agreement: the DUP analysis vindicated' (Belfast: DUP, 2003).

Chapter 4

(Re) Claiming Unionism

The present system increases nationalist and Republican
confidence because it offers them progress ... The same cannot be said for the unionist community. This present
Agreement is built upon the same faulty foundation that has
been tried before ... Unionists need convincing that an
Agreement is capable of addressing unionist concerns and
grievances.

Gregory Campbell[1]

When we got there we discovered an organised demonstration by the DUP, who had been tipped off that we were coming, probably by a sympathiser in the police. The crowd was
mostly made up of 'Hell's Grannies', whose contorted faces
as they shouted 'traitor' and threw rubber gloves at Tony
(Blair), saying he should wear them to shake hands with a
murderer like Gerry Adams, were disconcerting if not really
frightening. But their anger was real all right; they could not
believe that the Prime Minister had been talking to terrorists.

Jonathan Powell[2]

Throughout the contemporary period the DUP has consistently claimed
to be best positioned to interpret the 'true' political consequences of
government initiatives, to recognise the duplicity of Westminster and to
defend the Union against all comers. As a result the party has also
asserted to be legitimate heirs to the mantle of what they termed 'traditional unionism'. In so doing the DUP provides an important outlet for
the expression of Protestant unionist ethno-cultural identity as introduced in Chapter 2. That does not mean that the DUP can be understood simply as a direct form of politicised Protestantism. Certainly
while at least half of all the DUP's senior political representatives belong

to the Free Presbyterian Church,[3] its numerical strength remains small, with only around 3 per cent of Northern Ireland's Protestants being members.

Beyond this, however, the DUP has provided a coherent focus for resistance to political change and an outlet for the expression of those who see the need to strongly defend Ulster as being at the core of their politics. This oppositional mode, which lies deep within the politics and machinations of the DUP, needs some further context. Unionists at many levels have continued to express concern for their future political position, and indeed at times, the Union itself.

What requires explanation is how and why this resistance has crystallised around the DUP. One aspect surrounds the perceived credibility in the claims made by the DUP to represent unionism's most authentic voice. Peter Robinson made this explicit when he claimed that the:

> ... UUP is not the inheritor of the mantle of Carson and Craig. Their lineage continues with those who espouse traditional unionism not the pretenders who squat within the structures of the Ulster Unionist Council.[4]

The framing of such values has long been central to the self-image of the DUP, but their prominence within unionism is not a given and even in the contemporary period a leadership role for the DUP was far from assured. Initially, following the Agreement anti-accord unionists, and particularly that faction led by Ian Paisley, were largely dismissed as representing bygone values and the politics of former times. Unionist opposition to the Agreement quickly grew, however, and increasingly such views were effectively corralled by the DUP.

FROM SUNNINGDALE TO BELFAST AGREEMENTS

Much of the strength of the DUP's appeal rests upon a discourse specifically constructed over the past thirty years involving contemporary politics being understood as 'a final conflict for Ulster'. The importance of this framing of politics to the DUP is readily seen in the following statement by Ian Paisley on the party's thirtieth anniversary in 2001. In it he claims that the DUP emerged in a time of need as a direct response to the demand for a strong voice to defend the interests of the Union, in direct opposition to the UUP, which the DUP claimed has long misrepresented the unionist people. It is worth considering the rest of the statement at some length:

> Thirty years and what a toll it has taken on Ulster's People and

Ulster's democratic freedoms. The nest of traitors at Whitehall have seen to that, and tombstones are the milestones which have marked their surrender to murdering thugs of Irish Republicanism. If the UDUP had not been in existence, then Northern Ireland would not have been in existence. This Party and this Party alone, led the Ulster people to save the Union.[5]

Crucial in the period before the re-establishment of a working Assembly was the framing by the DUP of a narrative of peace process as something that ran counter to the will of the democratic majority in Northern Ireland. In part at least this reflected growing feelings within unionism that the whole of their social and political world was in danger. The DUP thus presented the view that the UK government had forsaken unionists[6] and that the 'feigned new peacemaker image' of IRA/Sinn Féin was a ploy 'to extort bottomless concessions from the government'.[7]

This resulted in what Neil Southern identifies as a self-perception of unionists as increasingly marginalised across the interconnected arenas of politics, culture and physical space, and the growing prominence of the notion of alienation within mainstream unionist ideology.[8] While Southern rightly points out that the feelings of alienation differed across class factions within unionism,[9] the broad concerns of unionism were highlighted and harnessed by the DUP.

One consequence was the construction of a particular frame of understanding, whereby the notion of untrustworthiness was applied to almost all other political groupings involved in Northern Irish politics, both within unionism and far beyond. Such views highlight consistencies in the DUP's approach throughout its existence and its continued promotion of the view that the Union is in danger of erosion and unionists must remain eternally vigilant against betrayal from within or without.

The framing of politics in this way has long been typical of the DUP. Since the early 1970s, the party has actively promoted itself as the bearer of unionism's traditional values, expressed in circumstances where Northern Ireland moves from one crisis to the next, due mainly to the lack of political guidance from the unionist leadership and the duplicity or weakness of successive British governments.

It is hardly innovative to point out that since its formation one of the main arguments emerging from the DUP has been that the Union is under threat, and that the DUP is its most true and able defender. It is, however, important to identify clearly how such arguments are formulated in ways that encourage support to be drawn to this position, especially after the Agreement, when the notion of alienation has been directly drawn upon to reinforce the politics of cultural unionism.

(RE) PRESENTING THE CRISIS?

So how does the DUP do this? In its formal presentation the notion that Northern Ireland faces a constitutional crisis has been openly represented in all DUP election manifestos since the formation of the party. Indeed, since the 1980s, every DUP election manifesto has been seen to adopt an identifiable style. So, for example, if we briefly consider the DUP's election manifesto from the 1982 Assembly election, it displays an almost contemporary feel in declaring that 'the DUP offers the surest guarantee' [and the] 'firmest stand against all attempts to force Ulster down the Dublin Road'. The section concludes: 'You know where you stand with the DUP', which in turn became the main slogan for the party in the election.[10] Having established its resolve to tackle Ulster's enemies, however currently defined, the manifesto then moves on to a wide-ranging series of proposals on broader social and economic issues.

In framing such views, the DUP set a pattern readily transferable to later periods and events. During the peace process the party made clear its belief that any grouping willing to engage with the politics arising from the Agreement merely demonstrated their feebleness, and that anyone seeking to pursue the agenda outlined by Tony Blair was engaged in little other than appeasement of the IRA. Further, for Paisley the government's plan was:

> ... to sacrifice Ulster's constitutional position on the altar of political expediency is part of a cowardly, underhand deal with the IRA to escape a mainland bombing campaign. To achieve this the issue of consent has been surreptitiously divested of any geographical or numerical definition, so that the government could connive to omit completely the issue of the union from the most recently concocted road map pointing to Dublin, namely the Heads of Agreement proposals, in which the detested, rejected and unworkable Framework Document returns to the stage adorned in a robe of unionist-friendly deception.[11]

To understand this analysis we need to return to the basic DUP perspective surrounding the politics of the peace process. Jim Cusack and Henry McDonald point out that from the outset the DUP took a more 'apocalyptic view' of the proposals of others.[12] At its onset the party pasted graphic posters across the Province, showing Northern Ireland being lifted out of the UK and moved towards a united Ireland. For the DUP the events surrounding the search for an accord merely highlighted how 'terrorists' were being rewarded for ending their campaign, while the real 'victims' were being ignored.

There are further examples of this: witness the DUP's approach to the Forum election in 1996, where it stood on an abstentionist ticket, claiming that the whole process was designed to negotiate away the very future of Ulster.[13] Hence, they argued that no unionist should be holding negotiations with the government or the SDLP, let alone with Sinn Féin. Instead, and in typical DUP style, it offered an unbreakable covenant with the Ulster People, to ensure that Northern Ireland's constitutional position was recognised without ambiguity. Ian Paisley put it in the starkest of terms: for him and many others the Union simply 'is not negotiable'.[14]

SLIPPERY SLOPES AND MISGUIDED FRIENDS

The public face of the DUP has remained remarkably consistent for over three decades, following its formation as an expression of dissatisfaction with the direction and policies of the UUP.[15] Throughout that time the party has drawn on current cultural and political anxieties to repeatedly claim that Northern Ireland was facing its gravest threat to date. In typical DUP style the 1997 UK general election became the 'most important election since the setting up of the Ulster state'.[16]

This re-emphasised the claim from the DUP that any agreements involving republicanism merely marked further calibrations along the path to a united Ireland.[17] Elsewhere, the DUP promoted what it claimed was the establishment of more democratic and accountable structures of government for Ulster, demanding that IRA/Sinn Féin dismantle its terrorist machine, while arguing that the main need was the defeat of terrorists, 'not some accommodation with them'.[18]

Some of the consistencies within DUP perspectives were again revealed at the time of the 2001 election, when the party manifesto described the DUP as the sole protector of unionists from both the republican movement and the duplicity of the UK government. Another message of the 2001 DUP manifesto was that the UUP simply could not be trusted as defenders of the Union. Indeed, at times Trimble's new unionist message was presented by the DUP as offering almost as much of a threat to the Union as that of Irish nationalism and republicanism. In offering a counter position to the UUP, Peter Robinson defended what he called the 'traditional unionism' of the DUP as representing majority rule, while further suggesting that while power sharing may be possible, it should only be between Unionist parties with the DUP in the lead.[19]

From within the DUP worldview, the peace process was underpinned by three key criteria. First, a conditional surrender to the IRA; second, a denial of democratic control to the majority within Northern

Ireland; and finally, the creation of all-Ireland bodies with executive powers to bring about harmonisation of politics and policy within the island of Ireland. The DUP made clear from the outset its belief that the intention behind the peace process was to weaken, if not destroy, Northern Ireland's constitutional position, Ian Paisley Jnr claiming: 'What you have is not a peace process but a "piece by piece" process and the actual agenda is "Irish unity by stealth".'[20]

Such a discourse has been reproduced throughout the contemporary period, creating anxiety and alarm across all factions of the Unionist bloc. At the onset of the contemporary period, Peter Robinson, the DUP deputy leader, outlined what for him were some of the results of the political process:

> The National Anthem, the Union Jack, the Queen's portrait, Orange culture and unionist traditions have become targets for extinction and demonisation. Even the act of remembering our gallant dead of two world wars is subject to a nationalist veto.
>
> Unionists must be made to feel guilty – embarrassed to expound unionist principles. Wholesome unionist values taught and nurtured for generations are rendered sectarian, right-wing, old fashioned, extreme and backward.[21]

These ideas increased in strength and influence across unionism. While many still subscribed to the familiar tenets of unionist thinking, the DUP repositioned its followers within a broader, more loyalist understanding of culture and identity. The broad thrust of these perspectives can be seen in many statements issued at the time by the DUP. Peter Robinson, for example, suggested that: 'Step by step, unionists are conditioned to become accustomed to "Irishness" rather than "Britishness" to prepare them for their intended destination.'[22]

These twin notions of betrayal and treachery have been drawn upon by the DUP again and again in the contemporary period, as the following illustrates:

> The majority of Ulster's unionists have given the Ulster Democratic Unionist Party the custodianship of our Province. They have charged us with the trust deeds of our future. We have a solemn and terrifying responsibility. Every evil force which seeks the destruction of our Province, the betrayal of our heritage, the abolition of the Union and the final victory of our enemies, is united to achieve that goal.
>
> This is war, war waged in every sphere. It is a fight where no Queensbury Rules are honoured. It is a battle where no international agreements are upheld. It is a struggle for the very existence of democracy. Every evil force is harnessed to the chariot of the

vilest treachery and diabolical deception. Destruction of Ulster is the aim and the IRA is the instrument of the entire Judas Iscariot strategy. Treachery is their order of the day.[23]

Part of the strength of the DUP appeal rests upon a discourse specifically constructed around themes of betrayal that engage directly with apprehensions that are never far below unionism's political surface. By focusing on such notions in the way it does the DUP effectively positions its members within an already understood unionist culture that imposes specific meanings, solutions and possibilities onto contemporary political events.

The discourses that have emerged are broad (concerning the demise of unionism and fear for the constitutional position), and remain core in mobilising unionists and demand public expression from its supporters through voting behaviour, meetings, rallies or other forms of public events. This statement from Ian Paisley just before the 2001 UK general election illustrates well the construction of such a discourse:

> Ulster's future within the Union cannot be secured under the terms of the Belfast Agreement. The Agreement is the drip-feed of IRA/Sinn Féin to take us into a fascist Irish Republic where the Protestant population has already been decimated ... Ulster is to be made a prey to Republican domination. It is vital that a body blow is struck now against the conspiracy and treachery afoot.[24]

FRAMING CULTURAL UNIONISM

Central also to the DUP's construction of politics is the notion that all those who do not fully support the DUP view are weakening the Union and are traitors to the unionist cause. This view has been repeated increasingly by the DUP; its clearest projection, however, has been seen in hostility toward the UUP, which the DUP has claimed was on a sell-out programme and looked upon at various times as a soft touch by the UK government, the Dublin administration, the White House, the IRA, and the Pan-Nationalist Front. According to the DUP, the UUP had proved to be an 'Achilles heel in this time of trial',[25] allowing republicans to dictate terms.[26]

Another clear example of this was revealed in October 2003 when, following another attempt to revitalise the peace process, Ian Paisley challenged the UUP leader David Trimble in the following terms:

> He was willing to accept a manifestly inadequate set of words from Republicans. The language used by Gerry Adams and the IRA singularly failed to state that the war was over or the IRA

would disband. Indeed today's statement is yet another fraud on the people of Northern Ireland. Whilst there is no precision about what the IRA has done, the government spells out in detail each and every concession to the IRA.[27]

Importantly, in making such arguments the DUP are able to draw on a perceived continuity across several generations of unionists and to invoke meanings that plumb deeply embedded cultural and political memories. A direct link is suggested between contemporary UUP leaders such as Reg Empey and David Trimble and previous UUP leaders such as Terence O'Neill, Brian Faulkner and James Molyneaux. All, according to the DUP, have been proved incorrect in their political judgement and claims that the Union was secure.

This perspective is secured and made meaningful across many factions of unionism and located in everyday expressions. Take, for example, this newspaper description of an encounter between Trimble and a Shankill Road pensioner in November 2003:

> Clutching her plastic shopping bag, 71-year-old Margaret Beattie was lying in wait for David Trimble. 'You're a puppet for the IRA,' she screamed, her face red with anger and the decibel level of her voice increasing with each shriek. 'Ulster's not for sale. You told us lies. Traitor!'[28]

It is here that the legitimacy of unionist politics is bounded and made real. This is not to argue that the DUP can directly determine the actions of its followers. Rather, much of the strength of the DUP framing is that it is subtle and wide ranging, constructing a lens through which people perceive and make sense of their political world. Importantly, however, to gain authority such a frame must be seen to be credible and its source must be seen as authentic.[29]

One set of responses by cultural unionism has therefore been to try to return unionism to its understood rudiments, that which is seen as 'commonsense' and unquestionable by many unionists. In so doing the DUP seek to frame contemporary events as linked directly to the past and their response as representing the authentic voice of unionism. The public discourse of the DUP offered an understanding of the peace process as primarily designed to dilute the unionist position and the DUP as the best guardians against the unionist 'birthright' being sold out.

Central to this comprehension of unionism is a political discourse of resistance. Ian Paisley made this very clear in the following claim:

I have no intention of surrendering. Have you? I have no intention of negotiating with the armed IRA/Sinn Féin. Have you? I have no intention of accepting any bribe. Have you? I have no intention of bowing to any occupant of Washington's White House. Have you? I have no intention of insulting the memory of Ulster's honoured dead. Have you? I have no intention of going back on my resolve to keep Ulster from Dublin rule. Have you? I have no intention of lowering the Union flag. Have you? I have no intention of stopping from singing the national anthem. Have you? That being so, I use the words of our founding father, Lord Carson, and I say to this government – You may betray us but you will never deliver us bound into the hands of our enemies. We will defend and retain our liberties and Almighty God will defend the right.[30]

There are several further discourses around which the DUP has restructured and reframed the notion of traditional unionism, in particular the concept of the 'democratic process' (largely taken to mean majority rule in Northern Ireland) and its refusal to capitulate to 'terrorism'. This constant in DUP discourse is further revealed by the following speech by Ian Paisley to the Labour Party conference almost a decade later:

The Secretary of State tells us that Sinn Féin is ready to do a deal. Indeed he would like them to be in our government. In fact, he will not countenance a government without them. The question on our lips is, are they fit to assume that responsibility? Having a mandate is not a qualification of a democrat. Talking the talk of democracy is not the qualification of a democrat. But walking the walk is what unionists will examine. By their example and actions we will know them. Unionists judge Sinn Féin by the cover given to them by the atrocities carried out by the IRA, even in this very city.[31]

Such discourses tap further into broader unionist mindsets. Especially important in the political reaction to the peace process is the perceived strength of the DUP claim to be the only party capable of taking the necessary action to defend the Union. Paisley also draws directly on images and events from the past to claim contemporary legitimacy for the actions of the DUP. Most often this is by direct reference to the leadership of Carson, the 1912–14 home rule crisis, or the formation of Northern Ireland as representative of the will and ability of Ulster Protestants to resist political change.[32]

Thus, the DUP construct a clear lineage and direct links with the past. One of the strongest of these discourses is of betrayal. From a

DUP perspective all those who initially involved themselves in the peace process, in the signing of the Agreement and its aftermath, had been taken in, or had sold out, to the point where they can either no longer have a genuine interest in the Union or have become dupes of a pan-nationalist inspired conspiracy. The DUP has drawn on the above oppositional forms in ways that are recognisable and more importantly meaningful to many unionists. Further, it does so in ways that are capable of highlighting the core principles of unionism, and identifying and mobilising support. Amid the continuing periods of suspension of devolved government, such views found increasing political support across various factions within unionism.

As subsequent chapters will show, particularly following the signing of the Agreement, these interpretations were drawn upon by ever widening factions of unionism to fall behind and provide support for the DUP position.[33] In standing down in favour of the DUP, during the 2005 elections Robert McCartney, leader of the UKUP and former MP for North Down, declared himself satisfied that the DUP was the party best placed to resist any weakening of the Union. Another manifestation was the open hostility expressed by many DUP members towards the UUP for its – albeit limited – support of the Agreement.

These criticisms reflected both ideological and political differences, and rested on two core DUP beliefs. First, that the UUP has been ineffectual in its tactics and commitment to the defence of unionism, and second, that the UUP remains distant from the 'ordinary' unionist people, for whom the DUP claim to speak. The response centred on the claim that only the DUP effectively stood in the way of what it called 'Trimble's betrayal policy'. Against this backdrop it is the DUP which has sought most directly to mobilise anti-Agreement forces, claiming from the outset that the real intentions behind the peace process were clear, and that the government of the UK had sought to betray the Union and the unionist people.

This has led to another key strand of DUP discourse around which unionism has restructured, that the UK government's intentions cannot be viewed uncritically, as it seeks to structure events to meet the demands of the republican movement.[34] This even led to claims that republicans were being allowed to prescribe the terms of the political debate[35] and that the UK government had 'psychologically abandoned Northern Ireland', planning a total withdrawal as soon as circumstances allowed.[36]

Alongside this ran the belief that the settlement would sacrifice British identity in Northern Ireland. As Ian Paisley put it when responding to the Joint Declaration:

> This ... is the latest in a long chain of events designed to drain

away the Britishness of Ulster. I have described it as British Ulster hung, drawn and quartered. Its contents are nothing short of a litany of concessions to IRA/Sinn Féin. Law abiding citizens in the Province will not tolerate reductions in security, freedom for ruthless terrorists on the run and the delivery of a Ministry of Justice to Gerry Kelly. If implemented it will put Sinn Féin/IRA permanently in government, it will give a full role of the Dublin government in the internal affairs of Northern Ireland and ensure IRA/Sinn Féin has complete control of policing and criminal justice![37]

UNIONIST FEARS INTO REALITY

One crucial question to answer of course is why unionists find the political vision of the DUP appealing. Why did the rhetoric of the DUP seem increasingly seductive to many unionists, and what is the basis of support for the DUP's politics of opposition? At the core of reactions from unionists are expressions that the political and cultural rights of unionism have been put under direct challenge by contemporary events. The open articulation of this by the DUP proved meaningful to many unionists,[38] who felt the 'pain of parity to be unbearable'.[39]

One clear location of this was found in unionist reactions to the Patten Report on the future of policing. The report was far reaching, making some 175 recommendations, including the change of the force's name to the Police Service of Northern Ireland (PSNI). At the same time it also recommended that Catholic representation be increased from 8 to around 30 per cent and that within ten years the force's size should be reduced from 11,400 to 7,500.[40] The proposals brought widespread anger from across unionism, much of which rested on the view that changing the structure and name of the RUC represented a concession to the republican movement that it had been unable to achieve during thirty years of conflict.

Unionist reaction to the disbanding of the RUC was only one example of the expressions of fear felt by many Protestants that the political process had put in jeopardy their essential identity[41] and that they were subject to a 'hollowing out [of] Ulster's Britishness'.[42] For some what was feared to be underway was an attempt to have 'everything British ... expunged from the Province's daily life'.[43] Hence, a survey conducted in November 2002 by the *Shankill Mirror* (a community newspaper based in Belfast's Shankill Road) found that fewer than one in ten supported the Agreement and 88 per cent believed that they could not trust Tony Blair to look after the interests of the unionist people.

Within this context certain political discourses increasingly dominated

unionist political life. Many unionists and loyalists perceive their core
identity of Britishness as increasingly threatened by contemporary
events Ulster.[44] This is given credence through the construction of a
unionist history that brings together a wide range of events that collectively are seen to point to the constant demise of unionism. Hence, all
of the major political initiatives of recent times designed to bring about
political settlement are projected as 'betrayal'.[45]

Central to the strength of the position of the DUP is its claim to have
most clearly recognised, made public and resisted such trends. The lexicon of the DUP's response reveals the strength of its belief that what
was underway was a negotiation of the very future of Ulster.[46] The
framing of the DUP as unwavering sentinels against the enemies of
Ulster allows the further construction of an oppositional discourse that
suggests that it is the DUP, and only the DUP, which has recognised the
'truth' and has effectively mobilised. This is set in contrast to the perceived political weakness by other unionists. Ian Paisley as usual put
this forcibly when he said:

> True unionism, unionism cleansed and delivered from the soft-
> ness of political expediency, has arisen and is on the march. Let all
> prevaricators tremble, for truth will always win. Let all compro-
> misers retreat, for I hear the marching feet of the enlarged and
> regenerated battalions of traditional unionism.[47]

Peter Robinson further clarified the DUP position when he claimed
that ordinary unionists sought a resolute approach from their politicians,[48] a self-projection that remains at the core of the DUP's political
discourse and public engagement. Such arguments have been used as
an organisational focus for wider factions of unionism.[49] Robert
McCartney has, for example, linked directly to this discursive frame,
suggesting that senses of Britishness within Northern Ireland have
been deliberately diluted as part of a wider strategic thrust towards
'Irishness' designed to negate opposition to Irish unity and ensure the
Greening of Northern Irish political identity.[50]

Much of this has also been taken on board by the leadership of the
Orange Order, who suggest that:

> It is the traditional enemies of Protestantism and Unionism – Irish
> nationalism and Republicanism – which is spearheading this
> attack on Northern Ireland's loyal ethos. But it is being aided and
> abetted by Government policies which can only have one out-
> come – a weakening of Northern Ireland's position within the
> United Kingdom.[51]

In response many unionists feel they must challenge what they regard as an insidious propaganda directed at subverting their political allegiance to the UK.[52] This perspective emphasises an identifiable notion of tradition within unionism, clearly seen in the way in which the DUP represent the continuity of threat to Northern Ireland's constitutional position.

AWAKENING UNIONISM

So how have the DUP drawn on these understandings to establish the dominant perspective within unionism? Throughout the immediate post-Agreement period, an increasing number of unionists were beguiled by the argument that the UK government had 'sold out' to a republican-set agenda and that republicanism had benefited most from the peace process.[53] The construction of this frame can be easily seen if we consider any of the public utterances of Ian Paisley.

Table 3: Content Analysis of Speech by Ian Paisley, 2004

Issue	No. of Times Featured	(%)
Unionism betrayed by UUP/Trimble	8	21
Ulster as distinct entity	6	16
DUP as true representatives of traditional unionism/leaders of unionism	6	16
IRA/Sinn Féin as synonymous	6	16
Unionism betrayed by UK government	3	8
DUP halting concessions to enemies	3	8
Looking to God for guidance	2	5
IRA as terrorists 2	5	
Demise of unionist culture	2	5

Take, for example, the address in Rasharkin to the Independent Orange Order on 12 July 2004 (outlined in Table 3), which identifies the key issues of the day as projected by Paisley.

If we analyse this in slightly more detail we can see the concentration on three core themes: that unionists represent a distinct people; that those people are or have been betrayed, they are under threat and their identity is being undermined; that the DUP is the only group that can effectively resist the threats and bring about a halt to the decline.

This interpretation allowed the DUP to position itself as the advance guard to those within unionism increasingly formulating opposition to the Agreement. Unifying these groups and individuals was a belief in the impending demise of the Union unless people could be made aware of political realities, awoken to the imminent danger and organised to resist.[54] From within this frame there is just one reasonable interpretation open to the audience, that unionism could only be successful if it took on board what the DUP presented as traditional unionist political values, those that it claimed to take to St Andrews some years later to renegotiate the Agreement.

THE SUCCESS OF CULTURAL UNIONISM

The overarching frame of the DUP's understanding is that what is at stake in contemporary politics is a conflict around the attempt to 'eradicate all traces of ... British sovereignty'[55] from Ireland. Vital to the political success of the DUP, however, is their ability to convince others that unionist culture and politics are under attack, against which the DUP brand of cultural unionism offers a buttress. Moreover, at the core of the DUP's contemporary success is its ability to frame itself as a failsafe firewall against Irish unity.

In harnessing this, the DUP has been able to draw directly on long-standing frames of understanding within unionism and on many of the central notions of cultural unionism outlined in Chapter 2. If we refer to Table 4 we can see a growing belief among DUP supporters (firmly located within the working class) that nationalists had benefited most from the Agreement and minority support for compromise. Although around three-quarters of DUP identifiers supported the workings of an Assembly, this is probably best explained as a belief from within the DUP that they would best secure the Union without compromise and to counter Sinn Féin in any devolved Assembly.

Table 4: Characteristics of DUP Voters in 1998 and 2003

	1998 (%)	2003 (%)
Believe that nationalists have benefited a lot from the Agreement	66	72
Support North–South bodies	21	39
Support Assembly	69	73
Support power sharing	35	71
Support the guarantee that NI will remain part of the UK as long as the majority of people in NI want this	98	97
Voted 'yes'/would vote 'yes' to the Agreement now	15	20
Believe that the DUP leaders should be willing to compromise	30	38
Aged 18–30	24	14
Self-perceived working class	75	77

Source: Dowds and Lynn[56]

By the election of 2003 these perspectives were widespread across unionism and DUP discourses were embedded across sections of the Orange Order (see previous chapter), elements of the UUP and other factions across unionism and loyalism.[57] It even found support from former Northern Ireland secretary, Peter Mandelson who has accused Tony Blair, when prime minister, of 'conceding and capitulating' to republican demands.[58]

The growing political support for the DUP was evident at all levels throughout Northern Ireland. In the 2003 local district council elections the DUP increased its number of councillors by 52 to 182, amassing 208,278 votes (almost 30 per cent of all first preferences cast). In contrast the decline in support for the UUP was stark. It won only 115 seats with a mere 126,317 votes, around 18 per cent of those cast. It marked the worst ever performance for the UUP, with the DUP gaining seats in twenty-one of twenty-six councils, while the UUP lost seats in all but seven of the councils in which it stood candidates.[59]

Within the Belfast hinterland results for the DUP were particularly impressive; the party made eight gains in the previous UUP stronghold of Lisburn, and overall control in Newtownabbey and Ards councils. Even in the UUP heartland of North Down, the DUP made significant advances (although this was partly attributable to the disappearance from local government of the UKUP, which then actively promoted support for the DUP). Following the election it was only in the four council areas of Fermanagh, Down, Moyle, and Newry and Mourne that the UUP had more seats than its erstwhile junior rival.

CONCLUSION

Crucial to their success was the ability of the DUP to construct a convincing frame of analysis for unionists. This suggested that the actions and beliefs of the UUP and other pro-Agreement unionists were directly undermining the soul of unionism and threatening the very existence of the Union. As this chapter has made clear, although initially self-excluded and marginalised (because of its resistance to the Agreement), the DUP became increasingly core to the overall unionist response to the Agreement and later post-Agreement politics (see Chapter 7).

Central to the strengthening of the DUP's position was its ability to harness the mounting feelings of marginalisation expressed by unionists, and the views that they had lost out to a 'concession conveyor belt'[60] driven by the apologists of armed IRA terror in government. Throughout the period of the peace process the DUP drew heavily on constructions of cultural unionism to position itself outside the main structures arising from the agreed settlement and to organise around a discourse of opposition to political and social loss. Reactions to such issues were also important in the development of distinct loyalist responses, both in party political expressions and on the streets.

NOTES

1. Campbell, G., cited in *Belfast Telegraph*, 8 January 2002.
2. Powell, J., *Great Hatred, Little Room: Making Peace in Northern Ireland* (London: The Bodley Head, 2008), pp.16–17.
3. Southern, N., 'Ian Paisley and evangelical Democratic Unionists: an analysis of the role of evangelical Protestantism within the Democratic Unionist Party', *Irish Political Studies*, 20, 2 (2005), pp.127–45.
4. Robinson, P., 'David Trimble is "barking mad"'. Archived at: http://www.peterrobinson.org/KeyArticles.asp?Article_ID=225
5. Paisley, I., 'Statement by party leader', DUP 30th Anniversary Conference 2001, p.7.
6. *The New Protestant Telegraph*, June 1995.
7. *Irish News*, 26 January 1998.
8. Southern, N., 'Protestant alienation in Northern Ireland: a political, cultural and geographical examination', *Journal of Ethnic and Migration Studies*, 33, 1 (2007), pp.159–80.
9. Southern, 'Protestant alienation in Northern Ireland'.
10. *The Voice of Ulster*, October 1982, p.8.
11. *Irish News*, 26 January 1998.
12. Cusack and McDonald, *UVF*, p.325.
13. Democratic Unionist Party, *Our Covenant with the Ulster People: Manifesto for the Forum Election* (Belfast: DUP, 1996).
14. *Irish Times*, 1 December 1997.
15. See Moloney, E. and Pollak, A., *Paisley* (Swords: Poolbeg Press, 1986); Nelson, S., *Ulster's Uncertain Defenders: Loyalists and the Northern Ireland Conflict* (Belfast: Appletree Press, 1984).
16. *New Protestant Telegraph*, March 1997, p.1.
17. McAuley, J.W., 'Fantasy politics? Restructuring unionism after the Good Friday Agreement', *Eire–Ireland*, 39, 1/2 (2004), pp.189–214.
18. Democratic Unionist Party, *The Unionist Team You Can Trust: Forum Election Communication* (Belfast: DUP, 1996). See also Democratic Unionist Party, *Election Special* (Belfast: DUP, 1996); Democratic Unionist Party, *The Framework of Shame and Sham: Yes the Framework Document is a One-Way Road to Dublin* (Belfast: DUP, no date).
19. BBC, *Hearts and Minds*, 15 May 2001.
20. *Observer*, 11 January 1998.
21. Democratic Unionist Party, Press Release, 27 October 1997.
22. Robinson, P., 'Call to unionists', *News Letter*, 31 October 1997.
23. Paisley, I., 'Leader's speech at DUP annual conference 2004, the Ramada Hotel, Belfast'. Archived at: http://www.dup.org.uk
24. Paisley, I., 'Vote DUP: eve of poll message'. Archived at: http://www.dup.org.uk
25. Democratic Unionist Party, Press Release, 24 March 1997.
26. *Belfast Telegraph*, 22 October 2002.
27. Paisley, I., 'IRA move yet another cynical gesture in latest agreement farce'.
28. Cited in O'Brien, C., 'Trimble is serenaded by Shankill shoppers', *Irish Times*, 11 November 2003.
29. See Druckman, J.N., 'Evaluating framing effects', *Journal of Economic Psychology*, no. 22 (2001), pp.91–101; Druckman, J.N., 'On the limits of framing effects: who can frame?', *Journal of Politics*, no. 63 (2001), pp.1041–66.
30. *Irish Times*, 1 December 1997.
31. Paisley, I., 'Speech to Labour Party conference 2006'.
32. Moloney, E., *Paisley: From Demagogue to Democrat?* (Dublin: Poolbeg Press, 2008), pp.282–3.
33. See works in Foster, *The Idea of the Union*; McCartney, R., *Reflections on Liberty, Democracy and the Union* (Dublin: Maunsel and Company, 2001).
34. Democratic Unionist Party, *Towards a New Agreement: DUP Analysis Vindicated* (Belfast: DUP, 2003).
35. Thornton, C. and McAdam, N., 'DUP warns of "fantasy politics"', *Belfast Telegraph*, 22 October 2002.
36. *The New Protestant Telegraph*, June 1995.
37. Cited in Thornton and McAdam, 'DUP warns of "fantasy politics"'.

38. McAuley, J.W., 'Whither new loyalism: changing politics after the Belfast Agreement', *Journal of Irish Political Studies*, 20, 3 (2005), pp.323–40.
39. Murray, D. (ed.), *Protestant Perceptions of the Peace Process in Northern Ireland* (University of Limerick: Centre for Peace and Development Studies, 2000), p.4.
40. BBC News Online, 'Concern Over Policing Reforms'. Archived at: http://news.bbc.co.uk/1/hi/in_depth/uk/2000/ruc_reform/default.stm
41. Dunn, S. and Morgan, V., *Protestant Alienation in Northern Ireland: A Preliminary Survey* (Coleraine: Centre for the Study of Conflict, University of Ulster, 1994), pp.20–1.
42. Lucy, G. and McClure, E. (eds), *Cool Britannia? What Britishness Means to Me* (Lurgan: Ulster Society, 1999).
43. Democratic Unionist Party, Press Release, 27 October 1997.
44. See Brown, K. and MacGinty, R., 'Public attitudes toward partisan and neutral symbols in post-Agreement Northern Ireland', *Identities: Global Studies in Culture and Power*, no. 10 (2003), pp.83–108.
45. See Grove, M., *The Price of Peace: An Analysis of British Policy in Northern Ireland* (London: Centre for Policy Studies, 2000); Robinson, P., *The Union Under Fire: United Ireland Framework Revealed* (Belfast: published by the author, 1995).
46. Democratic Unionist Party, 'The framework of shame and sham' (Belfast: DUP Headquarters, no date).
47. Paisley, 'Leader's speech at DUP annual conference 2004'; Chrisafis, A., 'Triumphant Paisley vows to defeat Ulster roadmap', *Guardian*, 10 May 2004.
48. Robinson, P., 'So, what now for unionism?', *Belfast Telegraph*, 12 June 2001.
49. See Grove, *The Price of Peace*; Roche, P.J., *The Appeasement of Terrorism and the Belfast Agreement* (Ballyclare: Northern Ireland Unionist Party, 2000).
50. McCartney, R., 'Gerry pandering?' *Belfast Telegraph*, 4 October 2001.
51. *The Orange Standard*, April 1999.
52. Morrow 'Nothing to fear but …? Unionists and the Northern Ireland peace process'
53. See material in McCartney, *The McCartney Report on Consent*; McCartney, *The McCartney Report on the Framework Documents*.
54. Robinson, P., 'Speech at the Young Democrat conference 2000'.
55. *Belfast Telegraph*, 11 June 2002.
56. Dowds, L. and Lynn, B., 'The changing face of unionism: evidence from public attitude surveys', *ESRC Devolution and Constitutional Change Programme, Research Briefing*, 32, August 2005.
57. Paisley, I. *The Fruits of Appeasement* (DUP press statement, 3 September 1998).
58. Watt, N., Wintour, P. and Bowcott, O., 'Blair guilty of capitulating to Sinn Féin – Mandelson', *Guardian*, 13 March 2007.
59. Wilson, R. and Wilford, R., *The 2005 Westminster and District Council Elections in Northern Ireland* (ESRC Research Programme on Devolution and Constitutional Change, briefing no. 30, October 2005), p.2.
60. Campbell, G., 'Suppression of unionist community unacceptable', *Belfast Telegraph*, 29 September 2005.

Chapter 5

The Politics of New Loyalism

The conceptual structure of Loyalism was powerfully reinforced by the experience of communal conflict ...
Contemporary events were seen in terms of images of the
past: Protestants were being pushed out of their traditional
areas and workplaces, they were under siege, subject to
genocidal attack, forced to retaliate. Only loyalist organisation, vigilance and militancy could defend the Protestant
population.

Joe Ruane and Jennifer Todd[1]

Loyalism today stands for the political empowerment of the
people. It stands for an end to deprivation in Protestant
working-class areas. Loyalists look forward towards the
future for Northern Ireland – a future in which society will
be equitable and just. Today, Loyalism is the only credible
alternative to the bankrupt traditional political establishment – a positive, vibrant, innovative and courageous form
of Unionism.

New Ulster Defender[2]

The contemporary shape of loyalism emerged following growing political tensions in the mid to late 1960s, the reactions of sections of the
Protestant working class to the emergence of the civil rights movement,
and the outbreak of political violence from the end of that decade
onwards, heralding growing fears by many Protestants of the onset of a
republican plot to 'destroy Ulster'.[3] The reactions to these events saw
unionism fragment,[4] one leading figure arguing that loyalism was really
only defined when as a result of mounting violence other unionists
initiated a process of ideological and political separation from the

Protestant working class.[5] As Farrington clearly reminds us, although the boundaries between unionism and loyalism are hazy, they certainly exist and remain meaningful to all concerned; the clearest lines of demarcation remain those of class and the social circumstances within which most loyalists live.[6]

One response from contemporary loyalism[7] saw the formation of paramilitary groupings, including those prepared to organise and engage in direct conflict.[8] Although the histories, tactics and leadership values of loyalist paramilitaries differ,[9] all expressed the common concern that Northern Ireland's constitutional position was under direct threat from militant republicanism, and made clear a willingness to counter this with physical force if deemed necessary.

As the conflict took shape and lengthened, the overt goal of tackling republicanism remained intact, but the definition of who or what constituted republicanism (and hence, in the terms of the loyalist paramilitaries, who was seen as a legitimate target) became increasingly more nebulous and ill determined.[10] For some this mattered little and, as a result, many:

> ... of their targets were innocent Catholics. Some Loyalists viewed this as appropriate because they saw all Catholics as either Republicans or republican supporters and therefore traitors to the State: each Catholic killed was one less threat to the Union. Others thought it was strategic to attack innocent Catholics because it gave the message to the wider nationalist community that they would pay a price for IRA actions. They hope that this would lead to pressure on the IRA from within the Catholic community.[11]

THE POLITICS OF LOYALISM

Loyalism, however, cannot be reduced simply to a militant physical force tradition. Rather, loyalist identity is constructed by drawing on a wide range of reference points that bind together social and political interpretations, and which are broader than paramilitarism (see also Chapter 7). It is therefore more meaningful to understand loyalism as an expression of unionism seen through the prism of Protestant working-class life. The resulting experiences have given rise to a series of political responses that include, but are not exclusively contained in, paramilitarism. Indeed, throughout the contemporary period both the UDA and UVF (the two biggest paramilitary groupings) have produced political representatives and ideas that have offered glimpses of a political imagination far beyond that of the established unionist leadership.

Paramilitary representatives have continued to set about framing

and explaining contemporary events and to engage in offering differing political understandings of those events. So what is the contemporary outcome? To begin to answer this question it is important to consider the room for flexibility in contemporary constructions of loyalist
identities. In particular this chapter will discuss how that which was
dubbed 'new loyalism' emerged from within loyalist paramilitary
organisations to reflect specific experiences, the backgrounds of those
involved in the conflict, and the communities from which they
emerged.[12]

Part of this involved constructing a more socially aware and inclusive politics, which at times has been seen to offer direct challenges to
the established unionist leadership.[13] The allegiance of the Protestant
working class has always been central to unionist politics. Take, for
example, the following account from a young man, growing up over
sixty years ago in the Hammer district of the Shankill Road in Belfast:

> The orator raised a hand ... Voice breaking, he bellowed: 'The
> men and women of the Hammer have sense, they are not easily
> gulled by their enemies; they are not going to be dragged into the
> land of Popery. They are sons and daughters of great people; peo-
> ple who fought dearly for Ulster, and now like their forebears they
> are going to prove that they have fire in their bellies. They are
> going to vote for right!'[14]

The positioning of the Protestant working class became core to a
political culture resting on the marginalisation as disloyal and untrustworthy of all those who questioned the workings of the Northern
Ireland state. The situation was never monolithic, however. Although
not always given the attention they merit, there have always been
autonomous voices from within working-class Protestantism. In more
recent times such voices were again heard as political debate and
expression opened up within many loyalist communities.

This witnessed the surfacing of community groupings and the
active participation of various community representatives drawn from
a range of individuals, including politicised paramilitary members, former paramilitary prisoners, councillors, community activists, women's
groups and other concerned local people. Some within working-class
Protestant communities began 'directing their energies into a radical
reappraisal of where they have come from and where they are going'.[15]
Although for many their mobilisation was not to be long term, such
grouping demonstrated a degree of self reflection not commonly found
within the unionist population, and certainly not always observable
within working-class loyalism.

The outcome of this was seen in particular through the political positioning of the PUP, which increasingly sought to establish distance from other sections of unionism through claims to be moving away from tribalism towards a more pluralist expression of working-class politics.[16] Further, the PUP made representations that mainstream unionist politicians consistently misrepresented the views of working-class unionists.[17] In response, while the PUP strongly and consistently restated its commitment to the Union, initially often describing itself as a 'socialist unionist' party, it also presented a pluralist notion of politics, claiming the legitimacy of any group seeking democratic and peaceful constitutional change 'regardless of religious, cultural, national or political inclinations'.[18]

PARAMILITARISM, POLITICS AND THE PEACE PROCESS

But how broadly did such views reflect wider paramilitary circles? Certainly in the immediate wake of the IRA ceasefire announcement loyalist paramilitaries did not fall in line with the wider political response. Some, at least, within loyalism believed that the IRA ceasefire was merely tactical; for others it was a sign of weakness, that republicans were on the back foot and that the loyalist military campaign should continue until Irish republicanism was completely defeated or there was evidence of IRA capitulation. More thought that while they may have reached the point of compromise, loyalist paramilitaries should not move until republicans declared a complete and public surrender.

As the IRA ceasefire held, however, the loyalist paramilitaries were forced to present a more measured response, not least because, as many within paramilitarism had long argued that their prime motivation was as a repost to republican violence, their core motivation now seemed to be removed. It took just over six weeks of intense debate among paramilitary and prisoner groupings, in a process brokered by a Presbyterian cleric, the Reverend Roy Magee, before the CLMC announced that loyalism would also bring a halt to its campaign, and that their ceasefire would be permanent unless republican paramilitaries resumed violence.[19]

While there was internal opposition, the dynamic across loyalist paramilitarism shifted towards those promoting a political dimension. As both UDA and UVF/RHC groupings accepted the need for a more positive and brazen involvement in the peace process, the voice of new loyalism increasingly began to be heard. But there were still other perspectives on offer within loyalism, and its orientation and alignment remained contested.

These developments will be explored throughout this chapter, which addresses some of the major perspectives of both the PUP and UDP groupings, and highlights important differences between these political groupings and the other major representatives of loyalism and unionism. It then considers some of the resulting tensions within loyalism, particularly in relation to the search for a political settlement. The remainder of the chapter identifies the different voices seeking to structure loyalism, in part at least, as an expression of resistance to mainstream unionism. Indeed, some would claim that the politics of the PUP and UDP could only be understood as part of a wider political project to redefine loyalism.

THE POLITICS OF THE PUP

So what form did this attempted reconstruction take? One example can be found directly in the expanded role of the PUP,[20] which from the early 1980s had begun to give expression to that understanding of politics developed by the UVF. Specifically this was driven by some of those UVF members made more socially aware and politically astute by the experiences they had undergone while in jail.[21] Although it was a far from uniform or universal process among loyalist prisoners, most of the UVF members who became active in, and later formed the leadership of, the PUP trace their inspiration and their developing interest in politics directly to their interaction with Gusty Spence and their political 'schooling' in prison.[22]

Spence had been the first loyalist in the contemporary period to be arrested for the murder of a Catholic, in 1966, but his subsequent personal political journey took some unexpected turns. For example, while serving his life sentence he wrote, sending his condolences, to the widow of the Official IRA (OIRA) leader Joe McCann, who had been shot dead by the British army on 15 April 1972. He then led some thirty UVF prisoners in a joint protest with OIRA inmates to demand political status. Shortly afterwards he issued a statement claiming that he 'deplored sectarian assassination, and that the unionist party had got the loyalists of Northern Ireland into "one hell of a mess"'.[23]

As commander of the UVF grouping in the prisons[24] Spence was instrumental in promoting political debates and discussions among prisoners and organising formal political discussions.[25] From around the mid-1970s he began to introduce the notions of 'politicising the paramilitaries' and 'putting fighting aside'.[26] His own politicisation was to affect not just his fellow inmates but also the direction of loyalist politics more broadly. Although 'the majority [of UVF prisoners] were little moved by his democratic socialism or his acceptance of Catholics in the Northern Ireland state',[27] he was able to draw on support from a number of committed followers, who were to become influential within the organisation.

Many of the views they expressed within the prisons, albeit in often extremely embryonic form, resurfaced to find greater political maturity and representation years later.[28] Indeed, Spence and the grouping he led could claim with justification to have acted as midwife to new loyalism.[29] This precipitated the formation of a politics which later found expression in those he influenced directly and in the policies of the PUP (especially following Spence's release from prison).[30] Kate Fearon describes the development of the situation as follows:

> The debates in prison had not been specifically about the Progressive Unionist Party per se. They were more about analysing Unionism and reflecting on being in prison. Many of those debates were too much, too soon for UVF members, but now there was an opportunity to present those discussions as an idea whose time had come.[31]

As the views of this grouping began to take shape it became clear that while the party's commitment to the Union could never seriously be challenged (either from within or without), the PUP began to demonstrate a willingness to promote a more inclusive form of unionism.[32] The party articulated support for a political break with what had gone before, promoting the view that it was mainly the ordinary people from both communities who had suffered during the period of Stormont rule. This theme can be clearly identified in the following statement:

> It has been mostly working-class people who have borne the brunt of the violence over these past twenty-five years and more and they are sick and tired of political sabre-rattling and mischievousness from whatever quarter. There can never, ever, be a return to the awful political and social abuses of the past and Stormont as we knew it is dead and gone, never to be resurrected.[33]

Increasingly, the PUP developed and promoted a distinct political platform, one that included open scepticism of the established unionist leadership and promoted a willingness to engage directly with political adversaries.[34] Alongside this the PUP offered expressions of a distinct 'leftist' position within unionism, especially on social and economic issues and an articulation of class, and to a lesser extent gendered readings of loyalism.

All of these were reflected in the promotion of a broad pluralist politics[35] repositioning loyalism through a restatement of the cultural values of working-class Protestantism set against the backdrop of a broad social democratic platform. In part this drew on deep-seated tenets from within the Protestant working class. In the view of Aaron Edwards, for example, 'the efforts of loyalist activists to reshape unionist political ideology from the "bottom up" echoed the challenges thrown down to traditional unionism by NILP politicians in the 1950s and 1960s.'[36] Both were driven and organised by an organic leadership[37] that sought to locate politics directly in the loyalist working-class communities, claiming that their views were at best under-represented by the unionist leadership.[38]

Thus, the PUP sought to mark itself off from traditional unionism, both in terms of its involvement in leadership and community development and through its willingness to engage with what other unionists openly dismissed in both ideological and political terms.[39] This gave rise to the development of a 'civic loyalism' promoting citizenship as the core of a solution. Thus, in the contemporary period the PUP has argued, for example, that the unionist leadership needed 'to wake up and give people hope rather than [a] constant sense of dismay',[40] reflecting broader findings that working-class Protestant communities felt increasingly isolated from and marginalised by the political process and that their traditions and culture were under threat.[41]

ENGAGING THE POLITICS OF THE ABSURD

At the heart of unionist ideology has always been its denial of the legitimacy of the political demands of Irish nationalism. Sometimes, as in the works of Aughey, where primacy of modernised civic unionism is asserted over the pre-modern character of ethno-religious nationalism, these denials are extremely sophisticated; at other times, as in the discourse of the DUP, they are much less complicated in presentation; and in the everyday expressions of some sections of loyalism they are forthright and unreconstructed.

Counter to these frames of reference, however, a clear signifier of the PUP's emergence was the willingness to promote engagement with representatives of Irish republicanism.[42] Indeed, as long ago as 1983, the PUP called for all-party talks to be organised to include Sinn Féin.[43] This marked the initial steps in the development of a politics by the PUP seeking to reflect the lived realities of the everyday in working-class areas, where community activists were often working side by side, and where cross-community dialogue and involvement in cross-community projects had been established.

Moreover, the PUP has sought to identify some form of collective recognition of common social and economic positions with their counterparts in nationalist areas and highlight how they have been subject to the same political forces (see Chapter 6). Part of the reconstruction of loyalism undertaken by the PUP was its consideration of, and attempts to centre, political issues beyond the constitutional position. The PUP has, for example, often emphasised the need for direct state intervention in areas such as health and social security services, urban regeneration, funded community development[44] and a strong interventionist state to provide social welfare policies in areas such as social housing, health and, in particular, education.[45]

Hence, for the PUP support for political accommodation, the introduction of a power-sharing devolved Assembly and a written constitution in Northern Ireland, have featured as longstanding commitments.[46] The development of these policies drew a harsh retort from other unionist political representatives. The DUP in particular, which was also seeking to position itself as the voice of working-class Protestantism, reacted strongly. One leading member of the PUP summarised the wider political dynamics between the two groups as follows:

> From very early days the inability of the Unionist Party and Sinn Féin to deliver undermined the Agreement. The PUP worked hard for the Agreement ... went head to head with the DUP on occasions which was difficult. Many people in the Party suffered emotional strain. It is not easy to constantly be referred to as 'Judas' and 'traitor'.[47]

RESTRUCTURING UNIONISM

While the political development of the PUP can never be divorced from the experiences of paramilitarism, its emergence also marked links with other recognisable social forces, and in particular with a history of Labour politics that has existed for many decades within the Protestant working class.[48] In the rapidly changing social relationships following the paramilitary ceasefires the expression of a more community-based, even class-aware, politics that reflected the everyday life of loyalists moved to the forefront. This resulted in the promotion of a policy direction that bore much similarity to the post-war 'Old Labour' and pre-Blairite British Labour Party.[49]

Some within the PUP also openly expressed views on the gendered nature of Northern Irish society. This again set it apart from other Unionist parties. Within unionism, the dominant tendency towards conservative social and political values,[50] fundamentalist interpretations of Christian ideology[51] and 'sectarian patriarchal relations'[52] have combined to reinforce the socially subordinate position of women.[53] This has seen women from a unionist background largely excluded from participation in political life[54] and from any conspicuous history of unionist politics.[55] Eilish Rooney suggests this is part of a broad process, the 'invisibility of women', reflected in 'the absence of gender awareness in the established literature on the Northern Irish conflict'.[56] Rooney further argues that, within unionism, although women have provided crucial resources[57] they have remained relatively hidden, a point reinforced by Rachel Ward, who identifies how the main projection of unionist women has largely remained confined to that of 'teamakers'[58] in support of politically active men.[59]

What changed, at least to some degree, in the immediate post-ceasefires period was that much of the activity involving women became more prominent and apparent at the community level. This was indicative of the rapidly changing social circumstances in the immediate aftermath of the ceasefires, where the relative absence of overt paramilitary violence and the drive for peace opened up space for more community-based expressions of political desires. It also reflected the 'alternative cultural environment' created by many women throughout the conflict to cope with 'the insidious atmosphere of sectarianism and violence ... death and injuries of loved ones ... and the destruction of normal family life'.[60]

While the majority experience for most women continued to be exclusion from any discernible presence in the public arena,[61] there was evidence this was being challenged, and those loyalist women created the opportunity to discuss their social relations in a more meaningful way. In the mid-1990s the rapid growth of campaign groups based around women's issues undoubtedly made some difference at a local level.[62] Such processes were, in part at least, enabled by interactions with the PUP and other community activists who reinvigorated localised politics at the time.

Of course, not all women from loyalist backgrounds are politically progressive in their outlook.[63] The story of the roles played by loyalist women during the conflict is only beginning to emerge,[64] although the evidence that is available suggests at best ambivalence towards women's involvement in paramilitarism from within the broader Protestant community, where 'gender equality and emancipation have been less evident'.[65]

The PUP's circle of influence expanded rapidly in the post-Agreement period. In particular, the PUP leadership argued that Protestant working-class politics needed to be set against a background recognising that the old heavy industry economy, which afforded small, if sometimes significant, privileges to the Protestant working class, was no more and that the politics emerging from that section of society should be repositioned within a broad framework of social democratic values. The PUP leadership also expressed an acute awareness of the situation of the Protestant working class as a group increasingly alienated, economically and socially, by contemporary political change.

Given their background, the leadership of the PUP was empathic to the mounting sense of alienation within working-class Protestant communities, where on the eve of the peace process 'a quarter of a century of violence, civil unrest and constitutional uncertainty [had] made worse the Unionist insecurity which led to partition and discrimination'.[66] As a result the PUP sought to highlight social and economic issues[67] and to focus on class relations and the centrality of community as core points of reference within unionism. It was this which was to provide the PUP with much of its vigour in the period following the ceasefires and which has remained central to the political potency of the party.

THE ULSTER DEMOCRATIC PARTY

The other main outlet for political expression based in the paramilitaries was the UDP. It too, for some time at least, found wider support within working-class Protestant areas. Like the PUP, the group emerged in its original form during the political ferment of the mid-1970s. The New Ulster Political Research Group (NUPRG)[68] strongly promoted the idea of a negotiated independent Ulster (within the European Union and the Commonwealth) as a political solution to the conflict. Details of the proposals were revealed in their policy document, *Beyond the Religious Divide*.[69] By the mid-1980s the UDA had established a more formal political organisation, the Ulster Loyalist Democratic Party (ULDP), which in 1989 became the UDP, winning a local council seat in Londonderry.

Throughout the 1970s and 1980s, the strength and form of political organisation, and the desire to find some form of public political expression, varied considerably, often determined by broader paramilitary reactions to the conflict and levels of violence in the wider society (in which, of course the UDA was centrally involved). Throughout that time, however, the UDA continued to promote some notion of a 'shared identity' as the basis for conflict resolution. Following the AIA of 1985, the UDA drew heavily on a reworking of *Beyond the Religious Divide* by two paramilitary leaders, John McMichael[70] and Harry Smallwood, for its political direction. This was republished as the *Common Sense* document,[71] among the central proposals of which were the establishment of a devolved power-sharing government in Northern Ireland. Although both McMichael and Smallwood were killed during the course of the conflict, the political direction outlined in *Common Sense* remained central to the political agenda of the UDA.

The UDP was also seeking to represent itself as an alternative location for unionist votes. Hence, in campaigning for the 1996 Forum election the UDP argued that it offered a new direction[72] to counter unionist politicians who had failed to provide effective leadership[73] and set out what it termed a democratic framework for government to be enshrined in a new written constitution.[74] Representatives from key areas of UDA strength (such as North Antrim and Londonderry) continued to openly challenge the peace process,[75] and in January 1998 the UDP chose to withdraw from all-party talks (ahead of its imminent expulsion) because of increasing levels of violence by the UDA.[76]

The UDP leader Gary McMichael was forced to issue a threat to resign if the UDA came out against the Agreement,[77]and it was increasingly clear that the electoral path of the UDP was far from secure. While the special circumstances surrounding the Forum election based on inclusivity allowed the UDP to take two seats, in the subsequent elections to the first Assembly the UDP failed to secure any representation or any worthy level of support from the electorate. The election was a watershed for the UDP. Not only did the results illustrate the size of the gap between the party and the voters; it also highlighted that the UDA could not even look directly to its heartlands for electoral support.[78] The result magnified increasing tensions between the UDA and UVF, precipitated by differing levels of success in the public representation of their respective politics. Such frictions were exacerbated by direct contrast with the fortunes of the UDP and the PUP, for which David Ervine (East Belfast) and Billy Hutchinson (North Belfast) won seats in the new Assembly.[79]

By the mid-1990s the belief that British citizenship had been undermined by the Agreement and that the Union was less secure than before the peace process were widespread within the ranks of the UDA. Such ideas were to become consistent, and growing reference points for the UDP. Indeed, Frankie Gallagher was later to claim that the rank-and-file membership of the UDA was never pro-Agreement, and that any positive expression towards it was always leadership-led rather than located in the ordinary membership.[80]

Many UDA members also believed that their political representatives were being increasingly marginalised from important political discussions and excluded from any meaningful political decision-making roles. By the end of the decade sections of loyalism were increasingly disenfranchised from the political consequences of the peace process. This notion began to become embedded within UDA thinking as early as 1996, as the following statement in reaction to the *Framework Document* illustrates:

The British Establishment's project is not to throw us out of the

United Kingdom, nor do we believe it is to hasten a United Ireland, but to dilute our citizenship and direct our future towards some form of Irish confederation. The centre of gravity of this document is not Unionist in terms defined by the Prime Minister for other UK regions. The Union may remain safe in the purely constitutional sense, but in the context of Northern Ireland it is far from satisfactory.[81]

The weight of such views among the rank and file, the drift of UDA leadership away from 'politics' as a central goal and the perceived exclusion of the UDP from the main political arena brought growing apathy, if not open hostility, towards the whole political project,[82] resulting in fourteen branches splitting from the UDP because of its pro-Agreement stance. Even at its highpoint few in the UDA voted for the UDP, preferring to give votes to anti-Agreement candidates before their own party.[83] Such tensions resulted in an increasing failure to mobilise support and a level of chaos and disorganisation within the party ahead of the May 2001 elections, which meant that the UDP failed to register in time to take part in the contest.[84]

Moreover, the UDA was increasingly being pulled in different directions by internal feuds, conflicts surrounding its political stance, arguments over the future direction of the organisation and ever mounting tensions among its leadership. In July 2001 the UFF released a statement claiming that it could 'no longer remain silent [concerning] criticisms of an agreement, which our membership have continuously voiced their opposition to, and which the vast number of the loyalist community have grown to despise'.[85] Reports emerged that at least five out of the six brigades who made up the UDA leadership opposed the peace process[86] and were actively promoting an end to the loyalist ceasefire.[87]

Antagonisms were also coming to the fore over the continuing involvement of the UDA in a web of criminality, extortion and drug trafficking. As the organisation sought to resolve its internal tensions the UDA returned to more familiar roles. The UDP was dissolved, supposedly fragmenting over ideological disagreements, but in reality having little choice following demands from the inner council of the UDA that it cease operating. One pro-inner council UDA magazine, *Warrior*, said the following:

> The change of tactics by the pan-nationalist front caught the UDA on the back foot and while republicans had a clear view of what they wanted to achieve out of the so-called 'peace process' the UDA had no strategy whatsoever for a peace-time scenario. Instead they were to rely on a political analysis by a weak and

incompetent leadership from within the Ulster Democratic Party which proved to be disastrous for the Organisation.[88]

The UDP was replaced by the Ulster Political Research Group (UPRG), largely comprised of those much more sympathetic to UDA leadership and charged with providing political analysis rather than acting as a political party or seeking a mandate.[89] The changes directly reflected the overall goals of the UDA at the time, and it was no coincidence that sectarian violence from within sections of loyalism became more commonplace and everyday.[90] By late 2001, amid heightening sectarian tensions, an upsurge in attacks on Catholic homes, intra-loyalist violence, the bombing of SDLP offices in Belfast and mounting criminal activities, the UK government had little option but to withdraw official recognition for the UDA ceasefire,[91] further weakening the position of those seeking to promote a more political stance.

CHANGING LOYALISM?

Although the UDA called another twelve-month ceasefire in early 2003 and urged the UPRG to 'steer the organisation down a diplomatic path',[92] it was not until early 2005 that the UPRG began to produce anything that might be considered coherent in terms of political direction for the organisation.[93] Following UPRG assurances that the UDA was now supportive of all aspects of the peace process, including the eradication of all paramilitarism, official recognition for the UDA ceasefire was restored.[94] Further, the UDA leadership claimed that it would seek to develop politics and to implant new initiatives based on political reconciliation across the ranks of the organisation.[95]

Against this background, the UPRG began to develop an identifiable political direction through its engagement with the notion of conflict transformation.[96] Some of the implications of this will be outlined in the next chapter. Broadly, however, in loyalist working-class districts, a combination of political forces, including former paramilitary prisoners, other community activists and members of the UDP and PUP, have sought to re-identify post-conflict politics, offering, in particular, a community-based challenge to the hegemonic position of the DUP. As one commentator put it:

> UDA members are possibly right that most 'Unionist leaders still seek to use paramilitaries for their own benefit' ... the DUP refuse to overtly talk with paramilitaries while negotiating indirectly behind backs. They prefer that loyalists remain enslaved in their boxes and fear lest they get up off their knees to challenge DUP hegemony.[97]

The contours of the material produced, however, did in part dispute that hegemony. It was largely both self-critical of unionism and pluralistic in approach and was expressed well by the Shankill Think Tank,[98] which argued forcibly that inter-community dialogue was the most realistic basis from which to develop a solution to the conflict. Partly in response to such community feelings, the UDP and PUP sought to increase the distance between themselves and the representatives of traditional unionism (while never claiming to question the existing constitutional position). This was reflected in claims to directly challenge the roles played by 'outdated' unionist politicians, because the 'Protestant people have woken up to [their] phoney politics'.[99]

Such arguments stretched the existing ideological space within loyalist working-class communities,[100] particularly through subsequent discussions involving the nature and form of Protestant and unionist culture and politics, and its possible future direction.[101] Certainly there were indications that the loyalist parties were willing to contest the legitimacy of the DUP and to formulate a new political approach. This took different forms; while the PUP strongly advocated devolved government, the UDP at times reflected a more integrationist stance. During the negotiations leading up to the Agreement, for example, the UDP argued that traditional unionism should adopt a much broader vista, by directly linking more fully with politics in the rest of the UK. Hence, the following:

> Unionism must decide what it believes is the best way forward for the people of the United Kingdom in coming years. It must seriously consider throwing in its lot with those who would democratise the state, destroying the power of the Establishment to deny the people of Northern Ireland their rights.[102]

Gary McMichael once highlighted what he saw as the importance of recognising loyalism as a distinct political force, arguing that republicans:

> ... must learn that it is not the British government with whom peace shall be negotiated, it is the other democratic representatives who disagree with Sinn Féin's analysis ... it is people like me ... with whom they must learn to share Northern Ireland, it is me and the rest of the population who will not accept the analysis and will not accept Irish unity.[103]

It is also possible to see another tendency emerging from within loyalism at this time, one that expressed growing social concern and that recognised a broader view of the causes of social and economic

marginalisation. Such factors have served to expose further incon-
gruities in relationships between some Protestants and the state. The
PUP and UDP thus provided reference points and discourses to challenge the existing unionist leadership along political, social and economic lines. Moreover, in the Forum election the UDP and PUP attract-
ed almost 10 per cent of the overall unionist vote, marking by far the
highest level of support ever achieved by politicised paramilitary
groups within loyalism.

REFRAMING LOYALISM

While levels of political support for new loyalism were never sustained,
the development of the PUP and UDP represented a crucial attempt by
loyalists to refine the parameters within which they interpreted and
sought representation for their political world.[104] Importantly, this was
only possible after the PUP convinced its supporters that the
Agreement had secured the Union and that the existing constitutional
link remained the priority for the party. The issue was much more contested within the UDP/UDA grouping, which was less able to persuade
its followers that the Union was solid or that its representatives could
ensure a leading role in the organisation in political negotiations.

The PUP presented a more coherent analysis, resting on the notion
that the Protestant working class were doubly disadvantaged: marginalised during the period of Stormont rule, (never having occupied the
privileged arena suggested by their opponents) and, in the contemporary period, having lost out politically, socially and economically. This
interpretation of an increasingly peripheral Protestant working class
forms the bedrock from which the PUP seeks to reconstruct and rein-
terpret loyalism's political past and to reposition Protestant working-
class politics in the future. As David Ervine once expressed it: 'The so-
called "good old days" represented little more than a sectarian system,
where everybody knew his or her place and forelock touching was the
norm.'[105]

Hence, the PUP positioned itself to 'oppose as strongly as anyone
else a return to that partisan system of government'.[106] Such perspectives proved important in processes that nurtured introspection among
key elements of the Protestant working class and in developing the
promotion of a 'shared responsibility' as a perceived mechanism for
reducing sectarian social relations.[107]

The PUP in particular was relatively successful in drawing support
for its position and presenting itself as a new voice within unionism.
They also proved capable of convincing others, both within the UVF
and the wider Protestant working class, of the validity of a political

path. Crucially, some 80 per cent of the expanding PUP membership had never previously joined a political party in Northern Ireland,[108] leading one commentator to describe the emergence of the PUP as the 'unshackling of loyalism'.[109]

Central to the broad development of loyalist politics has been an articulation from both the UDP and PUP that unionism was tactically limited. In particular both groups found themselves in conflict with the DUP over the claim to be the legitimate representatives of working-class loyalism. The then UDP leader Gary McMichael, for example, accused the DUP of 'failing in its duty', while David Ervine of the PUP claimed the DUP had deserted Northern Ireland in its greatest need.[110]

While some of the above clearly indicated political movement, serious questions remained as to whether the views of the UDP and PUP marked a permanent rupture within unionist ideology or were merely some fleeting expression of loyalist community concerns. This was especially problematic as they sought to draw support from a unionist community that has consistently expressed outrage against 'crimes supposedly committed in support of a community that likes to contrast itself with the nationalists by claiming to be especially loyal and law-abiding'.[111] Hence, support for the transition towards a new politics offered from loyalist paramilitaries proved difficult to sustain.

In particular, the DUP reacted strongly, seeing the growing eminence of new loyalism as a direct challenge to its self-appointed status as representatives of working-class loyalism. This was increasingly reflected in the lexicon of the DUP's response, which will be discussed more fully in later chapters. Briefly, however, representatives of the loyalist paramilitaries and the DUP came into direct competition for the allegiance of loyalists, reflecting not just growing ideological differences between the two groups but an increasingly moral stance expressed by the DUP in its public utterances towards loyalist paramilitaries, and more pragmatic conflicts between the two groups over resources and public representation of loyalist communities.

NEW LOYALISM ON THE WANE

Following the Agreement the PUP (and to a lesser extent the UDP) developed wider political programmes, and a sense of the political encompassing those who traditionally were excluded from such engagement. This period of expansion for the PUP was, however, relatively short. As Stephen Bloomer argued, while the PUP was a 'high impact' party, they were unable to put in place the organisational structures to lay the bedrock for longer-term electoral expansion.[112] As the sense of perceived crisis within loyalism deepened, the DUP succeeded in articulating more straightforwardly the broader concerns of work-ing-class loyalism through a discourse that was more easily recognis-able.

The UDP self-imploded as a political force, while it quickly became clear that the electoral base of the PUP was largely geographically restricted to identifiable sections of working-class loyalism. There is lit-tle to suggest that the PUP was able to look to the UVF for direct polit-ical support or organisational involvement. Indeed, as one party activist explained, the UVF grouping 'don't provide any economic or electoral support to the PUP. Most of them don't even vote for it. Many back the DUP instead.'[113] The limit to the PUP's constituency was fully revealed by the 2003 Assembly election results. Overall, the PUP vote was cut in half to just over 1 per cent of the turnout and this marginal electoral position of the PUP was confirmed in the 2007 Assembly elec-tion when only Dawn Purvis (standing in East Belfast) was elected.[114]

The regression of the PUP as an electoral entity had, however, been apparent for some time. Like all political representatives of loyalist para-militaries, the PUP ran up against the buffers of political legitimacy and credibility. Further, the PUP often found itself defending an Agreement from which many living in working-class unionist areas felt disenfran-chised, especially in what they saw as their position relevant to work-ing-class republicans and growing feelings of cultural and political insecurity across the Protestant working class.[115]

Taken alongside its limited organisational structure this did not bode well for future electoral expansion. Finally, as I have argued else-where, any hopes held by the PUP of expanding its electorate were at best severely dented in the summer of 2000 with the bloody conflict between the UDA and UVF.[116] Within the wider unionist community any chance of sustained growth for the PUP evaporated completely with subsequent paramilitary feuds within loyalism.[117] Despite the undeniable political talent of his replacement, Dawn Purvis, the task of recovery was not made any easier by the untimely death of the then party leader, David Ervine, in January 2007. Loyalism had lost the most articulate spokesperson of a generation and its most approachable and engaging public figure.

CONCLUSION

Following the 1994 ceasefires and the signing of the Agreement, the political response from within loyalism highlighted directly the main experiences of that section of society. The coming to public prominence of the PUP and UDP marked the revelation of a clear political dynamic representing distinctive ideological positions firmly rooted within the experiences of Protestant working-class communities. It proved difficult, however, for new loyalism to maintain that political momentum or for new loyalism to take root in the form envisaged by its originators and leading proponents.

Core ideologies provide loyalists with points of orientation, values and pre-suppositions that allow them to make sense of the world to accept a particular political perspective as valid. Although new loyalism drew heavily on these, there was no direct overlay. The meanings assigned to contemporary events by new loyalism could not breech the dominant frame of unionism. Indeed, within a decade, the transforming frame created by the PUP in the mid 1990s rapidly closed, as they failed to establish either an ideological or electoral bulkhead within unionism. Loyalism was becoming ever more fragmented as sections within it appeared increasingly unable, or unwilling, to change. The UDA in particular were reluctant to engage with the politics created in the post-Agreement era. Some of the reasons for this will be examined more fully in the next chapter, as will broader responses across loyalism and the repositioning of the political representatives of loyalism.

NOTES

1. Ruane and Todd, *The Dynamics of Conflict in Northern Ireland*, pp.94–5.
2. *New Ulster Defender*, no. 4 (December 1997), p.13.
3. Dixon, *Northern Ireland: The Politics of War and Peace*, p.86.
4. Tonge, *Northern Ireland: Conflict and Change*, pp.39–40.
5. Ervine, D. 'Redefining loyalism: a political perspective', in D. Ervine and J.W. McAuley, *Redefining Loyalism*, IBIS working paper no. 4 (University College Dublin: Institute of British Irish Studies, 2001), p.4.
6. Farrington, 'Loyalists and unionists: explaining the internal dynamics of an ethnic group', pp.28–30.
7. Hopefully it has been made clear throughout the book that loyalism can take a variety of forms and expressions. To emphasise the point, however, see, Aughey, A., 'The character of Ulster unionism', in P. Shirlow and M. McGovern (eds), *Who Are 'The People'?*, pp.16–33.
8. See McDonald, H. and Cusack, J., *UDA: Inside the Heart of Loyalist Terror* (London: Penguin, 2004); McAuley, J.W., '"Not a game of cowboys and indians": loyalist paramilitary groups in the 1990s', in A. O'Day (ed.), *Terrorism's Laboratory: Northern Ireland* (Dartmouth: Dartmouth Press, 1995), pp.137–58.
9. See Cusack and McDonald, *UVF*; Wood, *Crimes of Loyalty*.
10. Wood, *Crimes of Loyalty*, pp.100–77.
11. Lennon, B., *Peace Comes Dropping Slow*, p.25.
12. McAuley, J.W., 'The emergence of new loyalism', in J. Coakley (ed.), *Changing Shades of Orange and Green*, pp.106–22.
13. I have sought to trace this in some detail in McAuley, J.W., 'Very British rebels: politics and discourse within contemporary Ulster unionism', in P. Bagguley and J. Hearn (eds), *Transforming Politics: Power and Resistance* (Basingstoke: Macmillan Press, 1999); McAuley, J.W., 'Still "no surrender"? new loyalism and the peace process in Ireland', in J.P. Harrington and E.J. Mitchell (eds), *Politics and Performance in Contemporary Northern Ireland* (Amherst: University of Massachusetts Press, 1999); McAuley, J.W. 'Mobilising Ulster unionism: new directions or old?', *Capital and Class*, no. 70 (2000), pp.37–64.
14. Sims, J.Y., *Farewell to the Hammer: A Shankill Boyhood* (Belfast: White Row Press, 1992), pp.21–2.
15. Hall, M., *Ulster's Protestant Working Class: A Community Exploration*, p.27.
16. McAuley, J.W., '"Just fighting to survive": Loyalist paramilitary politics and the

Progressive Unionist Party', *Terrorism and Political Violence*, 16, 3 (2004), pp.522–44.
17. Progressive Unionist Party, *Manifesto for the Forum Election* (Belfast: PUP, 1996).
18. Progressive Unionist Party, *Support the Progressive Unionists* (Belfast: PUP, 1996).
19. Combined Loyalist Military Command (CLMC), 'Ceasefire Statement, 13 October 1994'. Archived at: http://cain.ulst.ac.uk/events/peace/docs/clmc131094.htm
20. The name was taken by a grouping of former UVF prisoners to consciously rework the name of the organisation that previously existed in the late 1930s as a vehicle for Protestant working-class radicalism. See Harbinson, *The Ulster Unionist Party*, pp.219–22.
21. McAuley, J.W. and Hislop, S., '"Many roads forward": politics and ideology within the Progressive Unionist Party', *Études Irlandaises*, 25, 1 (2000), pp.173–92.
22. See McKay, S., 'Diverging from the shadow of the gunmen', *Sunday Tribune*, 26 May 1996; Sinnerton, H., *David Ervine: Uncharted Waters* (Dingle: Brandon, 2002); Whitfield, D., 'Gusty Spence: heretic on the Shankill', *Morning Star*, 7 February 1997.
23. Moody, T.W., *The Ulster Question, 1603–1973* (Cork: Mercier Press, 1980), p.64.
24. Spence was later replaced by Billy Hutchinson who after his release was also to become a leading figure in the PUP.
25. Fearon, K., 'The conflict's fifth business: a brief biography of Billy Mitchell', unpublished (2002), pp.1–72.
26. Rowan, B., 'Loyalist ceasefire 10 years on'. Archived at: http://news.bbc.co.uk/1/hi/northern_ireland/3738146.stm
27. Bruce, S., 'Terrorists and politics: the case of Northern Ireland's loyalist paramilitaries', *Terrorism and Political Violence*, 13, 2 (2001), p.28.
28. Taylor, P., *Loyalists*, p.141.
29. See Garland, R., *Gusty Spence* (Belfast: Blackstaff Press, 2001); Stevenson, J., *'We Wrecked the Place': Contemplating an End to the Northern Irish Troubles* (London: The Free Press, 1996).
30. See Rowan, B., 'Decades after they met in jail, Gusty Spence remembers his protégé', *Belfast Telegraph*, 12 January 2007.
31. Fearon, 'The conflict's fifth business', pp.52–3.
32. See Braid, M., 'The Protestant pretenders', *Independent*, section two, 8 March 1995; Gallagher, M., 'Beyond the bullwark? The fringe loyalist parties and the future', *An Phoblacht/Republican News*, 19 January 1995; White, B., 'A loyalist's view from the hub', *Belfast Telegraph*, 5 October 1995.
33. Progressive Unionist Party, 'Submission to the Northern Ireland Office by the Progressive Unionist Party on the question of political prisoners and prisons', reproduced in *Journal of Prisoners on Prisons*, 7, 2 (1996), pp.31–57.
34. Progressive Unionist Party, *Manifesto for the Forum Election*.
35. McAuley, '"Just fighting to survive"', pp.522–43.
36. Edwards, A., 'Democratic socialism and sectarianism: the Northern Ireland Labour Party and the Progressive Unionist Party compared', *Politics*, 27, 1 (2007), pp.24–31.
37. Cassidy, K.J., 'Organic intellectuals and the new loyalism: re-inventing Protestant working-class politics in Northern Ireland', *Irish Political Studies*, 23, 3 (2008), pp.411–30.
38. Interview with author, Belfast 2006.
39. Progressive Unionist Party, 'How long are you prepared to wait for benefits to our community – election communication' (Belfast: PUP, 2003).
40. Cited in Rowan, B., *Paisley and the Provos* (Belfast: Brehon Press, 2005), p.170.
41. Shannon, A., *Report of the Taskforce on Protestant Working-Class Communities* (Belfast: Department for Social Development, 2005).
42. Progressive Unionist Party, *Support the Progressive Unionists*.
43. Purvis, D., 'British left: straddling the nationalist fence', in Progressive View Editorial Team, *Breaking the Mould* (Belfast: PUP, no date).
44. See Progressive Unionist Party, *Manifesto for the Forum Election* (Belfast: PUP, 1996); Progressive Unionist Party, 'Submission to the Northern Ireland Office by the Progressive Unionist Party on the question of political prisoners and prisons', *Journal of Prisoners on Prisons*, 7, 2 (1996), pp.11 – 24; Progressive Unionist Party, *Support the Progressive Unionists* (Belfast: PUP, 1996).
45. Progressive Unionist Party, 'How long are you prepared to wait for benefits to our community?'
46. Progressive Unionist Party, *Support the Progressive Unionists*.
47. Colin Robinson, cited in A. Edwards and S. Bloomer, *A Watching Brief?*, p.17.
48. See McAuley, 'Very British rebels'; Edwards, A., 'Democratic socialism and sectarianism:

the Northern Ireland Labour Party and Progressive Unionist Party compared'.

49. McAuley, '"Just fighting to survive"'.
50. Jacobson, R., 'Whose peace process? Women's organisations and political settlement in Northern Ireland, 1996–1997' (University of Bradford: Department of Peace Studies, Peace Studies Papers, 9/97).
51. McWilliams, M., 'Women in Northern Ireland: an overview', in E. Hughes (ed.), *Culture and Politics in Northern Ireland: 1960–1990* (Milton Keynes: Open University Press, 1993), pp.81–100.
52. Moore, R. 'An exploration of the impact of sectarianism and gender on the experiences and identities of Protestant women in Northern Ireland' (paper presented at Queen's University Belfast, 17–18 February 1995).
53. See Edgerton, L., 'Public protest, domestic acquiescence: women in Northern Ireland', in R. Ridd and H. Calloway (eds), *Caught Up in Conflict* (Basingstoke: Macmillan, 1986); Morgan, V. 'Bridging the divide: women and political and community issues', in P. Stringer and G. Robinson (eds), *Social Attitudes in Northern Ireland: The Second Report 1991–1992* (Belfast: Blackstaff Press, 1992); Morgan, V., 'Women and the conflict in Northern Ireland', in A. O'Day (ed.), *Terrorism's Laboratory: The Case of Northern Ireland* (Aldershot: Dartmouth, 1995); Walker, L., *Godmothers and Mentors: Women, Politics and Education in Northern Ireland* (Belfast: December Publications, 1997).
54. See Democratic Dialogue, *Report Number 4: Power, Politics, Positionings: Women in Northern Ireland* (Belfast: Democratic Dialogue, 1997).
55. See Sales, R., *Women Divided: Gender, Religion and Politics in Northern Ireland* (London: Routledge, 1997); Sales, R., 'Gender and Protestantism in Northern Ireland', in Shirlow and McGovern (eds), *Who Are 'The People'?*, pp.140–57; Sales, R., 'Women, the peace makers?', in J. Anderson and J. Goodman, *Dis/agreeing Ireland: Contexts, Obstacles, Hopes* (London: Pluto Press, 1998), pp.141–61.
56. Rooney, E., 'Intersectionality in transition: lessons from Northern Ireland', *Web Journal of Current Legal Issues*, no. 5 (2007). Archived at: http://webjcli.ncl.ac.uk/2007/issue5/rooney5.html
57. Rooney, E., 'Women in Northern Irish politics: difference matters', in C. Roulston and C. Davies (eds), *Gender, Democracy and Inclusion in Northern Ireland* (Houndmills: Palgrave, 2000), pp.164–86.
58. Ward, R., 'Invisible women: the political roles of unionist and loyalist women in contemporary Northern Ireland', *Parliamentary Affairs*, no. 55 (2002), pp.167–78.
59. See Racioppi, L. and O'Sullivan, K., 'Ulstermen and loyalist ladies on parade: gendering unionism in Northern Ireland', *International Feminist Journal of Politics*, 2, 1 (2000), pp.1–29; Racioppi, L. and O'Sullivan, K., '"This we will maintain": gender, ethno-nationalism and the politics of unionism in Northern Ireland', *Nations and Nationalism*, 7, 1 (2001), pp.93–112.
60. McWilliams, M., 'Violence against women and political conflict: the Northern Ireland experience', *Critical Criminology*, 8, 1 (1997), pp.79–92.
61. Rooney, E., 'Women, community and politics in Northern Ireland: -isms in action', *Journal of Gender Studies*, 1, 4 (1992), pp.475–91.
62. Sales, R., *Women Divided: Gender, Religion and Politics in Northern Ireland* (London: Routledge, 1997).
63. See Jacobson, R., 'Women and peace in Northern Ireland: a complicated relationship', in S. Jacobs, R. Jacobson and J. Marchbank (eds), *States of Conflict* (London: Zed Books, 2000), pp.179–98; Morgan, V., 'Peacemakers? Peacekeepers? Women in Northern Ireland 1969–1995', professorial lecture, given at the University of Ulster, 25 October 1995; Morgan, V. and Fraser, G., 'Women and the Northern Ireland conflict: experiences and responses', in S. Dunn (ed.), *Facets of the Conflict in Northern Ireland* (Basingstoke: Macmillan Press, 1995), pp.81–96.
64. Potter, M. and MacMillan, A., 'Unionist women active in the conflict in Northern Ireland' (Belfast: Training for Women Network, no date); Alison, M., 'Gender, small arms and the Northern Ireland conflict', paper presented to the International Studies Association annual conference, March 2005; McEvoy, S., 'Women loyalist paramilitaries in Northern Ireland: duty, agency and empowerment – a report from the field', paper presented to the International Studies Association annual conference, March 2007.
65. Potter and MacMillan, 'Unionist women active in the conflict in Northern Ireland', p.35.
66. McKittrick, D., 'Protestants left isolated as roles are reversed', *Independent*, 5 October 1993.

67. Cusack and McDonald, *UVF*, p.117.
68. See McAuley, J.P., 'Cúchulainn with an RPG7: the ideology and politics of the Ulster Defence Association', in E. Hughes (ed.), *Culture and Politics in Northern Ireland* (Milton Keynes: Open University Press), pp.44–68; McAuley, J.P., 'Contemporary developments in a loyalist paramilitary group in Northern Ireland – back to basics?', *Etudes Irlandaises*, 21, 1 (1996), pp.165–82.
69. New Ulster Political Research Group, *Beyond the Religious Divide* (Belfast: NUPRG, 1979).
70. McMichael, J., 'A jigsaw puzzle for the queen's loyalist rebels', *Fortnight*, no. 224 (1985); McMichael, J., 'Are Ulster loyalists now at a critical cross roads?', *Fortnight*, no. 236 (1986).
71. Ulster Political Research Group, *Common Sense* (Belfast: UPRG, 1987).
72. See Ulster Democratic Party, *The Unionist Team You Can Trust: Election Communication* (Belfast: UDP, 1996); Ulster Democratic Party, *Special Election Communication* (Belfast: UDP, 1996); Ulster Democratic Party, *Look to the Future: Election Communication* (Belfast: UDP, 1996).
73. Ulster Democratic Party, *Special Election Communication – Forum Election* (Belfast: UDP, 1996).
74. *Irish Times*, 26 May 1996.
75. Wood, I., 'Loyalist paramilitaries and the peace process', in B. Barton and P.J. Roche (eds), *The Northern Ireland Question: The Peace Process and the Belfast Agreement* (Basingstoke: Palgrave Macmillan, 2009), p.182.
76. Turner, J., 'Expulsion calls routine since UDP's inception', *Irish News*, 27 January 1998.
77. Gillespie, G., 'Noises off: loyalists after the Agreement', in M. Cox, A. Guelke and F. Stephen (eds), *A Farewell to Arms? Beyond the Good Friday Agreement* (Manchester: Manchester University Press, 2006), p.145.
78. Crawford, C., *Inside the UDA: Volunteers and Violence* (London: Pluto Press, 2003), p.95.
79. See McAuley, J.P., 'Contemporary unionist understandings of the peace process', *The Global Review of Ethnopolitics*, 3, 1 (2004), pp.60–76; McDonald and Cusack, *UDA*.
80. Cited in Garland, R., 'UPRG may hold loyalists' key to moving forward', *Irish News*, 31 March 2003.
81. Ulster Democratic Party, 'Response to government Framework Documents'.
82. BBC News, 'Loyalist party split over peace accord'. Archived at: http://news.bbc.co.uk/1/hi/northern_ireland/1132648.stm
83. McDonald and Cusack, *UDA*, p.304.
84. Party representatives 'forgot' to register the UDP as a political party under new laws. As a result the UDP had no legal status and its name could not appear on ballot papers. This forced outgoing councillors to stand as independent candidates.
85. Cited in Rowan, *The Armed Peace*, p.214.
86. *Belfast Telegraph*, 11 January 2001.
87. Murray, A., 'UDA truce "teetering on brink"', *Sunday Life*, 18 January 2004.
88. Cited in Hutchinson, W., 'Gary Mitchell's "talk process"', *Études Anglaises*, 56, 2 (2003), p.209.
89. *East Belfast Observer*, 13 May 2004.
90. Langhammer, M., '"Cutting with the grain": Policy and the Protestant community: What is to be done?', paper to the secretary of state for Northern Ireland and the Northern Ireland Office team (Belfast: published by the author, 2003).
91. BBC News, 'UDA upsurge in violence'; Archived at: http://news.bbc.co.uk/northern_ireland/1120534.stm
92. Johnston, I., 'Loyalist groups to swap guns for votes', *Ireland on Sunday*, 23 February 2003.
93. BBC News Online, 'Murphy "recognises" UDA ceasefire'. Archived at: http://news.bbc.co.uk/go/pr/fr/-/1/hi/northern_ireland/4006221.stm
94. Rowan, B., 'Helping loyalists "find their way"'. Archived at: http://news.bbc.co.uk/go/pr/fr/-/2/hi/uk_news/northern_ireland/3024240.stm
95. Rowan, B., 'Political door reopens for UDA'. Archived at: http://news.bbc.co.uk/go/pr/fr/-/2/hi/uk_news/northern_ireland/4011303.stm
96. See Breen, S., 'UPRG influence grows as politics replaces violence', *Sunday Life*, 2 July 2006; Breen, S., 'Men bringing UDA in from cold', *Sunday Life*, 30 July 2006.
97. Garland, R., 'Loyalists must take responsibility for themselves', *Irish News*, 9 October 2006.
98. Shankill Think Tank, *A New Beginning* (Newtownabbey: Island Publications, 1995).
99. *Irish Times*, 24 March 1997.
100. See Ballymacarret Think Tank, *Puppets no More* (Newtownabbey: Island Pamphlets, 1999); Ballymacarret Think Tank, *Beyond King Billy?* (Newtownabbey: Island Pamphlets,

1999); Seeds of Hope Ex–Prisoner Project, *Seeds of Hope* (Newtownabbey: Island Pamphlets, 2000).

101. See Ballymacarret Arts and Cultural Society, *Orangeism and the Twelfth: What it Means to Me* (Newtownabbey: Island Pamphlets, 1999); Belfast Community Economic Conference, *Conference Proceedings* (Newtownabbey: Island Publications, 1995); Shankill Think Tank, *A New Beginning* (Newtownabbey: Island Publications, 1995).
102. Ulster Democratic Party, 'The Anglo-Irish Agreement – it hasn't gone away you know!', UDP Press Release, Belfast, 19 November 1996.
103. *Irish Times*, 24 February 1997.
104. McAuley, J.P., 'Fantasy politics? Restructuring unionism after the Good Friday Agreement,' *Eire–Ireland*, 39, 1/2 (2004), pp.189–214.
105. Interview with author, May 2001.
106. Ibid.
107. See Ervine, cited in McAuley, J.P. 'The emergence of new loyalism', in J. Coakley (ed.), *Changing Shades of Orange and Green*, pp.106–22.
108. McAuley, J.P. and Tonge, J., 'The role of "extra-constitutional" parties in the Northern Ireland Assembly', final report to the ESRC, ESRC award L327253058, January 2001.
109. Stevenson, J., *'We Wrecked the Place': Contemplating an End to the Northern Irish Troubles* (New York: The Free Press, 1996), p.196.
110. *Belfast Telegraph*, 23 July 1997.
111. Bruce, 'Terrorists and politics', p.47.
112. Bloomer, S., 'Bridging the militarist–politico divide: the Progressive Unionist Party and the politics of conflict transformation', in Edwards and Bloomer (eds), *Transforming the Peace Process in Northern Ireland*, pp.97–113.
113. Cited in Clarke, L., 'PUP to rethink ties with UVF', *Sunday Times*, 9 October 2005.
114. CAIN, 'Results of elections held in Northern Ireland since 1968'.
115. Southern, 'Protestant alienation in Northern Ireland'.
116. McAuley and Hislop, 'Many roads forward', pp.173–92.
117. McAuley, 'Fantasy politics? Restructuring unionism after the Good Friday Agreement'.

Chapter 6

Transforming Loyalism?

Thatcherism and globalisation removed Belfast's heavy industry, and with it the old culture of guilds and trade unions. All that is left for the [Protestant working class] is contempt from the Protestant middle class, loathing from a confident Catholic working class, hatred from the police, and siren voices offering leadership to an almost mythological Protestant state that vanished before they were born.

John O'Farrell[1]

We have once again witnessed, on the part of the British government, a reluctance to accept Loyalism as having a legitimate culture. Time and time again Nationalists/Republicans have been appeased by the governing bodies who seem to believe that acts of Nationalism stem from a wide cultural base, but anything Loyalist is simply sectarian.

Combat[2]

Beyond the elite level of governmental accords, party political agreements, policy formulation and institution building offered by the Agreement, it also needed to find support at street level and to lay foundations in everyday social and political relations. Within unionism this met with several challenges, including highly visible examples of resistance to political change surrounding events such as the disputed Orange parades at Drumcree, continuing paramilitary involvement in street confrontations and 'community policing', open feuding between (and occasionally within) loyalism and persistent criminal activity from sections of paramilitarism.

All of these were reflected in the often confused and sometimes contradictory response of loyalism to the peace process and post-conflict politics. This chapter highlights some of the key responses within loyalism on the ground and some of the political consequences of the alternatives being offered within contemporary loyalism. It also questions whether, and in what sense, it is possible to talk of long-term change within the ideology and structure of loyalism. To begin to answer this it is necessary to identify some major points of self-reference within loyalism. Class divisions within unionism remain at the core of its social relationships[3] and at the heart of the ideological and political relationships formed across loyalism and unionism.

CLASS STRUCTURE AND UNIONISM

The class structure of contemporary unionism was empirically demonstrated in the Noble Index of economic deprivation for 2002, which suggested that more Protestant areas were suffering high levels of economic deprivation than were Catholic ones.[4] Only the predominantly Catholic electoral wards of Falls and Whiterock matched the levels of deprivation found in Protestant working-class areas such as Crumlin, Shankill and Woodvale. Horgan suggests that 25 per cent of Protestant households live in poverty (compared to 36 per cent of Catholic households), and that the 'difference between the number of poor Protestants and poor Catholics is reducing – not because Catholics are more well off, but because Protestants are less well off'.[5] All this against a background where the poorest (both Protestant and Catholic) were worse off in 2006 than a decade earlier.[6]

Moreover, there has been an increasing recognition within many working-class Protestant strongholds that they have clearly failed to take advantage of, or fully participate in, educational opportunities. David Hanson, the social development minister, reported in 2006, for example, that of the fifteen wards performing worst in educational attainment, thirteen were in Protestant working-class parts of Belfast,[7] while in Northern Ireland as a whole, a greater proportion of Protestants than Catholics left school with no qualifications.[8]

Such factors, combined with shifting demographics, have created diminishing senses of political, psychological, economic and sometimes even physical security within Protestant communities, underpinned by strong beliefs that loyalist communities 'are perceived as having less value and importance' than their republican counterparts.[9] Given this, it is hardly surprising that Protestant working-class responses to contemporary political events have sometimes been convoluted. Underpinning many of the concerns of working-class loyalism are beliefs that they have not benefited socially in the post-Agreement period; that they have failed to improve their increasingly marginalised economic position, and that they have lost out to republican demands and organisation in the political arena.

Further, Horgan shows that the gap between rich and poor within the Protestant community is widening.[10] This gives further weight to Mitchell's claim that the Protestant middle classes 'have enjoyed high standards of living and educational achievement, rising levels of equity in property and bountiful jobs in the public sphere'.[11] Indeed, Morrow suggests that from the 1980s it has been possible to identify a grouping of middle-class 'contented' unionists which had distanced itself from unionist politics and symbolism and was composed of those who 'were generally supportive of British governmental efforts to establish economic and social stability' and who 'experienced their Britishness as an identification with the mainstream of British cultural life'.[12]

In a similar vein the Faith and Politics Group identified those middle-class unionists who 'opt out and seek to coast along in a private world of material prosperity'.[13] The politics of this group rests on a sense of unionism (identified in Chapters 2 and 3) that largely represents those who see themselves as fully integrated, both economically and socially, within the rest of the UK. Those who position themselves in this way are more likely to draw on some broad notion of civic nationalism and construct a notion of citizenship as resting within a broader UK state rather than identify with cultural unionism.

Anecdotally it draws support from those who feel more comfortable reading the *Daily Mail* than the *Belfast News Letter*, or who are more concerned with the fortunes of Arsenal than Linfield Football Club. Moreover, they most strongly disassociate themselves from traditional unionist institutions (such as the Orange Order), not least because these can no longer guarantee social status.[14] If they vote at all, they are often prepared to cast their mark for what they see as liberal unionism.[15] Hence, from within loyalism there are increasingly strong feelings expressed that the Protestant middle class have 'pulled the ladder up behind them and ignored working-class Protestants'.[16]

In response to this, loyalists increasingly talk of what they term 'middle unionism' in detrimental and often oppositional terms. Central to the construction of contemporary loyalist identities, therefore, are widespread expressions that they have lost out politically from recent events and that the concerns they raise are ignored by other unionists.[17] Jack Holland reflects this directly when he says:

> A deep sense of betrayal characterized the feeling many loyalists harboured towards the Protestant middle class who, they believed, reaped most of the benefits of the state while condemning and dissociating themselves from the paramilitaries who 'defended' it.[18]

Dominic Murray suggests that many working-class Protestants feel that they have given much and received very little in return from the peace process,[19] while Hall notes continuing uncertainties within the Protestant working class concerning the benefits from the Agreement.[20] It is, of course, within exactly that faction of society where paramilitarism is most deeply rooted and the construction of loyalism most intensely contested. This is represented by struggles within loyalist paramilitarism to formulate a political response and broader conflicts concerning the legitimacy of paramilitarism. Such disputes continue to structure crucial areas of political response. As Julie Healy argues, locality matters, suggesting that unless space is made for working-class understandings and interpretations then the hegemony of middle-class worldviews will never be challenged.[21]

LOYALISM, POLITICS AND PARAMILITARISM

Competition around claims to represent the 'true voice' of loyalism manifest daily at the micro-level. To gain legitimacy, such leadership must be seen to have considerable integrity, trustworthiness and standing, hence the continuing struggles for authority within and between the paramilitaries, between the DUP and loyalist groupings, and between the DUP, paramilitaries and other community-based representatives. A defining factor of working-class loyalism remains the relationship with paramilitarism. In trying to unpack this it must be understood that loyalist paramilitary groups and post-paramilitary organisations such as former prisoner groups remain engaged in a complex set of social and political relationships with the communities in which they are found.

Such organisations have existed in their contemporary forms for the past four decades, during which time they have played a variety of roles, from organised violence to the articulation of political perspectives, and from the reproduction of sectarian ideologies to the presentation of social and economic grievances and community development. Loyalist paramilitaries have always occupied a number of different roles within working-class communities.[22] Central to any of these roles, however, has been the need to gain the level of legitimacy to operate within loyalist areas.

During the period of overt conflict, this was relatively straightforward. Loyalist paramilitaries sought to validate their existence by suggesting that they shared the same objectives as the state, but that they were more committed than the state in taking the 'war' to the enemy. Hence, one of the major stated objectives of loyalist paramilitaries was always to bring to 'justice' active republicans, especially as they perceived the police and army as unable, or unwilling, to do so. Beyond this, however, the relationships between working-class Protestants and paramilitaries are most often determined and contested by everyday events, usually at a highly localised level.

INTERNAL DISPUTES

Not all in the loyalist paramilitaries supported the political turn that followed the Agreement. Those factions of loyalist paramilitarism which sought to reassert the conflict or at least contradict and challenge the proposed political settlement, continually questioned the stance of those politicised paramilitary groupings in favour of the Agreement. Primary among such groupings was the LVF, formed by the late Billy Wright in the mid-1990s, when the mid-Ulster faction of the UVF that he led broke away from the main organisation in dismay at their support (albeit sometimes tacit and backroom) for the peace process.

The split demonstrated just how deeply rooted some of the opposition was within loyalism to political accommodation. Wright openly denounced the peace process as delusion and sham and constantly decried the Shankill-based UVF leadership and the PUP (especially David Ervine and Billy Hutchinson) as under the influence of communists and left-wing extremists.[23] The position adopted by Wright also reflected views in currency within some elements of the UDA at the time[24] and drew further support from dissident UVF members in Belfast and from other loyalist paramilitary groups discontent with the path taken by political representatives and the peace process in general. Broadly, Wright and his followers claimed that politicians were selling out loyalists through a 'surrender deal' and accused unionist politicians in general and the PUP in particular of having lost touch with grassroots loyalism. The coalescing of more fundamental elements of the UDA and UVF around the LVF focused on one strand of loyalist reaction and precipitated several sectarian killings in Northern Ireland.[25]

Such a response had widespread political implications and, as Gordon Gillespie recognised, posed serious questions about the 'modernisation' of loyalism.[26] Throughout the formative peace process and in the period following the Agreement most loyalist paramilitaries fell in line with their politicised leadership of the PUP and UDP. At a minimum they were disinclined to disagree in public. This sometime reluctant consensus ended with the dissolution of the UDP on 28 November 2001. Clearly although the UDP leader Gary McMichael still strongly supported the Agreement, the leadership of the UDA and an increasing number of UDA members did not. While the PUP position was stronger, support was far from absolute within UVF ranks. As early in the process as July 1999 the UVF were expressing concerns regarding the maintenance of their ceasefire and the PUP being left out of the 'political loop' by government.[27]

The paramilitary response was also structured by developing concerns around the extent of loyalist involvement in criminality,[28] often located within the murky world of personality-driven fiefdoms[29] and used as a way of acquiring money both 'for organisations ... and personal gain'.[30] Although it cannot be dealt with at any length here, sections of loyalist paramilitarism continued to engage in gangsterism, including 'soliciting donations for so-called charitable organisations, using pubs and clubs to raise and launder money, providing "security" services, exploiting government grants and counterfeiting documentation'.[31] This resulted in huge financial turnover and, often, large personal gain for those involved.[32]

The negative effects of drug dealing, extortion and racketeering on loyalist working-class communities cannot be disputed. As Steve Bruce explains, such criminality 'further demoralizes neighbourhoods that [already] feel threatened by Catholic expansion and suffer high levels of economic deprivation'.[33] Indeed, the Loyalist Commission (comprising representatives of the UDA, UVF, RHC, UFF and Protestant Church and community representatives) claimed that racketeering and gangsterism was in danger of destroying investment and economic growth in working-class Protestant areas.[34] Brian Rowan suggests that at times loyalist paramilitaries polluted the places where they live with drugs,[35] and at one point it was claimed that the growing drug culture had demoralised loyalists more than had thirty years of the Troubles and the open threat of republican violence.[36]

Loyalist paramilitarism was also destabilised by its factionalism. The UVF and UDA have been involved in a series of bloody conflicts in the post-Agreement period. The most intense of these occurred during the summer of 2000, when seven people were killed and hundreds forced to relocate to houses within their respective 'safe' areas of what became a recognised physical interface between UVF and UDA supporters on the Shankill Road.[37] This was not the only outbreak of such violence in recent times. Another feud occurred in 2001, when the UVF and LVF each killed one member of the opposing organisation.

A particularly vicious feud broke out in the summer of 2005 in areas of east Belfast and north Down. At its end four LVF members had been killed by the UVF, following which the LVF announced it was 'standing down'. The faction of the UDA led by Johnny Adair, supporting the LVF, were eventually forced to flee Northern Ireland, 'expelled' by others within the organisation.[38]

The catalysts for post-Agreement conflicts within loyalist paramilitarism have varied.[39] They have included tensions over support for, or resistance against, the political process; support from some members of the UDA for the LVF (challenged by the mainstream UVF); localised power struggles seeking to further demarcate territory; and disputes involving criminality, drugs and the trading of illegal goods.[40] Broadly, however, such divisions 'crystallised into two broad camps – pro-conflict transformation and those who wished to regress'.[41]

Here there were some important differences in the public representation of the two main groupings. Ian Wood explains it as follows:

> ... the PUP, like Sinn Féin had been much better at creating a distance between itself and its paramilitary wing. Marjorie Mowlam's January talks with leading UDA/UFF men had reinforced many people's view of the UDP as a party which could take no serious initiatives without the support of convicted killers. Conversely, Billy Hutchinson had taken care to make it clear that even if UVF prisoners had come out against the peace process it would have made no difference to his party's [PUP] stance in the Stormont negotiations.[42]

The interplay across and between these positions often combined in differing ways to influence the political positioning of loyalist representatives in the post-Agreement era.

INSIDE LOYALISM'S COLDHOUSE

Within this context, the PUP continued to project its pro-Agreement stance, seeking to build a political platform to harvest support largely from within the Belfast urban area. Did this mean the UVF were fully on board? Relationships between the PUP and UVF remained complex and were certainly not necessarily as direct as some outside commentators suggested. However, although it was not until late 2005 that the UVF agreed to fully commit to a process of disarmament and conflict transformation, by and large they remained supportive of the PUP throughout the contemporary period (at least to the point where they undertook a non-interventionist stance).

That is not to say that the UVF was always completely at one with the PUP,[43] or that the political analysis of the PUP leadership and the action of the UVF has always dovetailed.[44] A clear example of this was seen in 2002 when the UVF leadership openly questioned the broad political direction that the PUP was taking. The resulting tensions were enough for the UVF to overtly question its confidence in the peace process[45] and its political consequences,[46] claiming that the outcome was 'increasingly biased towards the demands of Sinn Féin'.[47]

The political positioning of the UVF at the time involved the negotiation of a path between assuring its members that the Union was safe while at the same time reflecting its concerns surrounding the broader political consequences of the Agreement.[48] The tensions between these positions often became apparent, such as in early 2003 when the UVF claimed loyalists were being 'airbrushed' out of the process and that the British and Irish governments were continuing to make 'unilateral concessions to republicans'.[49]

The UVF was not alone in expressing such concerns, and the increasing disillusionment of many Protestants about the non-constitutional agenda was openly recognised by the then secretary of state, John Reid, when he suggested that a 'cold house' had been created for unionists.[50] The depth of this understanding within unionism was graphically represented in a large mural that appeared in Vicarage Street in east Belfast, which proclaimed: 'Since the Signing of the Good Friday Agreement in April 1998 the Following Concessions have been Given.' These were listed as follows:

LOYALISTS
• Prisoners Released
• Visas to the USA

REPUBLICANS
• Prisoners Released
• Visas to the USA
• Seats in government
• Facilities in Westminster
• Army/Police Stations Closed
• Home Battalions of the RIR Disbanded
• On the Runs Allowed to Return
• Columbia 3 Remain at Liberty
• Bias Against Protestants in Employment Practices
• Seán Kelly Child Murderer Set Free
• Increase in Investment
• Access to Shared Roads Denied
• Loyalist Culture Eroded
• £26.5 Million Pay Off

In response the following demands are made on behalf of the 'Loyalist People of East Belfast':

• Equality
• Parity of Esteem
• Shared Access to Main Arterial Routes

- No Bias in Employment Practices
- Cultural Equality
- Equal Investment
- Effective Accountable Policing

Finally, an overarching statement framing the mural declares: 'This is not equality – This is not parity of esteem – This is not what the Good Friday Agreement was meant to deliver.'

That the perceived benefits to republicanism were seen as widespread compared to those of loyalism is reflective of the thinking behind the production of the mural. That republican gains are seen as seven fold in relation to those given to unionism is not untypical of the views of many. Such views have continued to frame the response to contemporary events.

CONTESTING LOYALISM

So what is the likely future direction of loyalism? The answer is not straightforward. Loyalism still frames daily interactions and behaviour by offering a meaningful interpretation of the everyday world, so that this can be understood in ways that guide responses to differing situations. Different frames currently on offer contribute to the construction of loyalist identity, at both personal and collective levels. Some seek to redefine relationships within loyalist working-class communities positively, others less so, such as those that focus increasingly on exclusive forms of loyalist identity.

RACE AND ETHNICITY IN NORTHERN IRELAND

One contemporary manifestation of this reveals itself through the changing social relations of race and ethnicity and the rise of what has been termed by some as a 'new sectarianism'.[51] Several writers have pointed to the widespread populist belief that because the number of people from ethnic minorities in Northern Ireland is few, issues of race and ethnicity have been deemed of little relevance.[52] This is perceived as especially so in a society dominated by political conflict over the constitutional issue; and because divisions around national identities are easily recognised, there has until quite recently been a disinclination to see racism as a public problem.[53] The position has quantifiably changed. Although still far from mainstream concerns, Aidan McGarry, Paul Hainsworth and Chris Gilligan note the increasing attempts by political parties in Northern Ireland to address ethnic minority needs in election manifestos.[54]

Not all engagement has been so positive. Alongside expansion in the size of ethnic minority groups in recent years, however, has come a growth in the number of reported incidents of racism, racist harassment and hate crimes.[55] This came to world attention in early summer 2009 when, following a series of attacks on up to twenty Romanian families living in the loyalist Village area of Belfast, they were first of all forced to flee their homes and move into temporary accommodation, and then felt compelled to leave Northern Ireland for good.[56]

The use of violence against the growing number of immigrants to Northern Ireland marks a further inward turn by some towards an intensely defensive construction of loyalism as part of a 'legacy of intolerance'.[57] As Desmond Bell once pointed out, at the heart of loyalism are deeply developed personal bonds that link individuals to their localised community,[58] and in that respect the resistance offered within some sections of working-class Protestant communities to outsiders marks continuity rather than a break in the construction of loyalism.

Paul Connolly locates racism within wider processes of attitude formation that are found across the population.[59] Most, although not all, of the main perpetrators of racist incidents are young men, often acting in groups.[60] So how broadly are such attitudes held? Connolly and Michaela Keenan reveal that within their sample of 1,267 drawn from across Northern Ireland around a quarter did not want people of Asian, African Caribbean or Chinese ethnic origin living in their area.[61]

Around a further third (34 per cent) were reluctant to have ethnic minorities in the same workplace, while a small majority (53 per cent) would not want a close family member to marry a Chinese person.[62] Such broad attitudes manifested directly in the opposition of local residents to a proposed Chinese cultural centre in Belfast[63] and are supported by results from the *Northern Ireland Life and Times Survey* suggesting that around 25 per cent of the population recognised that they were prejudiced against 'people of ethnic minority populations'.[64]

IS UNIONISM RACIST?

How does this prejudice manifest itself? Chris Gilligan has provided evidence to suggest that, given the rapid rise in Northern Ireland of members of ethnic minority communities (from 534 in 2000 to 12,225 in 2005) compared to the number of recorded racist attacks, the risk of being involved in such an incident is less today than it was at the turn of the century.[65] It is nonetheless important to ascertain how such events are distributed across the population and to note that between January 2005 and September 2006 more than 90 per cent of all racist attacks (64 in total) occurred in loyalist areas.[66]

As Christine Steenkamp notes, however, a hostile response towards ethnic groups is far from universal and 'many Loyalist communities are generally welcoming to immigrants',[67] while the attacks on the Romanian families outlined above also engendered 'anti-racist' protests from those living within loyalist districts. So is there a predisposition within unionism to racism? In the years between 1994 and 2005, Gilligan also reports that the proportion of Catholics who saw themselves as racially prejudiced doubled (from 9 to 18 per cent). Over the same period, however, the level of Protestants reporting such views almost trebled, from 12 to 33 per cent.[68]

How can we begin to interpret this? All racist sub-cultures exist within a particular context. Following Connolly and Keenan[69] it is possible to suggest that in Northern Ireland those people who identify most strongly with the cultural tradition from which they come, and centre Irish or British nationalism as a core belief, are also likely to consider being 'White' as core to their sense of identity. Thus, for Connolly, rather than being marginal to the collective identities of unionism and nationalism, race is a fundamental (if often implicit) aspect of them.[70]

So what role, if any, does racial prejudice play in the construction of unionist identities? Unionist identity reconstructs and repositions in relation to political, economic, social and cultural circumstances. Relationships with ethnic minority groupings do not remain constant, and for many this relationship has been constructed as oppositional. Indeed, one of the conclusions that Connolly and Keenan draw is that 'people in Northern Ireland are far more willing to accept someone from the other main religious tradition than someone from an ethnic minority community'.[71] At times such prejudice may result in confrontation and racist-motivated violence,[72] as with the series of co-ordinated attacks[73] on the Chinese community in south Belfast that took place in 2003 and 2004.[74]

Is it possible to locate such prejudice within particular sections of society? The findings by Connolly and Keenan also suggest that if there is any correlation between age, religion, residence and a person's level of prejudice it is only a very weak one.[75] Overall, levels of prejudice tend to be slightly higher among the Protestant population compared to Catholics, while those living in rural districts exhibit slightly higher levels of prejudice than those living in urban areas.

Within Connolly and Keenan's analysis, neither gender nor social class register as key variables in relation to the level of racial prejudice. These social variables are important. As Máirtín Mac an Ghaill points out, racism itself is not fixed by time and develops differently in particular contexts and over time in the same society.[76] Both racism and sectarianism clearly show the strength and development of strong communal values and reflect ignorance, and sometimes fear, of others' life patterns and behaviour.

While some of the processes of sectarianism do mirror racism and vice versa, to argue that sectarianism is racism is to misunderstand.[77] Embedded sectarianism can be extended into other communities and individuals who are seen to differ in faith, ethnic or cultural background,[78] but as William Connolly points out, all identity 'requires difference in order to be, and it converts difference into otherness in order to secure its own self-certainty'.[79] This does not make racism any more acceptable, but understandings of both racism and sectarianism within the construction of unionist identity must be categorised with precision, not collapsed into a common category of bigotry. Again, this is not to say that racism or sectarianism cannot be part of the construction of loyalism; sometimes they are overtly so. However, senses of loyalist identity are fluid, and loyalists draw upon and seek to harness different sets of references at different times and in different circumstances to construct a coherent identity.

LOYALISM AND IDENTITY

There are several examples in recent history of the contested nature of loyalist identities. In the late 1970s, for example, it manifested through the promotion of an independent Ulster and the adoption of *Cúchulainn* as a cultural icon by the UDA.[80] More recently the promotion of Ulster Scots culture has come to the fore as the basis for a distinct identity among Ulster Protestants.[81] While it remains challenged,[82] there are a series of narratives constructed within Ulster Scots discourse, including a linking of the past with present through the 'Scottish connection', most often through the plantation, or even through the creation of alternative myths of origin around the existence of pre-planter Scots in Ulster.[83]

Although the connection is understood as having physical, cultural, social and genealogical aspects, the primary aspect of the movement has been the promotion of a distinct language[84] as the core of identity, often seen as a counterweight to what is perceived as an increasingly self-confident Irish nationalist culture.[85] Contemporary unionism and loyalism adopts several points of reference from within overlapping social, cultural and political categories and dialogues.[86] Increasingly these draw on what Graham suggests are the 'jaundiced attitudes held by many loyalists towards the Union'.[87] One expression of this at street level was seen in the formation of the 'Love Ulster' campaign.

LOVING ULSTER

The initial focus of Love Ulster was a special edition of the *Shankill Mirror* published in August 2005 with the front page banner headline 'Ulster At Crisis Point'. Its editorial made overt the concerns of sections of the loyalist population it addressed when it said:

> Make no mistake, be under no illusions, the Ulster you love today faces a crisis of potentially fatal proportions. Devious political liars plot to destabilise our community, suppress our culture, weaken our resolve and lead us down the road towards a United Ireland ... We will not accept being forced into a Republic – either by decades of Republican terrorism, or years of cowardly British policy.[88]

One of the most eye-catching pages drew directly on the famous poem attributed to Pastor Martin Niemöller following his imprisonment by the Nazis, which, in the special edition of the *Shankill Mirror*, was transmuted to:

> In the 1970s they came for the B Specials – I did nothing;
> in the 1980s they came for the UDR – I did nothing;
> in the 1990s they came for the RUC – I did nothing;
> 2005, and they've come for the RIR – what can I do?

On 29 October 2005 behind the banner 'Enough is enough!', several thousand took part in a rally at Woodvale Park in Belfast.[89] The organisers claimed that this was part of a campaign to 'demand to respect the rights of the unionist community'. In an attempt to express 'unionist unity' the demonstration, which included victims' groups, was addressed by several speakers, including the Belfast county grand master of the Orange Order, Dawson Baillie. In declaring his support for the project, Robert Saulters of the Orange Order pointed to the members of his organisation who he believed had been murdered 'just for being a Protestant and an Orangeman'.[90]

Such views of victimhood and discrimination have found several other outlets in recent times, including those represented by Families Acting for Innocent Relatives (FAIR) and a group calling itself Women Raising Unionist Concerns (WRUC), the declared aim of which was to 'save Loyalist culture, schools, traditions and Ulster' by engaging in direct peaceful action such as blocking roads during the rush hour.[91]

The Love Ulster movement lost much of its momentum after a parade it had organised in Dublin on 25 February 2006 was abandoned as a result of street violence and counter-protests. Love Ulster did however demonstrate that it was capable of bringing together representatives from a whole range of organisations around the notion that

Protestants had lost out directly in the post-peace process period and that their suffering during the Troubles had not been recognised. This was fanfared at its launch in a *News Letter* editorial pointing out that:

> The unionist community has been treated abominably by its own government and there is now a strong feeling in pro-Unionist circles that a determined push is on to achieve a united Ireland, coming not just from Republicans ... It is not surprising, therefore, that a campaign is being launched to co-ordinate unionists in opposition to a united Ireland and the 'crisis point' which many people believe has been reached for the Union.[92]

While never likely to become central to unionist politics, such campaigns did articulate the increasingly heard view from within unionism that the political process had acted to favour Irish nationalism, sometimes to the point where it was argued that unionists had become second-class citizens. Also central to the Love Ulster campaign was the desire to reinforce a collective cultural identity, underpinned by notions of Protestants as victims, and that there was a deficit within unionism, brought about by a bias in jobs towards Catholics, cultural and political marginalisation and dramatic underinvestment and spending in Protestant areas. Such themes have been consistently and prominently highlighted across loyalism in recent years, particularly by the DUP.

BACK TO CONFLICT I: THE 2005 RIOTS

Aside from the confrontations surrounding its sojourn to Dublin, Love Ulster was largely a non-violent expression of loyalist frustration. Not all organisations within loyalism have, however, sought to make their point by peaceful means in the post-Agreement period. In September 2005, several loyalist areas of Belfast erupted into sustained street violence, pitched at an intensity reminiscent of the worst days of the conflict. At its height, members of the PSNI exchanged gunfire with loyalist paramilitaries, and in direct response the Northern Ireland secretary Peter Hain withdrew recognition of the ceasefires of the UVF and the RHC, claiming that those groups had been central in organising and orchestrating the riots.[93]

The main perspectives represented in the media at the time were twofold: that loyalist paramilitaries had taken advantage of the situation to stage-manage the violence[94] and that the root cause lay in high levels of social and economic deprivation found in many loyalist working-class communities, reflecting the view that such areas had been 'neglected for 25 years'.[95] While both the involvement of paramilitaries and the social experiences of the Protestant working class were no doubt factors, there was another crucial aspect to consider. Feelings of political and cultural alienation within loyalism ran deep, reflecting a genuine disillusionment across the Protestant community surrounding the outcomes of the peace process and the consequences of the Agreement.

The overt trigger to the disturbances was seen to be the rerouting of an Orange Order parade in north Belfast. More realistically the violence came after weeks of mounting tension between loyalists and the state over the government's perceived haste in responding to the IRA's vow to disarm. Many also believed that too many concessions had been made to bring this about and that unionists were not being made fully aware of what was going on. Hence, David Ervine of the PUP described the disorder as a cry for recognition from 'ordinary Protestants who felt increasingly separated from the rest of Northern Irish society'[96] and the ramification of deep-rooted discontent from within the Protestant working class.

This rested on notions presenting the view that while working-class Catholic areas had directly benefited from the peace process, the opposite was true of many Protestant areas and within these the most deprived had suffered disproportionally in their lack of access to resources. For the PUP the cause of such turmoil and street confrontations rested in a 'sense that the Unionist community has been set aside while the [British] government plays footsie with the Republicans'.[97] Ervine further suggested that the roots of the 2005 riots were grounded in 'an ever growing sense of confidence in Catholic communities, and the reverse in Protestant districts'.[98]

Such perspectives were often self-reinforced through the reproduction of, and reference to, collective memories and political myths. These frames of understanding are used to interpret a rapidly changing social world through the development of a strong sense of 'territoriality' and long-term differences in cultural learning. Processes of political socialisation take place overtly through the ritual forms of political behaviour (one the most obvious being the parading tradition), and through less obvious informal influences such as family or other social networks within the community.[99]

BACK TO CONFLICT II: RETURN TO WAR?

Patterns of social and political behaviour are reproduced across loyalism. On Friday 24 November 2006 the Assembly met, supposedly yet again to plot a way forward and to progress the road map prepared by premiers Blair and Ahern. The precursor to this had been three days of intensive negotiations in Scotland, producing as an end result what became known as the 'St Andrews Agreement'. The prime reason for the Stormont meeting was to nominate prospective first and deputy first ministers. The DUP declined to take part in the nomination process, a clear rebuff widely read by supporters as presenting further lines of resistance to republicanism, which would only be removed when Sinn Féin accepted that the state had a legitimate role in policing.

Others, however, including the speaker of the Assembly, offered a much more positive interpretation, taking Paisley's admittedly somewhat ambivalent speech as an indication that he had not ruled out some future participation in a working Assembly. Amid the confusion, proceedings were suspended and the Assembly chambers evacuated as security staff forcibly intercepted an armed man[100] as he was repeatedly heard to call out 'no surrender' and that Paisley had sold out the Protestant people.[101] It later transpired that the intruder was Michael Stone, who first came to notoriety when on 16 March 1988 he attacked and killed mourners at a funeral of IRA volunteers shot dead by the SAS in Gibraltar.[102] In the process, Stone took on an almost iconic status within loyalism.

But the more recent action failed to even begin to merit anything like that reaction. Indeed, UPRG spokespersons almost immediately dismissed the action as a 'gimmick' designed to undermine what they described as 'real politics'. By marginalising Stone so quickly and directly, the contemporary UDA leadership made apparent comparisons between what they termed the old loyalism and those engaged in processes of political change. It was clear that not all those associated with the paramilitaries were seeking to play insular or backward-looking roles.

LOYALIST PARAMILITARISM AND COMMUNITY

How did such differences within paramilitary groups manifest at the community level? One key grouping determining the direction of loyalism at street level is former loyalist prisoners. A common experience involves altered views following their shared experiences in prison and their reintegration into society.[103] These experiences have helped reshape the political input from paramilitary groupings (often following individual reassessment of why they participated in the conflict).[104] This has led some to develop other approaches based on ideas of community engagement and developing community cohesion,[105] involving changing relationships both within and across loyalist communities.

One area where this can be seen surrounds the relationship of the paramilitaries to 'community policing', especially within those districts under their direct control. Throughout the Troubles community policing and enforcement by paramilitary groups was commonplace as a way of both maintaining internal control[106] and enforcing discipline in local districts,[107] where young people in particular were subjected to 'punishment beatings'.[108]

Even until quite recently, it was apparent that some within the paramilitaries still regarded such roles as legitimate. Take for example the following statement issued by the Belfast brigade of the UVF on 13 April 2005 regarding the level of petty crime in west Belfast:

> It is time for those involved in these acts to desist with immediate effect ... Protestants have suffered enough throughout the conflict with Republicans to endure hardships at the hands of local criminal scum ... We say this to criminals – take special heed, we will not tolerate your activities in any shape or form. Think carefully before roaming our estates![109]

Following the ceasefires, even as some within working-class communities were challenging (or at least questioning) their role in post-ceasefire society, the number of physical punishments meted out by loyalist paramilitaries grew, increasing from thirty-seven in 1993 to ninety-four a decade later. Christina Steenkamp points to important changes in the dynamic of loyalist violence during this time, from an 'inter' to an 'intra' focus, underpinned by an attempt to control territory and enforce localised social and economic control.[110]

Although there is evidence that, following the ceasefires, the use of firearms in loyalist punishments declined, the intensity of the beatings increased,[111] continuing at a rate almost twice that of their republican counterparts[112] and reaching a peak in 1996 (as did those by republican groups). From 2003, however, the frequency of such attacks began to decline. The first six months of 2005 saw the numbers of punishments meted out continue to fall steadily,[113] and while there were twelve paramilitary-style attacks by loyalists from July to December 2006 and eighteen in the first six months of 2007, by the end of June 2007 the number of such incidents recorded dropped to zero.[114] Although occasional attacks still did take place after that, such as the tarring and feathering of an alleged drug dealer in the late summer of 2007,[115] such events have all but disappeared from everyday life in loyalist communities.

LOYALIST PARAMILITARISM IN THE COMMUNITY

Understandings of the concept of community are extremely wide-ranging, and the term is used in a variety of ways across political, sociological, popular and social policy discourses and debates.[116]

Underpinning all of these understandings of community, however, are central ideas that include social order and disorder and the need for security and solidarity within marked communities (however defined). It would be naive therefore to suggest that there has not always been some degree of support for informal justice regimes within working-class loyalist areas as a perceived means of bringing about security.

It should also be said that during the conflict paramilitaries were at times under severe pressure from some within their own communities to bring an end to anti-social behaviour (especially in those areas where they projected themselves as self-appointed guardians and in the absence of 'normal' policing). Some members of the local community consistently gave at least tacit support to punishment attacks as a form of community justice.[117] One report published in the early 1990s noted the following situation in loyalist working-class communities:

> The police are not fulfilling their role of crime prevention and are more interested in anti-terrorist work. This has left a vacuum for the paramilitaries. They may be used by people in the community to get things done – for example, for house break-ins in which the police have failed to catch the culprits. It was stated that the police have recommended the use of paramilitaries for 'quick action' in cases like this.[118]

As Hall suggests, within tight-knit working-class communities, those who demanded that paramilitary organisations should 'deal with' anti-social elements were not inhumane ogres. Rather, he argues that they were ordinary people who felt isolated, helpless and angry by the inadequacy of official responses and who saw few other options open to them.[119] Such views support the findings of Colin Knox and Rachel Monaghan,[120] who argue that within loyalist areas community-based retributive justice developed because of the perceived inability of the police to deal with crime; the rise of petty crime in loyalist communities; and the perceived leniency of the formal criminal justice system.

But the legitimacy of the response of loyalist paramilitaries, even within the working class, was far from universal, particularly in the range and severity of physical punishments they utilised. The political response to the Agreement brought issues of criminal justice to the fore. At the macro level this led to issues such as the restructuring of policing and contestation around the nature and form of the criminal justice system. At the micro level, post-conflict life brought added dimensions, for example an increase in the amount of anti-social behaviour in working-class communities including drug abuse, binge drinking and joyriding. Running in parallel with wider issues surrounding the 'normalisation' process,[121] these behaviours raised core issues concerning community reactions.

This brought to the fore responses from sections of the paramilitaries seeking to re-enforce or redefine their self-identified roles as community protectors. Thus, some sought to promote different strategies through, for example, the introduction of schemes to counter physical punishments,[122] where community leaders and former combatants have sought to instigate non-violent alternatives to punishment beatings through schemes operating at a community level focusing on anti-social behaviour. One example is found in processes of restorative justice.

The concept of restorative justice is not new and it remains far from unitary in its interpretation or application.[123] Broadly, however, it involves bringing together those parties with an interest in a specific offence (for example victim, offender, perhaps the families of offender and victim, and often community and perhaps state representatives) with a view to dealing with all those affected by the crime committed.[124] Those involved in this 'collectively resolve how to deal with the aftermath of the offence and its implications for the future'.[125] This process often includes making some form of amends to their victim, engagement with forms of community reparation, and developing strategies for tackling social problems affecting a specific locality.[126] Most importantly, the offender is in some form obliged to take responsibility for his or her actions, and the victim and wider community are involved in defining the obligations placed on the offender.[127]

Since the late 1990s both republican and loyalist communities have been involved in operating restorative justice schemes. While there is much commonality in broad approach it is, however, important to identify the different dynamics at play within loyalist and republican communities. The informal system that emerged from within republicanism reflected the broad questioning of the state's legitimacy[128] and demanded the right to be run independently from the formal system and the police service (although the situation may alter with the entry of Sinn Féin unto policing boards). Nonetheless, Community Restorative Justice Ireland (CRJ) has claimed, with some justification, that if they were to engage with the PSNI they would lose much creditability in the communities within which they operate, where republican paramilitaries have historically provided a role in the absence of what is seen as a legitimate state police force.[129]

In loyalist areas, restorative justice programmes developed in a different context; less hostile to statutory law enforcement authorities, and seen as providing an alternative to the state rather than competing directly with it.[130] The primary restorative justice initiative operating within loyalist districts is 'Alternatives'. Most closely associated with the PUP grouping, it deals largely with young persistent offenders, whose

typical offences include theft, breaking and entering, shoplifting, bully-
ing, excess noise, graffiti and vandalism – that which is usually categorised in popular discourse as petty crime or anti-social behaviour.
One report suggests that just over 40 per cent of referrals came directly
from paramilitary organisations, around 27 per cent from other community-based groups, social services referred another 18 per cent and
around 13 per cent were self-referred.[131]

Binding together such projects is the belief that local statutory
organisations have often failed to fully comprehend dominant community values, and therefore underpinning restorative justice projects is
recognition that working-class communities have discrete histories and
cultures reflected in the strength of distinct political socialisation within those communities. As Brendan McAllister records:

> During the 1990s, in both republican and loyalist communities, a
> number of individuals, including people with links to paramili-
> tary organisations, helped devise mechanisms to deal with anti-
> social behaviour, particularly in inner city areas where sections of
> the community had grown used to paramilitaries dealing with
> offenders and using methods such as beatings, deportation,
> maiming and even shooting ... A number of schemes got off the
> ground. They involved individuals with a known background in
> paramilitarism, including time spent in prison.[132]

McAllister further notes that while such people bore high credentials
within paramilitary circles, those with a 'paramilitary background or
good working relationships with paramilitaries ... were highly suspect
in the eyes of other sections of the community'.[133]

Such provision remains contested. This draws on longstanding relationships of equivocation between paramilitaries and the wider
Protestant population. Thus, for example, only 3 per cent of Protestants
were supportive of the early prisoner release scheme under the terms of
the Agreement (compared to 31 per cent of Catholics).[134] Given the central
role played by former prisoners in such schemes, critics suggest that such
groups may simply act as a cover for continuing paramilitary influence in
local areas; others, that youths in loyalist working-class communities risk
being punished twice, once by the official justice system and then again
by the community or its representatives.[135] Even when such schemes are
seen to work effectively, there are tensions surrounding the 'ownership'
of such projects,[136] their funding sources and their relationship with official agencies, although four restorative justice schemes operating in loyalist districts were given government approval in May 2007.[137]

Restorative justice projects represent one aspect of the wide range of
non-pay-based and voluntary grouping engaged with conflict transfor-

mation work in loyalist areas.[138] While there are limitations to what can be achieved by such ventures, this should not downplay what has been brought about by those actively engaged in seeking to move away from violence towards processes of conflict transformation.[139] Alongside 'Alternatives', the list of organisations located within loyalist communities that seek to engage directly with civil society is long. It includes, for example, Local Initiatives for Needy Communities (LINC), the Inner East Forum, and the Ex-Prisoners Interpretative Centre (EPIC) as groupings focusing on community development, the facilitation of cross-community contacts and issues of common concern across a range of community groups and representatives in areas of social need and cohesion.

LOYALISM, CIVIL SOCIETY AND CONFLICT TRANSFORMATION

The broad dynamic for much of the above is provided through the concept of conflict transformation. As has been noted, conflict transformation 'operates both personally and spatially within and without (between) the respective communities'.[140] This has a specific meaning, as Smithey explains:

> A sustainable peace in situations of intractable conflict means that groups of people, distinguished from one another along familiar lines of ethnopolitical division, feel they have the wherewithal and opportunities for collaboration and opposition without resorting to violent coercion. Conflict is thus transformed, not simply resolved. Grievances, prejudices and collective identities hardened over decades of violent conflict cannot be quickly pacified or dissolved, especially among those who have borne the brunt of violent conflict.[141]

Although within sections of loyalism, particularly those associated with the PUP, broad ideas around conflict transformation have been established for over two decades,[142] the processes remain fluid and incomplete. Since late 2004 some form of transition to the political sphere has also become increasingly central to the thinking of the UDA and its political representatives in the UPRG. The internal relationships of the UDA grouping are complex and remain highly localised,[143] and while following the Agreement the organisation was certainly engaged in continued violence and criminal activity,[144] this should not mask the direction in which the organisation has turned.

At one level this involved a formal consultation process involving UDA members;[145] at another it reflected the direction of the political leadership provided by the revamped UPRG (see previous chapter) and mirrored changes in personnel within the leading ranks of the

UDA. Such processes were given increased momentum in July 2005 following the announcement by the IRA that their military campaign had ended. The broad response from the UDA membership reflected the view that the organisation needed to promote a process that would ensure the Union while recognising a move towards the primacy of politics and away from a military campaign.[146] Thus, Hall suggests that the dominant view from ordinary members is that while the IRA's military war might indeed be over, their political war certainly was not.[147]

There was a clear binary to this. The beliefs of a majority of UDA members still saw the need to 'defend Ulster', and their belief that loyalists remained 'a last line of defence' had not lessened.[148] Most UDA members also recognised, however, that they must now take the 'fight into the political arena'.[149] Hence the awareness as legitimate the role the UPRG now has in promoting a political perspective and the primacy of non-violent means to achieve the goals of the UDA.[150] This has led the leadership of the UPRG to again emphasise that mainstream Unionist parties are incapable of representing the needs of working-class Protestants. This found a political outlet through the 'Loyalism in Transition' initiative, and public expression in *A New Reality*, published by the UPRG in October 2006.

Hall has provided further details on discussions by the UDA membership[151] and the proceedings of an international workshop on conflict transformation.[152] Although the overt recognition by the UDA within the documents that 'they too have been part of the problem' is something new, not far below the surface are themes that have been consistently found since the formation of the UDA. In particular, the notion that politicians, especially the DUP, have used and abandoned 'ordinary Protestants' quickly resurfaces.

In response, the UPRG proposals highlight a number of key issues, including disaffection with the political fragmentation of unionism and the lack of strong community-level political leadership. The UPRG has also increasingly articulated concern regarding the social and economic conditions within loyalism, calling for government measures to counter poor employment opportunities and the lack of educational success in Protestant working-class areas. They also point to the fear of the diminution of their cultural heritage, through processes whereby Ulster Protestant identity is constantly challenged. This culminated in late 2008 with a UDA statement that they would seek to retrain members to engage in peaceful struggle 'on a new battlefield' of cultural politics to be fought out on the terrain of media presentation, education, politics, social and community work and business.[153]

LOYALISM AND CIVIL SOCIETY

The main contemporary thrust of loyalist paramilitary groupings has been to ensure a legitimate position within their immediate communities and to broaden this to the arena of civil society to engage with the state in what can commonly be understood as community development. This is far from universally accepted, not just because the origins of many of those involved lie within paramilitarism but also because the negative effects of an established culture across working-class Protestants of conservative social values, apathy, mistrust and opposition to anything even resembling socialist politics remain deeply rooted.

This is not to say that over several generations working-class Protestant communities did not develop some level of organic leadership or seek to organise their own systems of social support largely through an infrastructure centred on the Church, the Orange Order, and sometimes the organised labour or trades union movement. This found expression and outlet through various community organisations, including tenants associations, cultural and community arts, housing groups, Church-based youth organisations, Orange Widows, welfare organisations and so on.[154]

Much of the activity and influence of the grouping associated with the paramilitaries continues to operate at this community level. Any discussion of the concept of community takes us to a complex arena, made more so because, as Field suggests, many of the contemporary debates around the 'old' concept of community now tend to overlap with the 'new' one of social capital.[155] The concept of social capital has been made especially prominent through reference to the recent works of Robert Putnam[156] and James Coleman.[157] The widespread debates concerning the theoretical and practical parameters of social capital have seen it become central to many research and policy agendas. While definitions of social capital remain diverse,[158] its core aspects surround the building of relations of social trust through deepening social connections.[159] This manifests at the local level, but is also central in establishing connections across society.[160]

Putnam and Goss identify four distinct dimensions to social capital. These are: formal versus informal; thick versus thin; inward-looking versus outward-looking; and bridging versus bonding.[161] Levels of formal social capital refer to the level of organisation addressing social capital among groups. The distinction between 'thick' and 'thin' points to the degree to which social capital is 'interwoven' and 'multi-stranded' across an identifiable grouping (Putnam and Goss give the example of steelworkers who both work and socialise together).[162] 'Inward-looking' social capital promotes the social and material interests of group members, while 'outward-looking' connects groups with wider resources and public goods.

Finally, bonding capital strengthens the sense of belonging among those with common interests and social conditions, while bridging capital refers to those social networks that bring together those 'who are unlike one another'.[163] Putnam contends that the development of such shared social values provides the base for the creation and expansion of working civic institutions, through the development of bonding capital. In turn it is claimed that this helps generate bridging capital, which contributes positively to formulating broader identities and social relationships.

In considering such material it is clear that throughout Northern Ireland social bonding remains largely restricted to one's 'own' community[164] and that intra-community cohesion remains high.[165] Equally observable is the level of social division between communities, where high levels of distrust and an exclusive set of social relations constantly reinforce social distance from the Other, strengthening thick social bonds while weakening bridging capital and the possibility of social bonding.[166]

It must also be recognised that within the Protestant community core relationships to civil society were constructed in particular circumstances and in particular ways,[167] whereby any criticism of welfare provision was seen as a direct challenge to the state itself. This had consequences for the development of both inward-looking and thick social capital. Many of the core values of loyalism emerged and developed within traditional tightly knit industrial communities. But the development of politics during the Stormont years also inhibited working-class agitation for better social conditions and importantly robbed the Protestant working-class community of the development of much organisational and political skill.[168]

This also helped build a political culture within which any criticism offered of social and economic conditions or political direction was open to accusations of disloyalty from mainstream unionism, resulting in little or no anti-state activism by the Protestant working class.[169] A reluctance to engage fully with state welfare provision and other public services continues to have deep cultural resonance within working-class unionism, with poor levels of take up for funding programmes and a lack of capacity and confidence in dealing with external welfare agencies and public services.[170]

The refusal of many Protestants to declare themselves in public need was again highlighted at a major conference held in the early 1990s.[171] Almost a decade later Robson noted that within Protestant communities there continues to be a perception that 'community development' remains something that largely works to the benefit of nationalists, who are better at 'working the system' than their unionist counterparts, highlighting a continued reluctance within loyalism to organise to try to secure wider resources from the state.[172]

But there are those who sought to counter this trend. From their origin, individuals who joined paramilitaries were often also members of other groups active in civil society, local politics and community development.[173] The early days of the UDA saw the organisation filled with community and trade union activists,[174] alongside others holding status in working-class communities.[175] As Langhammer notes:

> A generation ago every street in Newtownards Road, Tigers Bay, Sandy Row, the Shankill or Rathcoole [all traditional working-class Protestant districts] would have had a convenor, or shop steward, or Health and Safety representative as a result of mass participation in the great, unionised manufacturing enterprises of shipbuilding, aircraft, engineering and textiles. This meant that every community had people with capacity for leadership, organisation and negotiation, learnt through the trade union movement.[176]

In recent years there has undoubtedly been much top-down effort seeking to empower civil society,[177] but this still is subject to interpretation and negotiation at the level of community structures. Even if we accept the assertion of Langhammer that civil society is much less developed within Protestant working-class areas than within similar Catholic districts,[178] this does not mean that politics and active civil society are somehow completely divorced in those areas.[179] There is observable activity, and among the key arenas are those activities where community activists and paramilitary groupings draw on the same resources, work side by side or indeed are one and the same people.

These lived experiences may explain the tendency for at least some within loyalism to recognise a broader view of the reasons for the conflict, and to seek to express a form of politics that looks to encompass the economic, social and cultural circumstances felt by working-class Protestants. This has drawn many of those involved to the notion of capacity building within communities, linking to broader ideas suggesting that:

> ... civil renewal, particularly in the neighbourhoods where people live, will not take place either as a result of well meaning volunteers from elsewhere or the state from above, but with the direct involvement of those who live there ... building the capacity of the dispossessed to help themselves, to change the circumstances in which they live from ones which blight their lives to ones which transform and liberate them.[180]

PARAMILITARIES AND CIVIL SOCIETY

While the negative and violent side of paramilitarism are apparent, as have been some of the residual consequences such as the levels of criminality for working-class areas, this should not blind us to changes that have taken place among loyalist paramilitary groupings,[181] in particular recognition that in the post-conflict period sections of the paramilitaries have also acted to develop local involvement in processes of conflict transformation and community development.[182] Importantly, as Tom Winston reminds us, paramilitaries 'are local people involved in organizations with long histories and family connections'.[183] Sections of the paramilitaries and former combatants remain embedded in the community and provide important leadership roles within it, for example through the negotiation for scarce social, economic and political resources on behalf of working-class communities rather than direct involvement in violence.[184]

As loyalist paramilitary (and post-paramilitary) organisations engage more fully with processes of conflict transformation it is likely that the impact will increasingly be felt across civil society, broadly defined as the arena of voluntary political activity outside formal state intervention and organisation.[185] Further, it is clear that paramilitaries, former prisoners and their associates have been involved in a range of activities aimed at conflict reduction and eliminating violence on the streets. These have included attempts to decrease confrontations at interfaces, the stewarding of bonfires, and the repainting of many of the more aggressive and militaristic loyalist murals with 'cultural' representations[186] and local icons and personalities, such as the Titanic, George Best or C.S. Lewis.[187]

While not denying that the relationships in loyalist communities towards paramilitarism and its associates remain inconclusive, it is still at the localised level of their ideological and physical heartlands that many who have been involved with the paramilitaries retain a high level of local status and are seen to have some legitimacy. Moreover, where paramilitaries retain some level of authority they often set the context and operate as 'mood music' for community development activities.[188]

Without doubt the violence perpetrated by paramilitaries was always a self-limiting factor in having their voices heard; since the ceasefires some sections of paramilitarism (notably former prisoners) have shown leadership in the transformation from cultures of violence towards other forms of political and social expression.[189] The political development of such groups has not taken place in a straight line, and will not do so in the future. Nor is this a simple case of 'good' and 'bad' paramilitaries, or oppositional groupings of 'hawks' and 'doves' within these organisations. As one former UVF member explains, there has always been fluidity in the tactics and positions taken by many within the paramilitary groups:

> People sometimes try and simplify the thing into hawks and doves, and it doesn't always work like that because people who might have approved of the fact that the Provos were getting a bloody nose at the time would also have realised that that wasn't the way to do business indefinitely and it couldn't go on like that.[190]

Hence, both ideological and pragmatic conflicts (and the intertwining of these) continue to surround the political positioning of groupings representing, or emerging from, the paramilitaries. In discussing peace processes and accords worldwide, John Darby highlights four major positions taken by former combatants. These are categorised as 'dealers' who are prepared to negotiate; 'zealots' whose major goal is to bring down or spoil a peace process by the use of violence; 'opportunists' who may be persuaded under certain circumstances to end violence; and 'mavericks' whose violence is primarily motivated by personal rather than political objectives.[191]

While it is clear that within loyalist paramilitarism there have been, and remain, members representative of all of these positions, it should not be assumed that these are fixed. Individuals may, and have, moved between these positions in response to wider political circumstances. What is important is to identify the balance between these dynamics at any point. Increasingly, former combatants have become 'centrally placed stakeholders' in embedding peace.[192] Clearly within the UVF/PUP grouping, those active in and seeking to develop a political emphasis were given a greater level of legitimacy (both internally and externally) much earlier than their equivalent in the UDA.

There is increasing evidence, however, that those prepared to engage politically (represented by the UPRG) have come to the fore within the UDA. This was clearly seen following the outbreak of violence by dissident republican groups in March 2009, when both of the main loyalist groups made clear in their initial responses that they remained committed to the political path and that a military response was not an option,[193] aiding the eventual move towards the decommissioning of loyalist paramilitary weaponry some three months later.[194]

Within loyalist communities, social connections and networks at the local level – what others have called bonding capital – remains strong.[195] Given their history it is clear that paramilitary groupings have played a role in building and maintaining social connections and networks within localised areas. Sometimes, as in the early 1970s, this was easily seen, as when the claims from the UDA to be defending particular communities led to the formation of the Ulster Community Action Group (UCAG), which for a short time became deeply engaged in development work, often accepting 'basic tenets of opposition to the state'.[196] More broadly it was all but impossible to organise community work within such areas without at least the tacit support of paramilitary groups.

In the contemporary period, while some paramilitaries and loyalist former prisoners are active in cross-community and conflict resolution processes, these still have had a limited impact in structuring the broader response from many loyalist communities, or in constructing extended links with the Other. Overall, within loyalist communities there is an identifiable weakness in any collective community or political actions designed at building levels of bridging capital.[197] The survey material, presented by Acheson et al, demonstrates just how deeply embedded most voluntary organisations are within their own communities. They also note that those organisations that straddle the community divide remain in a distinct minority.[198] As Van Til puts it, the strength of community in Northern Ireland 'rests most often in the realm of bonding and far too infrequently offers its members an opportunity to "bridge" or interact with those of different backgrounds or values'.[199]

LEARNING TO BE LOYALIST

Such relationships are crucial. The eventual positioning of Protestant working-class communities within civil society remains at the core of any lasting resolution. While a negotiated settlement may have been brought about, for it to last its legitimacy and effectiveness must be accepted not only by those prepared to make the accord but by future generations of loyalists. It must be developed and strengthened not just at the high table of politics but also at the everyday level.

Young loyalists experience society in a particular way. As elsewhere, young people in Northern Ireland experience multiple strands of marginalisation. In 1995, for example, around 37 per cent of children in Northern Ireland were living in poverty.[200] Even if not on the economic margins, they are certainly more likely than their elders to lack resources and to be excluded (to a greater or lesser degree) from social and political processes and institutions.[201] Moreover, the life experiences of young people in Northern Ireland are often territorially bounded,[202] with young people 'more likely to see invisible interfaces and lines of demarcation'.[203] Orla Muldoon points out that for over a generation young people in Northern Ireland grew up in a divided society, experiencing 'unchecked and pervasive sectarian prejudice'.[204]

So upon which political reference points do young people from a loyalist background draw and how integrated are they into the wider political process? A broad outline of the contours of life for young people growing up in loyalist districts can be gleaned from material produced by community groups[205] and academics.[206] Such evidence begins to confirm the characterisation of Protestant working-class youth culture as a hybrid identity constructed at the interface of other youth sub-cultures common across the UK and that sense of ethnic identification expressing various forms of attachment to 'Ulster'.[207]

Without denying the intensity or extent of an ever-present Americanised popular culture, the localised culture of loyalism, as an outlet for expressions of the everyday and the immediate, remains a key organisational focus in structuring identity. Importantly, it has been recognised that:

> Working-class youth inhabit, like their parents, a distinctive structural and cultural milieu defined by territory, objects and things, relations, institutional and social practices. In terms of kinship, friendship networks, the informal culture of the neighbourhood and the practices articulated around them, the young are already located by the parent culture.[208]

While anyone now aged under twenty-five can have little, if any, direct recall of the conflict, the importance of folk and collective memory in orientating political reactions in Northern Ireland cannot be understated.[209] As people's responses are always shaped by political socialisation and subjective orientations, memories of conflict, even if based in collective fiction or highly selective recollections, help shape contemporary perceptions.[210]

Such perceptions rarely fade quickly or spontaneously.[211] Indeed, throughout Northern Ireland such memories are increasingly reinforced by a whole calendar of commemorative events, public gatherings, displays and presentations.[212] Loyalists, as with many other collectives, draw upon forms of social memory and commemoration to provide individual reference points and to reinforce social solidarity and group identity.[213] This is used to interpret current circumstances and understandings of their political and social worlds through the creation of cultural landscapes[214] and reinforcement of political practices.[215] Crucially such processes help rank certain events as more important (or at least more central) to identity than others.[216]

The Agreement and devolved government have brought into relief issues concerning the extent to which in the future different political differences and attitudes may change or continue to be reinforced. This occurs within a context where, despite the broad societal transformations brought about by the peace process, there remain many areas where social relations have not significantly altered: economic hardship remains a facet of everyday life; the physical and political realities of sectarian division remain deeply felt. As Colin Coulter and Michael Murray express it, while Northern Ireland 'may no longer be at war with itself, neither can it be said to be genuinely at peace'.[217] Within the contemporary period many continue to look to highly specific political reference points that appear enduring and offer some sense of political stability and cultural reinforcement.

FUTURES FOR LOYALISM?

For loyalism, acute understandings of sectarian difference formed and reinforced by political conflict and violence run deep within the social being of Northern Ireland. Much of this constructed sense of difference continues to be presented as community-validated truths to children and young people.[218] These patterns of socialisation are central to the development of politics, especially in a society where around 36 per cent of the population are aged under twenty-five.[219] Connolly and Maginn show, for example, that from a very early age children develop an understanding of social differences between Protestant and Catholic[220] and begin to apply negative characteristics to the other group, while Lanclos provides evidence that by the time children reach primary school the understanding and 'telling' of difference is understood and embedded.[221]

Established patterns of political socialisation are central to the development of social identities by the young,[222] and the salience of group membership remains central to the formation of identity.[223] Marie Smyth and Mark Scott reveal a clear overlap between the political expression of young people and those of the adult population.[224] Indeed, their survey responses indicated that young people's views on the Agreement dovetailed almost directly with the wider population, with 77 per cent of Catholic and 45 per cent of Protestant youth surveyed offering support for the Agreement, and with around one in three young Protestant respondents claiming they would oppose the Agreement given the opportunity.

The stability and direction of post-Agreement politics rests in the acceptance of parity between Ulster unionist and Irish nationalist political traditions. The success, or failure, of this will reveal itself through positive involvement in and the development of civil society as outlined above. In achieving this, the level of support given by the next generation is, of course, vital to any continuing settlement. There is, for example, some evidence of a strengthening sense of 'Northern Irish' identity among young people.

When the views of young people and adults across Northern Ireland are compared there is a lower level of self-classification as 'British' among young Protestants (51 per cent) than in the adult Protestant population (75 per cent). They were, however, much more likely to describe their identity as 'Northern Irish' or 'Ulster' than the adult population.[225] Drawing on this, there is a further tendency to portray young people as offering 'hope for the future'[226] and as holding inherently progressive or liberal views. While there has been a growing trend across the population in Northern Ireland to identify as 'Northern Irish' or as 'British and Irish',[227] the claim that this marks a liberalisation of political views needs to be treated with caution. Deeply embedded processes of political socialisation continue to reinforce strong discourses of difference, which in many ways are self-perpetuating.

In turn this manifests in social and political differences emphasising competing sectarian values and national identities[228] through a variety of political, social and economic sub-cultures.[229] One example of this is found in a survey of young Protestants in north Belfast which indicated that the main reason they voted, or intended to vote, the way they did was because of religion (23 per cent), community tradition (20 per cent) and policies (19 per cent). Some 11 per cent voted the way they did because of family loyalty, while 7 per cent cast their vote because it was the same way as their friends.[230]

As Healy points out, sectarian patterns of segregation continue to directly influence the worldview and attitudes of those growing up in divided localities.[231] Sectarianism among young people continues to be experienced in the banal and the everyday[232] as well as the political set piece and public expressions of commemoration[233] used 'as part of the struggle to achieve the hegemony of one particular discourse at the expense of others'[234] and to reinforce existing social solidarities. Further, many believe that religious ethnic difference is always likely to impact on social and political relationships in Northern Ireland, often adopting strategies in order to avoid sectarian confrontation or abuse.[235]

Young people continue to learn about competing political structures in identifiable ways.[236] Although there is much need for further research into the political views of the post-conflict generation, existing evidence suggests that young people 'assume, all too readily, the political and religious mantles of their predecessors'.[237] They also become aware of how politics is orientated and experienced through inherited senses of difference[238] and come to easily understand everyday meanings of constructed social difference. There are important nuances within this, not least of which is that young Protestants remain more pessimistic about their future than do young Catholics or adult Protestants. For both old and young, engagement with party politics remains only a limited part of everyday loyalist culture.

CONCLUSION

While there are still many common bonds and reference points between unionism and loyalism, there is a growing sense from within loyalism that the main outcomes of past allegiance to traditional unionism have reinforced its position of social deprivation and political exclusion. Indeed, many feel as an outcome of the political process they have been twice marginalised, as loyalists and as working class. All of this influenced and continues to influence how people respond to wider political events. Political actions are often qualified by external circumstances, but they are also structured by enduring socialisation processes, which confirm and reinforce points of authenticity and difference buttressed by local memory, commemoration and acts of active remembering.

Loyalist culture clearly continues to reject much of unionism as middle-class, paternalistic, exploitative and unrepresentative. Communal experiences have found expression and outlets through a variety of social groupings, including family and friendship networks and religious and community associations, as well as paramilitary and formal political groupings. Loyalist reactions have been guided by a particular frame of understanding that in part recognises how loyalist communities have remained polarised, most obviously from republicans but also from other factions of unionism and from the wider society in Northern Ireland. Such communities, however, remain strongly bonded at the horizontal level. It is here that the nature of loyalism remains contested. Its future political direction will be determined, in part at least, by which of the multiple discourses available to them to interpret and develop are seen as most convincing by the next generation.

NOTES

1. O'Farrell, J., 'Payback time in Belfast', *New Statesman*, 19 September 2005.
2. *Combat*, Christmas issue 1997, p.5.
3. Ruane and Todd, *The Dynamics of Conflict in Northern Ireland: Power, Conflict and Emancipation*, p.61.
4. Northern Ireland Statistics and Research Agency, Noble Data 2006, Archived at: http://www.nisra.gov.uk. See also Noble, M. et al, *Measures of Deprivation in Northern Ireland* (Belfast: Northern Ireland Statistical Research Agency, 2005).
5. Horgan, G., 'Devolution, direct rule and neo-liberal reconstruction in Northern Ireland', *Critical Social Policy*, 26, 3 (2006), p.657.

6. 'Poorest worse off despite peace process', *Irish Examiner*, 14 September 2006.
7. Cited in McGill, P., 'Spending in Protestant areas: not what it says on the cover', *Scope* (June 2006), p.12.
8. Equality Commission for Northern Ireland, *Census 2001: Community Background in Northern Ireland* (Belfast: ECNI, 2006), p.24.
9. Shannon, A., *Report of the Taskforce on Protestant Working-Class Communities*, p.20.
10. Horgan, 'Devolution, direct rule and neo-liberal reconstruction in Northern Ireland', p.657.
11. Mitchell, C., 'For God and … conflict transformation? the Churches' disengagement with contemporary loyalism', in Edwards and Bloomer (eds), *Transforming the Peace Process in Northern Ireland*, p.149.
12. D. Morrow 'Nothing to fear but … ? unionists and the Northern Ireland peace process', pp.14–15.
13. Faith and Politics Group, *Transition* (Belfast: FPG, 2001), p.15.
14. Shirlow and Murtagh, *Belfast: Segregation, Violence and the City*, pp.106–7.
15. See Coulter, 'Direct rule and the unionist middle classes'; Coulter, 'The culture of contentment: the political beliefs and practice of the unionist middle classes'; Tonge, J. and Evans, J., 'Faultlines in unionism: division and dissent within the Ulster Unionist Council', *Irish Political Studies*, no. 16 (2001), pp.111–32; Tonge, J. and Evans, J., 'It's a family affair? attitudes to the GFA and the DUP within the UUP', paper presented to the Political Studies Association of Ireland, annual conference, October 2003.
16. Interview with author, 14 September 2005.
17. McKittrick, D., 'What makes the loyalists angry is seeing the other side doing so well', *Independent*, 17 January 2002.
18. Holland, J., *Hope Against History: The Ulster Conflict* (London: Hodder and Stoughton,1999), p.306.
19. See various contributions in D. Murray (ed.), *Protestant Perceptions of the Peace Process in Northern Ireland* (University of Limerick: Centre for Peace and Development Studies, 2000).
20. Hall, M., *An Uncertain Future: An Exploration by Protestant Community Activists* (Belfast: Island Pamphlet, 2002), p.3.
21. Healy, J., 'Locality matters: ethnic segregation and community conflict – the experience of Protestant girls in Belfast', *Children and Society*, no. 20 (2006), pp.105–15.
22. McAuley and McCormack, 'The protestant working class and the state in Northern Ireland since 1930', p.45.
23. McIntyre, A., 'Of myths and men: dissent within republicanism and loyalism', in Edwards and Bloomer, *Transforming the Peace Process in Northern Ireland*, p.127.
24. Wood, 'Loyalist paramilitaries and the peace process', p.183.
25. Anderson, C., *The Billy Boy: The Life and Death of LVF Leader Billy Wright* (Edinburgh: Mainstream Publishing, 2002).
26. Gillespie, G., 'Loyalists since 1972', in Boyce and O'Day (eds), *Defenders of the Union*, p.268.
27. Murphy, C., 'UVF to review stance on peace process', *Irish Times*, 17 July 1999.
28. See Eames, R. (2003) 'Loyalists must end criminality'. Archived at: http://www.news. bbc.co.uk/go/pr/fr/-/1/hi/northern_ireland/3021452.stm
29. See Anderson, *The Billy Boy: The Life and Death of LVF leader Billy Wright*; Wood, *Crimes of Loyalty*, pp.263–96.
30. Organised Crime Task Force, *Annual Report* (Belfast: HMSO, 2005).
31. Organised Crime Task Force, *Annual Report and Threat Assessment* (Belfast: HMSO, 2006).
32. In 2003 a report by the Northern Ireland Affairs Committee at Westminster claimed that paramilitaries were making up to £18 million per year through smuggling, extortion and armed robbery. Within this it was suggested that income from illegal activities organised by the loyalist paramilitaries totalled nearly £5 million.
33. Bruce, S., 'Turf war and peace: loyalist terrorism and political violence', *Terrorism and Political Violence*, 13, 2 (2001), p.518.
34. The IMC noted in 2006 that within sections of the UDA criminality remained 'endemic', and that in 2007, while UVF involvement in drugs had reduced, some individual members 'remained involved in serious crime for personal gain'. See, Independent Monitoring Commission, *Tenth Report of the IMC* (London: Stationery Office, 2006); Independent Monitoring Commission, *Fifteenth Report of the IMC* (London: Stationery Office, 2007). For a broad outline of loyalist paramilitary involvement in criminality, see Silke, A., 'In defence of the realm: financing loyalist terrorism in Northern Ireland – Part One: extor-

tion and blackmail', *Studies in Conflict and Terrorism*, 21, 4 (1998), pp.331–61; Silke, A., 'Ragged justice: loyalist vigilantism in Northern Ireland', *Terrorism and Political Violence*, no. 11 (1999), pp.1–31.
35. Rowan, *Paisley and the Provos*, p.16.
36. Loyalist Commission, 'Drugs and the loyalist community', document in possession of the author, no date; Thornton, C., 'Paramilitary gangs "still in business": moves to destabilise peace continue', *Belfast Telegraph*, 4 November 2004.
37. Persic, C. and Bloomer, S., *The Feud and the Fury ... The Response of the Community Sector to the Shankill Feud, August 2000* (Belfast: Springfield Intercommunity Development, no date).
38. Adair, J. with McKendry, G., *Mad Dog* (London: John Blake, 2007).
39. For good journalist accounts of some of the key figures within loyalist paramilitarism throughout this time, see Lister, D. and Jordan, H., *Mad Dog: The Rise and Fall of Johnny Adair and 'C Company'* (Edinburgh: Mainstream, 2003); Jordan, H., *Milestones in Murder* (Edinburgh: Mainstream, 2002), pp.197–204; McDowell, J., *The Mummy's Boys: Threats and Menaces from Ulster's ParaMafia* (Dublin: Gill and Macmillan, 2008); Rowan, B., *How the Peace Was Won* (Dublin: Gill and Macmillan, 2008).
40. Gallaher, C. and Shirlow, P., 'The geography of loyalist paramilitary feuding in Belfast', *Space and Polity*, 10, 2 (2006), pp.149–70; McAuley, '"Just Fighting to Survive"', pp.522–43; McAuley, J.W., 'Fantasy politics? Restructuring unionism after the Good Friday Agreement', *Éire–Ireland*, 39, 1/2 (2004), pp.189–214.
41. Gallaher and Shirlow, *The Geography of Loyalist Paramilitary Feuding*, p.155.
42. Wood, 'Loyalist paramilitaries and the peace process', p.184.
43. Murphy, C., 'UVF to review stance on peace process', *Irish Times*, 17 July 1999.
44. Edwards, A., 'Abandoning armed resistance? the Ulster Volunteer Force as a case study of strategic terrorism in Northern Ireland', *Studies in Conflict and Terrorism*, 32, 1 (2009), pp.146–66.
45. Ervine, D., 'Loyalist confidence in decline'. Archived at: http://news.bbc.co.uk/northern_ireland
46. UVF spokesperson cited in *Combat*, January 2003, p.3.
47. Cited in *Combat*, January 2003, p.4.
48. See Hall, M., *The Death of the 'Peace Process'? A Survey of Community Perceptions* (Belfast: Island Pamphlets, 1997).
49. *Irish Times*, 'Police chief worried by loyalist warning', 17 January 2003.
50. Northern Ireland Office, 'Northern Ireland must not become a cold place for Protestants – Reid, 21 November 2001'. Archived at: http://www.nio.gov.uk/northern-ireland-must-not-become-a-cold-place-for-protestants
51. Steenkamp, C., 'Loyalist paramilitary violence after the Belfast Agreement', *Ethnopolitics*, 7, 1 (2008), pp.159–76.
52. Hainsworth, P. (ed.), *Divided Society: Ethnic Minorities and Racism in Northern Ireland* (London: Pluto Press, 1998); Mann-Kler, D., *Out of the Shadows: An Action Research Report into Families, Racism and Exclusion in Northern Ireland* (Belfast: Barnardos, 1997).
53. Connolly, P., *'Race' and Racism in Northern Ireland: A Review of the Research Evidence* (Belfast: Office of the First Minister and Deputy First Minister, 2002); Connolly, P., '"It goes without saying (well, sometimes)": racism, whiteness and identity in Northern Ireland', in J. Agyeman and S. Neal (eds), *The New Countryside? Ethnicity, Nation and Exclusion in Contemporary Rural Britain* (Bristol: Policy Press, 2005).
54. McGarry, A., Hainsworth, P. and Gilligan, C., 'Political parties and minority ethnic communities in Northern Ireland: election manifestos 1994–2007', *Translocations: The Irish Migration, Race and Social Transformation Review*, 3, 1 (2008), pp.106–32.
55. See Jarman, N. and Monaghan, R., *Racist Harassment in Northern Ireland* (Belfast: Office of the First and Deputy First Ministers, 2003); Gallagher, E., 'Racism and citizenship education in Northern Ireland', *Irish Educational Studies*, 26, 3 (2007), pp.253–69.
56. McDonald, H., 'Belfast Romanians rehoused after race attacks', *Guardian*, 17 June 2009.
57. Rolson, B., 'Legacy of intolerance: racism and unionism in south Belfast', IRR News. Archived at: http://www.irr.org.uk/2004/february/ak000008.html
58. Bell, D., *Acts of Union: Youth Culture and Sectarianism in Northern Ireland* (Basingstoke: Macmillan, 1987).
59. Connolly, P., 'An examination of the nature and causes of racism in Northern Ireland', in R. Goldie (ed.), *Belfast: an Inclusive City? Exploring Issues of Racism and Diversity*, report on

The Irish Association spring conference (London: Institute of Governance Public Policy and Social Research, 2005).

60. See Connolly, P. and Keenan, M., *The Hidden Truth: Racist Harassment in Northern Ireland* (Belfast: Northern Ireland Statistics and Research Agency, 2001); Jarman, N. and Monaghan, R., *Racist Harassment in Northern Ireland* (Belfast: Office of the First Minister and Deputy First Minister, 2003).

61. Wojtas, O., 'Irish find room for racism', *Times Higher Education Supplement*, 21 April 2000.

62. Connolly, P. and Keenan, M., *Racial Attitudes and Prejudice in Northern Ireland* (Belfast: Northern Ireland Statistics and Research Agency, 2000).

63. Chan, S., '"God's little acre" and "Belfast Chinatown": cultural politics and agencies of anti-racist spatial inscription', *Translocations: The Irish Migration, Race and Social Transformation Review*, 1, 1 (2006), pp.1–13.

64. Gilligan, C., 'Racial prejudice in Northern Ireland', University of Ulster, press release, 21 June 2006.

65. Gilligan, C., 'Northern Ireland: the capital of "race hate"?', *Spiked*, 18 June 2009. Archived at: http://www.spiked-online.com/index.php/site/article/7043

66. McDonald, H., 'Loyalists linked to 90 per cent of race crime', *Observer*, 22 October 2006.

67. Steenkamp, 'Loyalist paramilitary violence after the Belfast Agreement', p.167.

68. Gilligan, 'Racial prejudice in Northern Ireland'.

69. Connolly, P. and Keenan, M., *Racial Attitudes and Prejudice in Northern Ireland* (Belfast: Northern Ireland Statistics and Research Agency, 2000).

70. Connolly, P., 'An examination of the nature and causes of racism in Northern Ireland', keynote address at 'Belfast: An Inclusive Society? Exploring Issues of Racism and Diversity' conference on The Irish Association, March 2005.

71. Connolly, 'An examination of the nature and causes of racism in Northern Ireland'.

72. Jarman, N., 'Victims and perpetrators: racism and young people in Northern Ireland', *Child Care in Practice*, 9, 2 (2003), pp.129–39.

73. Even here, however, things may not be straightforward, as the original dispute appears to have started between local paramilitary leaders and the Chinese business community over extortion demands.

74. Chrisafis, A., 'Racist war of the loyalist street gangs', *Guardian*, 10 January 2004.

75. See Connolly, P. and Keenan, M., *Racial Attitudes and Prejudice in Northern Ireland* (Belfast: Northern Ireland Statistics and Research Agency, 2000); Connolly, P. and Keenan, M., *The Hidden Truth: Racist Harassment in Northern Ireland* (Belfast: Northern Ireland Statistics and Research Agency, 2001).

76. Mac an Ghaill, M., *Contemporary Racisms and Ethnicities* (Buckingham: Open University, 1999).

77. See McVeigh, R., '"There's no racism here because there's no black people here": racism and anti-racism in Northern Ireland', in P. Hainsworth (ed.), *Divided Society: Ethnic Minorities and Racism in Northern Ireland* (London: Pluto, 1998); McVeigh, R., 'Is sectarianism racism? the implications of sectarian divisions for multi-ethnicity in Ireland', in R. Lentin (ed.), *The Expanding Nation: Towards a Multi-Ethnic Ireland (conference proceedings)*, Dublin: Trinity College, 22–24 September 1998; McVeigh, R. and Tomlinson, M., 'From Good Friday to good relations: sectarianism, racism and the Northern Ireland state', *Race and Class*, 48, 4 (2007), pp.1–23.

78. McGrellis, S., 'Pushing the boundaries in Northern Ireland: young people, violence and sectarianism' (Families and Social Capital ESRC Research Group, London South Bank University, 2004), p.29.

79. Connolly, P., '*Race' and Racism in Northern Ireland: A Review of the Research Evidence* (Belfast: Office of the First Minister and Deputy First Minister, 2002), p.64.

80. McAuley, 'Cúchulainn with an RPG7: the ideology and politics of the Ulster Defence Association'.

81. Stapleton, K. and Wilson, J., 'A discursive approach to cultural identity: the case of Ulster Scots', *Belfast Working Papers in Language and Linguistics*, no. 16 (Belfast: University of Ulster, 2003), pp.57–71.

82. MacPóilín, A., 'The linguistic status of Ulster Scots', submission to Belfast City Council, 1998.

83. Stapleton, K. and Wilson, J., 'Ulster Scots identity and culture: the missing voices', *Identities: Global Studies in Culture and Power*, no. 11 (2004), pp.563–91.

84. Nic Craith, M., *Plural Identities Singular Narratives: The Case of Northern Ireland* (Oxford: Berghahn, 2002).

85. Radford, K., 'Creating an Ulster Scots revival', *Peace Review*, 13, 1 (2001), pp.51–7.
86. Benhabib, S., *The Claims of Culture: Equality and Diversity in the Global Era* (Princeton, NJ: Princeton University Press, 2002).
87. Graham, B., 'The past in the present: the shaping of identity in loyalist Ulster', *Terrorism and Political Violence*, 16, 3 (2004), pp.483–500.
88. *Shankill Mirror*, 29 August 2005, p.2.
89. BBC News Online, 'Thousands join in unionist rally'. Archived at: http://news.bbc.co.uk/1/hi/northern_ireland/4388286.stm
90. Ulster TV Newsroom Online, 'Campaign opposed to united Ireland'. Archived at: http://u.tv/newsroom/indepth.asp?pt=n&id=64353
91. Breen, S., 'Loyalist women to bring city to a standstill', *Sunday Life*, 30 October 2005.
92. *News Letter*, editorial, 29 August 2005.
93. Connolly, K., 'Riots reveal a deeper resentment', http://news.bbc.co.uk/1/hi/northern_ireland/4246630.stm
94. *The Times*, 13 September 2005.
95. *News Letter*, 13 September 2005.
96. Interview with author, 14 September 2005.
97. Cited in O'Neill, B., 'The clashes in Northern Ireland expose the dangerous side to the politics of identity', *Spiked Online*, 14 September 2005. Archived at: http://www.spiked-online.com/Articles/0000000CAD5A.htm
98. Interview with author, 14 September 2005.
99. Murtagh, B., 'Social activity and interaction in Northern Ireland', *Northern Ireland Life and Times Survey Research Update*, no. 10 (February 2002).
100. Stone was convicted in December 2008 of the attempted murder of Sinn Féin leaders and jailed for sixteen years. His somewhat bizarre defence was that he had been taking part in a performance art event.
101. McKittrick, D., 'Loyalist Stone attempts Stormont attack', *Independent*, 25 November 2006.
102. BBC News Online, 'Michael Stone: Notorious Loyalist Killer'. Archived at: http://news.bbc.co.uk/1/hi/northern_ireland/848647.stm; Stone, M., *None Shall Divide Us* (London: John Blake, 2004).
103. For various background material, see Gormally, B., *Conversion from War to Peace: Reintegration of Ex-Prisoners in Northern Ireland* (Bonn: Bonn International Centre for Conversion, 2001); Irwin, T., 'Prison education in Northern Ireland: learning from our paramilitary past', *The Howard Journal*, 42, 5 (2003), pp.471–87; McEvoy, K., O'Mahony, D., Horner, C. and Lyner, O., 'The home front: the families of politically motivated prisoners in Northern Ireland', *British Journal of Criminology*, 39, 2 (1999), pp.175–97; Von Tangen Page, M., 'The early release of politically motivated violent offenders in the context of the republican and loyalist ceasefires in Northern Ireland', *Peace Studies Briefing*, no. 45 (University of Bradford: Department of Peace Studies, 1995), pp.1–24.
104. Shirlow, P., Tonge, J., McAuley, J.W. and McGlynn, C., *Abandoning Historical Conflict? Former Paramilitary Prisoners and Political Reconciliation in Northern Ireland* (Manchester: Manchester University Press, 2010).
105. Inter Action Belfast, *The Role of Ex-Combatants on Interfaces* (Belfast: Inter Action Belfast, 2006).
106. Neumann, P.R., 'The imperfect peace: explaining paramilitary violence in Northern Ireland', *Low Intensity Conflict and Law Enforcement*, 11, 1 (2002), pp.116–38.
107. McCorry, J. and Morrisey, M., 'Community, crime and punishment in west Belfast', *The Howard Journal*, 28, 4 (1989), pp.282–90.
108. Thompson, W. and Mullholland, B., 'Paramilitary punishment and young people in west Belfast: psychological effects and the implications for education', in L. Kennedy (ed.), *Crime and Punishment in West Belfast* (Belfast: The West Belfast Summer School, 1994), p.61.
109. *Combat*, no. 28, 2005.
110. Steenkamp, C.J., 'Loyalist paramilitary violence after the Belfast Agreement', *Ethnopolitics*, 7, 1 (2008), pp.159–76.
111. Nolan, P.C. and McCoy, G., 'The changing pattern of paramilitary punishments in Northern Ireland', *Injury*, 27, 6 (1996), pp.405–6.
112. Police Service of Northern Ireland, *Report of the Chief Constable 2002–2003* (Belfast: PSNI, 2003).
113. McCrory, M.L., 'Decrease in number of paramilitary-style attacks', *Irish News*, 5 August 2006.

114. *News Letter*, 18 July 2007.
115. Shaikh, T., 'Alleged criminal tarred and feathered in vigilante attack', *Guardian*, 29 August 2007.
116. For an introduction to the issue, see Mooney, G. and Neal, S., 'Community: themes and debates', in G. Mooney and S. Neal (eds), *Community: Welfare, Crime and Society* (Maidenhead: Open University Press, 2009), pp.1–33.
117. McWilliams, M., 'Masculinity and violence: gender perspectives on crime in Northern Ireland', in Kennedy (ed.), *Crime and Punishment in West Belfast*; Silke, A., 'Drink, drugs, and rock 'n' roll: financing loyalist terrorism in Northern Ireland – Part Two', *Studies in Conflict and Terrorism*, 23, 2 (2000), pp.107–27.
118. Community Development in Protestant Areas, p.30.
119. Hall, M., *An Uncertain Future: An Exploration by Protestant Community Activists* (Belfast: Island Pamphlets).
120. Knox, C. and Monaghan, R., *Informal Justice in Divided Societies* (Basingstoke: Palgrave Macmillan, 2002).
121. Higgins, K., Percy, A. and McCrystal, P., 'Secular trends in substance use: the conflict and young people in Northern Ireland', *Journal of Social Issues*, 60, 3 (2004), pp.485–506.
122. Schrag, L., 'Best practice in restorative justice', paper presented at the Centre for Restorative Justice, Vancouver (Vancouver: Simon Fraser University, June 2003).
123. Crawford, A. and Newburn, T., *Youth Offending and Restorative Justice: Implementing Reform in Youth Justice* (Cullompton: Willan Press, 2003).
124. See Goodey, J., *Victims and Victimology: Research, Policy and Practice* (Harlow: Longman Pearson, 2005), especially 'Restorative justice: victim-centred paradigm shift', pp.183–216; Marshall, T., 'Seeking the whole justice', in S, Hayman (ed.), *Repairing the Damage: Restorative Justice in Action* (London: ISTD, 1997), pp.10–17.
125. Marshall, T.F., 'Restorative justice: an overview', Home Office Research Development and Statistics Directorate (London: Crown Publications, 1999), p.5.
126. McEvoy, K. and Mika, H., 'Restorative justice in conflict: paramilitarism, community, and the construction of legitimacy in Northern Ireland', *Contemporary Justice Review*, 4, 3–4 (2001), pp.291–319.
127. Marshall, 'Restorative justice: an overview', pp.11–16.
128. McCorry and Morrisey, 'Community, crime and punishment in west Belfast'.
129. Monaghan, R., 'Community-based justice in Northern Ireland and South Africa', *International Criminal Justice Review*, 18, 83 (2008), p.86.
130. McEvoy, K. and Mika, H., 'Punishment, politics and praxis: restorative justice and non-violent alternatives to paramilitary punishment in Northern Ireland', *Police and Society*, 11, 3 (2001), p.282.
131. Smyth, M. and Campbell, P., 'Young people and armed violence in Northern Ireland' (Belfast: Institute for Conflict Research, 2009). Archived at: www.coav.org.br
132. McAllister, B., 'Peace-making efforts in Northern Ireland', paper presented at the fourth conference of the European Forum for Restorative Justice, Barcelona, Spain, 15–17 June 2006, p.9.
133. Ibid.
134. *Northern Ireland Life and Times Survey 2000*. Archived at: http://www.ark.ac.uk/nilt
135. Schrag, 'Best practice in restorative justice'.
136. Criminal Justice Review Group, *Review of the Criminal Justice System in Northern Ireland* (Belfast: HMSO, 2000).
137. These are: East Belfast Alternatives; Greater Shankill Alternatives; North Belfast Alternatives; and North Down Impact.
138. Gribbin, V., Kelly, R. and Mitchell, C., 'Loyalist conflict transformation initiatives', Research paper presented to the Office of the First Minister and Deputy First Minister (2005).
139. Shirlow, P. and McEvoy, K., *Beyond the Wire: Former Prisoners and Conflict Transformation in Northern Ireland* (London: Pluto, 2008).
140. Shirlow, P., Graham, B., McEvoy, K., Ó hAdhmaill, F. and Purvis, D., *Politically Motivated Former Prisoner Groups: Community Activism and Conflict Transformation* (Belfast: Report to the Northern Ireland Community Relations Council, 2005), p.18.
141. Smithey, L.A., 'Grassroots unionism and conflict transformation in Northern Ireland', *Shared Space*, no. 6 (2008), p.51.
142. Such views were first aired in Progressive Unionist Party, *War or Peace: Conflict or*

Conference, policy document of the Progressive Unionist Party (Belfast: no publisher, no date [circa 1985]); Progressive Unionist Party, *Agreeing to Differ for Progress* (Belfast: PUP, 1985); Progressive Unionist Party, *Sharing Responsibilities* (Belfast: PUP, 1985).
143. Wood, *Crimes of Loyalty*, pp.1–27; 57–78.
144. See Harris, L., 'Duck or rabbit? the value systems of loyalist paramilitaries', in M. Busteed, F. Neal and J. Tonge (eds), *Irish Protestant Identities* (Manchester: Manchester University Press, 2008); Harris, L., 'Exit, voice, and loyalty: signalling of loyalist paramilitaries in Northern Ireland', in A. Edwards and S. Bloomer (eds), *Transforming the Peace Process in Northern Ireland*, pp.79–98.
145. Hall, M., *Loyalism in Transition 1: A New Reality?* (Belfast: Island Pamphlets, 2006).
146. *Shankill Mirror*, October 2006, p.8.
147. Hall, *Loyalism in Transition 1*, p.10.
148. Garland, R., 'UPRG may hold loyalists' key to moving forward', *Irish News*, 31 March 2003.
149. *Irish News*, 8 March 2006.
150. Breen, S., 'UPRG influence grows as politics replaces violence', *Sunday Life*, 2 July 2006.
151. Hall, *Loyalism in Transition 1*, p.12.
152. Hall, M., *Loyalism in Transition 2: Learning From Others in Conflict* (Belfast: Island Pamphlets, 2007).
153. *News Letter*, 11 November 2008.
154. See Langhammer, 'Cutting with the grain'; Nelson, S., 'Developments in Protestant working-class politics', *Social Studies* (Winter 1976/77), pp.205–8; Weiner, R., *The Rape and Plunder of the Shankill* (Belfast: published by the author, 1975).
155. Field, J., 'Social capital and lifelong learning', *The Encyclopedia of Informal Education*. Archived at: www.infed.org/lifelonglearning/social_capital_and_lifelong_learning.htm
156. Putnam, R.D., *Making Democracy Work: Civic Traditions in Modern Italy* (Princeton, NJ: Princeton University Press, 1993); Putnam, R.D., 'Bowling alone: America's declining social capital', *Journal of Democracy*, 6, 1 (1995), pp.65–78.
157. Coleman, J.C., 'Social capital in the creation of human capital', *American Journal of Sociology*, no. 94 (1998), S95–S120; Coleman, J.S., *Foundations of Social Theory* (Cambridge, MA: Harvard University Press, 1990).
158. See Anheier, H. and Kendall, J., 'Interpersonal trust and voluntary associations: examining three approaches', *British Journal of Sociology*, no. 53 (2002), pp.343–62; Burt, R., 'The network structure of social capital', *Research in Organisational Behaviour*, no. 22 (2002), pp.345–423; Harper, R., *Social Capital: A Review of the Literature* (London: Social Analysis and Reporting Division, Office for National Statistics, 2001); White, G., 'Civil society, democratization and development: clearing the analytical ground', *Democratization*, no. 1 (1994), pp.375–90.
159. Pretty, J.N and Ward, H., 'What is social capital?', *World Development*, 29, 2 (2001), pp.209–29.
160. Beem, C., *The Necessity of Politics: Reclaiming American Public Life* (Chicago: University of Chicago Press, 1999), pp.22–3.
161. Putnam, R.D. and Goss, K.A., 'Introduction', in R.D. Putnam (ed.), *Democracies in Flux: The Evolution of Social Capital in Contemporary Society* (Oxford: Oxford University Press, 2002).
162. Ibid., p.10.
163. Ibid., p.11.
164. Bacon, D., 'Revitalising civil society in Northern Ireland: social capital formation in three faith-based organisations (FBOs)', paper presented at the 7th Researching the Voluntary Sector Conference (London: NCVO Headquarters, 2001).
165. Leonard, M., 'Bonding and bridging social capital: reflections from Belfast', *Sociology*, 38, 5 (2004), pp.927–44.
166. See, Cairns, E., Lewis, A. and Mumcu, O., 'Memories of recent ethnic conflict and their relationship to social identity', *Peace and Conflict: Journal of Peace Psychology*, 4, 1 (1998), pp.13–22; Niens, U., Cairns, E. and Hewstone, M., 'Contact and conflict in Northern Ireland', in O. Hargie and D. Dickson (eds), *Researching the Troubles: Social Science Perspectives on the Northern Ireland Conflict* (Edinburgh: Mainstream Publishing, 2003), pp.85–106.
167. See, Ditch, J., 'Social policy in "Crisis"? the case of Northern Ireland', in M. Loney, D. Boswell and J. Clarke (eds), *Social Policy and Social Welfare* (Milton Keynes: Open University Press, 1983), pp.58–82; Morrissey, M. and Ditch, J., 'Social policy implications of emergency legislation in Northern Ireland', *Critical Social Policy*, 1, 3 (1981), pp.19–39.

168. McKittrick, D., *Endgame: The Search for Peace in Northern Ireland* (Belfast: Blackstaff Press, 1994), p.6.
169. Inter Action Belfast, *The role of Ex-Combatants on Interfaces*.
170. Shannon, A., *Report of the Taskforce on Protestant Working-Class Communities*, p.8.
171. Community Relations Information Centre, *Community Development in Protestant Areas* (Belfast: Community Development in Protestant Areas Steering Group, 1992).
172. Robson, T., 'The community sector and conflict resolution in Northern Ireland', paper presented at The Role of Civil Society in Conflict Resolution Conference (Maynooth: National University of Ireland, 2001).
173. McAuley and McCormack, 'The Protestant working class and the state in Northern Ireland since 1930', pp.34–8.
174. Bruce, 'Terrorists and politics' (p.31) suggests for example that the framework for the emergence of the UDA in Derry rested on a loose network of shop stewards and union activists.
175. In the early 1970s much of the social structure of loyalist communities bore a strong resemblance to classical occupational communities. See, for example, Brown, R. and Brannen, P., 'Social relations and social perspectives amongst shipbuilding workers: a preliminary statement', *Sociology*, 4, 1 (1970), pp.71–84; Revill, G., '"Railway derby": occupational community, paternalism and corporate culture 1850–1890', *Urban History*, 28, 3 (2001), pp.378–404; Roberts, I., *Craft, Class and Control: The Sociology of a Shipbuilding Community* (Edinburgh: Edinburgh University Press, 1993).
176. Langhammer, M., 'Analysis of the Malaise in Protestant Heartlands'. Archived at: http://www.labour.ie/northernireland/NBN.html
177. Fitzduff, M. and Gormley, C., 'Northern Ireland: changing perceptions of the "other"', *Development*, 43, 3 (2000), p.65.
178. Langhammer, 'Cutting with the grain'.
179. See McCartney, C., 'The role of civil society', in C. McCartney (ed.), *Striking a Balance: The Northern Ireland Peace Process, Accord – An international Review of Peace Initiatives* (London: Conciliation Resources, 1999); Community Convention and Development Company, *Protestant, Unionist, Loyalist Communities; Leading a Positive Transformation (conference Report)* (Belfast: CCDC, 2006).
180. Atkinson, D., *Civil renewal: Mending the Hole in the Social Ozone* (Studley: Brewin Books, 2004), p.38.
181. Shirlow, Tonge, McAuley and McGlynn, *Abandoning Historical Conflict? Former Paramilitary Prisoners and Political Reconciliation in Northern Ireland*.
182. Petrigh, C., Review of *The importance of local involvement in conflict transformation* in *Journal of Peace Conflict and Development*, no. 10 (March 2007); Reich, H., '"Local ownership" in conflict transformation projects: partnership, participation or patronage', *Berghof Occasional Paper*, no. 27 (Berlin: Berghof Research Centre for Conflict Management, 2006).
183. Winston, T., 'Alternatives to punishment beatings and shootings in a loyalist community in Belfast', *Critical Criminology*, 8, 1 (1997), pp.122–8.
184. McEvoy, K. and Shirlow, P., 'Re-imagining DDR: Ex-combatants, leadership and moral agency in conflict transformation', *Theoretical Criminology*, 13, 1 (2009), pp.31–59.
185. The precise definition of 'civil society' is contested. For a variety of perspectives see Edwards, M., *Civil Society* (Cambridge: Polity Press, 2004); Ehrenberg, J., *Civil Society: The Critical History of an Idea* (New York: New York University Press, 1999); Kaviraj, S. and Khilnani, S. (eds), *Civil Society: History and Possibilities* (Cambridge: Cambridge University Press, 2001); Lederach, J.P., 'Civil society and reconciliation', in C.A. Cocker, H.F. Olser and P. Aall (eds), *Turbulent Peace: The Challenges of Managing International Conflict* (Washington, DC: US Institute of Peace, 2001); Pollock, G. 'Civil society theory and euro-nationalism', *Studies in Social and Political Thought*, no. 4, March (2001), pp.31–56.
186. Gribbin, Kelly and Mitchell, 'Loyalist conflict transformation initiatives'; Mitchell, C., 'The limits of legitimacy: former loyalist combatants and peace-building in Northern Ireland', *Irish Political Studies*, 23, 1 (2008), pp.1–19; Smithey, 'Grassroots unionism and conflict transformation in Northern Ireland'.
187. McKittrick, D., 'A makeover for the murals that depicted hate, violence and bigotry', *Independent*, 1 September 2008.
188. Acheson, N., Cairns, E., Stringer, M. and Williamson, A., *Voluntary Action and Community Relations in Northern Ireland* (Coleraine: University of Ulster, Centre for Voluntary Action Studies, 2007), p.68.

189. See McEvoy, L., McEvoy, K. and McConnachi, K., 'Reconciliation as a dirty word: conflict, community relations and education in Northern Ireland', *Journal of International Affairs* (Fall–Winter 2006); Shirlow and McEvoy, *Beyond the Wire*.

190. Colin Robinson, cited in Bloomer and Edwards, *A Watching Brief?*, p.8.

191. Darby, J., *The Effects of Violence on Peace Processes* (Washington, DC: US Institute of Peace Press, 2001).

192. Inter Action Belfast, *The role of Ex-Combatants on Interfaces*, p.3.

193. Gordon, D., 'Top loyalist praises McGuinness but warns of "Real UDA clowns"', *Belfast Telegraph*, 12 March 2009; Rowan, B., 'PUP leader urges loyalists not to react to killings', *Belfast Telegraph*, 10 March 2009.

194. Rowan, B., 'Loyalist groups UDA and UVF disarming after decades of terror and 1,000 deaths', *Belfast Telegraph*, 18 June 2009.

195. Cairns, E., Van Til, T. and Williamson, A., *Social Capital, Collectivism-Individualism and Community Background in Northern Ireland* (Report to the Office of the First Minister and Deputy First Minister, Coleraine: University of Ulster, 2003).

196. Deane, E., 'Community work in the 70s', in H. Frazer (ed.), *Community Work in a Divided Society* (Belfast: Farset Co-operative Press, 1981), p.15.

197. Garland, R., 'Loyalists must take responsibility for themselves', *Irish News*, 10 October 2006; McCarron, J.J., *Civil Society in Northern Ireland: A New Beginning?* (Belfast: Northern Ireland Council for Voluntary Action), p.2.

198. Acheson, Cairns, Stringer and Williamson, *Voluntary Action and Community Relations in Northern Ireland*, pp.46–8.

199. Van Til, J., *Breaching Derry's Walls: The Quest for a Lasting Peace in Northern Ireland* (Plymouth: University Press of America), p.19.

200. Save the Children Fund, *Poverty Pack* (London: SCF, 1995).

201. Borer, T.A., Darby, J. and McEvoy-Levy, S., *Peacebuilding After Peace Accords* (Notre Dame: University of Notre Dame Press, 2006), pp.41–2.

202. There is some evidence to suggest that everyday life is more localised for boys than for girls. See material reviewed in Healy, 'Locality matters: ethnic segregation and community conflict'.

203. Byrne, J., Hansson, U. and Bell, J., *Shared Living: Mixed Residential Communities in Northern Ireland* (Belfast: Institute for Conflict Research, 2006), p.12.

204. Muldoon, O.T., 'Children of the troubles: the impact of political violence in Northern Ireland', *Journal of Social Issues*, 60, 3 (2004), p.457.

205. See Belfast Interface Project, *Young People on the Interface* (Belfast: Regency Press, 1998); Hall, M., *Young People on the Interface* (Belfast: Belfast Interface Project, 1998); Newhill Youth Development Team, *Young People Speak Out*, Island Pamphlets, no. 20 (Newtownabbey: Island Publications, 1998).

206. See, for example, Kelly, B., 'Young people's views on communities and sectarianism in Northern Ireland', *Child Care in Practice*, 8, 1 (2002), pp.65–71; Leonard, M., 'Teens and territory in contested spaces: negotiating sectarian interfaces in Northern Ireland', *Children's Geographies*, 4, 2 (2006), pp.225–38.

207. See Gillespie, N., Lovett T. and Garner, W., *Youth Work and Working Class Youth Culture: Rules and Resistance in West Belfast* (Buckingham: Open University Press, 1992), p.163; Bell, D., 'Acts of union: youth culture and ethnic identity amongst Protestants in Northern Ireland', *British Journal of Sociology*, 38, 2 (1987), pp.158–83; Bell, D., *Acts of Union: Youth Culture and Sectarianism in Northern Ireland* (Basingstoke: Macmillan, 1990).

208. Gillespie, N., Lovett, T. and Garner, W., *Youth Work and Working-Class Youth Culture: Rules and Resistance in West Belfast* (Buckingham: Open University Press, 1992), p.9.

209. This has led some to call for the setting up of a 'truth commission' in Northern Ireland similar to that already found in South Africa and elsewhere. See, for example, Hamber, B. and Wilson, R.A., 'Symbolic closure through memory, reparation and revenge in post-conflict societies', *Journal of Human Rights*, 1, 1 (2002), pp.35–53; Healing Through Remembering, *Making Peace with the Past: Options for Truth Recovery Regarding the Conflict in and About Northern Ireland* (Belfast: Healing Through Remembering Group, 2006); Lundy, P. and McGovern, M., 'The politics of memory in post-conflict Northern Ireland', *Peace Review*, 13, 1 (2001), pp.27–33.

210. Herbert, D., 'Shifting securities in Northern Ireland: "terror" and "the troubles" in global media and local memory', *European Journal of Cultural Studies*, 10, 3 (2007), pp.343–59.

211. Fentress, J. and Wickham, C., *Social Memory* (Oxford: Blackwell, 1992).

212. See Leonard, J., 'How conflicts are commemorated in Northern Ireland', Central Community Relations Unit. Archived at: http://www.ccruni.gov.uk/research/qub/leonard97.htm

213. Wilson, J. and Stapleton, K., 'Voices of commemoration: the discourse of celebration and confrontation in Northern Ireland', *Text*, 25, 5 (2005), pp.633–64.

214. See, for example, Brockmeier, J., 'Remembering and forgetting: narrative as cultural memory', *Culture and Psychology*, 8, 1 (2002), pp.15–43; Wertsch, J., *Voices of Collective Remembering* (Cambridge: Cambridge University Press, 2002).

215. Graham, B. and Whelan, Y., 'The legacies of the dead: commemorating the Troubles in Northern Ireland', *Society and Space*, no. 25 (2007), pp.476–95.

216. Gamson, W.A. and Modigliani, A., 'The changing culture of affirmative action', *Research in Political Sociology*, no. 3 (1987), pp.137–77.

217. Coulter, C. and Murray, M., 'Introduction', in C. Coulter and M. Murray (eds), *Northern Ireland After the Troubles: A Society in Transition* (Manchester: Manchester University Press, 2008), p.21.

218. See, Fay, M.T., Morrissey, M. and Smyth, M., *Mapping Troubles-Related Deaths in Northern Ireland 1969–1998* (Londonderry: INCORE, University of Ulster, 1998); Fay, M.T., Morrissey, M. and Smyth, M., *Northern Ireland's Troubles: The Human Costs* (London: Pluto Press, 1999); Smyth, M., *Half the Battle: Understanding the Impact of 'the Troubles' on Children and Young People* (Londonderry: INCORE, University of Ulster, 1998); Smyth, M. and Fay, M.T. (eds), *Personal Accounts from Northern Ireland's Troubles: Public Conflict, Private Loss* (London: Pluto Press, 2000).

219. Kosic, A., *Promoting reconciliation through youth: inter-ethnic community mobilization project report* (Kingston: European Research Centre, Kingston University, 2005), p.4.

220. Connolly, P. and Maginn, P., *Sectarianism, Children and Community Relations in Northern Ireland* (Coleraine: Centre for the Study of Conflict, University of Ulster, 1999).

221. Lanclos, D., *At Play in Belfast: Children's Folklore and Identities in Northern Ireland* (London: Rutgers University Press, 2003).

222. See Burton, F., *The Politics of Legitimacy: Struggles in a Belfast Community* (Routledge and Kegan Paul, 1978); Ewart, S. and Schubotz, D., *Voices Behind the Statistics: Young People's Views of Sectarianism in Northern Ireland* (London: National Children's Bureau, 2004).

223. See Whyte, J., 'Young people and political involvement in Northern Ireland', *Journal of Social Issues*, 60, 3 (2004), pp.603–28; McAuley, J.P. 'Peace and progress? political and social change among young loyalists in Northern Ireland', *Journal of Social Issues*, 60, 3 (2004), pp.541–62.

224. Smyth M. and Scott, M., *The Youthquest 2000 Survey: A Report on Young People's Views and Experiences in Northern Ireland* (Londonderry: INCORE, University of Ulster, 2000).

225. Fullerton, D., 'Changing times – or are they?', *ARK Social and Political Archive Research Update*, no. 30 (2004), pp.1–4.

226. Horgan, G. and Rodgers, P., 'Young people's participation in a new Northern Ireland society', *Youth and Society*, 32, 1 (2000), pp.107–37.

227. 'Survey shows shift in Northern Irish identity', *Irish Times*, 2 December 2008.

228. Niens, Cairns and Hewstone, 'Contact and conflict in Northern Ireland', pp.123–40.

229. See Breen, R. and Devine, P., 'Segmentation and social structure', in P. Mitchell and R. Wilford (eds), *Politics in Northern Ireland* (Boulder, CO: Westview Press, 1999), pp.53–65; Darby, J., *Scorpions in a Bottle: Conflicting Cultures in Northern Ireland* (London: Minority Rights Publications, 1997), pp.41–70.

230. LINC Resource Centre, 'Young people and politics in north Belfast' (Institute for Conflict Research, June 2003), pp.1–10.

231. Healy, J., 'Locality matters: ethnic segregation and community conflict – the experience of Protestant girls in Belfast', *Children and Society*, no. 20 (2006), pp.105–15.

232. See McCully, A., 'Teaching controversial issues as a contribution to the peace process in Northern Ireland' (paper presented at BERA conference, Queen's University Belfast, 1998); Muldoon. O.T., Trew, K. and Kilpatrick, R., 'The legacy of the Troubles on the young people's psychological and social development and their school life', *Youth and Society*, 32, 1 (2000), pp.6–28.

233. Wilson, J. and Stapleton, K., 'Voices of commemoration: the discourse of celebration and confrontation in Northern Ireland', *Text*, 25, 5 (2005), pp.633–64.

234. Graham, B. and McDowell, S., 'Meaning in the Maze: the heritage of Long Kesh', *Cultural Geographies*, 14, 3 (2007), p.364.

235. Smyth and Scott, *The Youthquest 2000 Survey: A Report on Young People's Views and Experiences in Northern Ireland.*
236. Connolly, P., Smith A. and Kelly, B., *Too Young to Notice? The Cultural and Political Awareness of 3–6 Year Olds in Northern Ireland* (Belfast: Community Relations Council in Partnership with Channel 4, 2002).
237. Muldoon, Trew and Kilpatrick, 'The legacy of the Troubles on the young people's psychological and social development and their school life'.
238. Hughes, J. and Donnelly, C., 'Ten years of social attitudes to community relations in Northern Ireland', in A.M. Gray, K. Lloyd, P. Devine, G. Robinson and D. Heenan, *Social Attitudes in Northern Ireland* (London: Pluto Press, 2002).

Chapter 7

Unionism, Fragmentation and Loyalism

Go anywhere within unionism, from a UUP branch meeting in North Down to a drinking den in Taughmonagh, and you will hear the same talk of government betrayal and concessions.

Alex Kane[1]

Unionists have always felt themselves to be outnumbered. Facing betrayal, friendless, with only their own solidarity on which to rely. The question is, which competing strand of contemporary unionism will prevail – a defensive, power-maintaining, and exclusive identity focused on the past, or a pragmatic, pluralist, and inclusive identity focused on the future?

Patrick Mitchel[2]

The period following the Agreement witnessed fragmentation, disengagement and political reorganisation across unionism. Much of this was precipitated by a lack of confidence in the political outcomes of the accord, which in turn rested on the strongly held perception across unionism that Irish republicanism had delivered far more for its constituency than had unionist representatives for theirs. By 2005 only one per cent of Protestants thought that unionists had benefited more than nationalists from the Agreement, while 68 per cent believed that the reverse was true.[3]

But why was this seen to be so, and how can we explain the level of disenchantment across the unionist community surrounding the political consequences of the accord? In seeking to answer these questions, it is important to understand just how deeply rooted opposition was (and remains) within some sections of unionism. Immediately before the signing of the Agreement most unionists were, at best, extremely hesitant about any engagement with republicanism,[4] with fewer than half wanting their leaders to take part in any face-to-face talks with Sinn Féin representatives.[5] Thus, despite the public expressions of euphoria that were so obvious in the immediate wake of the signing of the Agreement the unionist community was divided over the settlement and many from within unionism continued to express scepticism.

UNIONISM AND POST-PEACE POLITICS

The divisions within unionism were illustrated by a *Belfast Telegraph* survey less than a year after the signing of the Agreement that showed another decline in unionist support for the accord. Another poll in September 1999 indicated that unionist support had fallen to under 40 per cent. The continuing depth of unionist disillusionment was further demonstrated when a Queen's University/Rowntree Trust poll in February 2003 indicated that just over one-third of Protestants claimed they would support the Agreement in another referendum, the lowest level for over five years.

At the time the levels of resistance within unionism even led Hall to suggest that the peace process was dead in the water.[6] While this was no doubt an overstatement, the responses from the Protestant community did at best indicate a growing lack of engagement with, and support for, the Agreement. MacGinty further highlighted important differences in communal perceptions of the Agreement (see Table 5).[7] For the vast majority of Catholics (some 77 per cent) the Agreement was inherently sound and offered the basis for settlement (although there was some difference in opinion whether it needed full implementation or renegotiation).

Within the Protestant unionist community, however, the view was very different and the divisions surrounding the merits of the

Table 5: Catholic and Protestant Views on the Agreement

	Catholic (%)	Protestant (%)
The Agreement is basically right and just needs to be implemented in full	41	10
The Agreement is basically right but the specifics need to be renegotiated	36	33
The Agreement is basically wrong and should be renegotiated	4	24
The Agreement is basically wrong and should be abandoned	2	17
Don't Know	17	16

Source: MacGinty[8]

Agreement remained stark; and while around 43 per cent thought the Agreement to be basically right, almost the same number (41 per cent) believed it was wrong, and that it required either full renegotiation or to be abandoned entirely. Only 10 per cent of Protestants thought that the basic problem lay in the failure to fully implement the terms of the Agreement as it stood, suggesting that a very large majority opposed the Agreement under any terms.

Unionist fears and antagonisms apparent within the poll were harnessed and given fullest expression in the rebuttal of the Agreement by the DUP, which throughout the mid-1990s continued to talk of a 'shameful engagement' and a politics designed at 'deluding the unionist people rather than defeating the IRA'. They also continued to highlight a peace process that had heralded a growing prominence for Sinn Féin (and eventually their place in the executive of a devolved government).[9] As one grouping of Protestant Church officials put it, for many unionists there was a sense of 'everything solid melting into air'. They further argued that the Agreement raised concerns as it created a fluidity and malleability about the Northern Ireland state, meaning that:

> ... the whole framework of society is altering. Further, the State and its institutions are being remodelled. The release of paramilitary prisoners has offended a community's sense of right and wrong ... A Party with paramilitary links is allowed to enter government. Thus, it appears, the moral universe is turned upside down.[10]

Within this framework of understanding, unionist anxieties manifest at the level of the everyday, where people's sense of identity draws directly upon their strength of belonging to an identifiable social group, often marked out by ethnic, social, cultural and economic boundaries. All of these operate at the community level to emphasise difference, to drive apart senses of social cohesion, to reinforce in-group social solidarity and to emphasise difference from the Other. In Northern Ireland this is most commonly understood and experienced as sectarianism.[11]

UNIONISM, LOYALISM AND SECTARIANISM

Given its centrality to political, cultural, economic and even physical and material relationships, sectarianism remains core to understanding the social world of Northern Ireland. A useful starting point in understanding what remains an under-theorised notion is provided through the following definition:

> It is about people's attitudes to one another, about what they do

and say and the things they leave undone or unsaid. Moreover, 'sectarianism' is usually a negative judgement that people make about someone else's behaviour and rarely a label that they apply to themselves, their own sectarianism always being the hardest to see.[12]

The construction of sectarianism in Northern Ireland mirrors social relationships found in ethnically divided societies elsewhere, including the negative construction of those seen as the oppositional group; the projection of the community with which people identify as superior to others; the demonising of enemies; and the attempt by political majority groups to curb the rights of minorities. As one grouping explains, sectarianism further involves:

> ... themes of power and powerlessness, of possession and dispossession, of advantage and disadvantage, of majority and minority, of violence and counter-violence, of loyalty and disloyalty, of injustice and justification, of grievance and insecurity, of siege and deliverance, of colonised and coloniser – all inter-playing with the role of religion.[13]

Such sectarian social relationships, in existence since the formation of the state,[14] led to the formation of identifiable cultural contexts of conflict,[15] which deepened and intensified throughout the Troubles beginning in 1968. Sectarian ideology was powerfully reproduced through day-to-day experiences and activities, through processes that continue to affect all aspects of Northern Irish society.[16]

For many people everyday social relationships remain as fractured as they were before the ceasefires,[17] while sectarianism continues to function as what Carlo Gébler suggests is a glass curtain separating the two communities.[18] Among others, Frank Burton,[19] Karen Lysaght and Anne Basten[20] have demonstrated how everyday interactions with sectarianism often involve people adopting various coping strategies and behaviour based on intricate knowledge of highly localised sectarian geographies. Madeleine Leonard has provided detailed information concerning how teenagers are intimately aware of, and negotiate boundaries in and around, interface areas in Belfast[21] and how both Catholics and Protestants attempt to 'appropriate space in sectarian ways'.[22]

The sectarian worldview permeates the entirety of Northern Irish society to the point where it 'can be and often is the reality of life'.[23] For David McKittrick the resulting separation means that some people experience lives almost entirely lived in parallel,[24] a view supported by John Farrell who describes the current situation as 'officially blessed apartheid'.[25] Certainly for some at least the sectarian divide remains deep and sectarian violence (albeit at a much lower and less intense level) remains an everyday experience,[26] evidenced by the 1,702 incidents and 1,470 sectarian motivation crimes recorded by the PSNI in 2006.[27]

The physical manifestation of everyday sectarian divisions[28] is illustrated in the continued physical separation of Protestant and Catholic communities by the many peace walls and gates located throughout Northern Ireland.[29] As Jarman points out, while such 'security architecture' may continue to give a 'sense of reassurance', it remains a clear indication of the distance still to be travelled before Northern Ireland may be considered a 'normal' society.[30]

Further, Jennifer Hamilton, John Bell and Ulf Hansson among others have provided compelling evidence about the effects of sectarianism on everyday life, ranging from the choices of places in which to socialise to which ATM to use to withdraw money or where to shop or take place in leisure activities.[31] Moreover, there is no strong indication of generational change, with evidence of continuing segregation even among those of compulsory school age.[32] Indeed, Bernadette Hayes and Ian McAllister[33] argue that levels of prejudice in today's generation may be up to three-quarters higher than that found among those who grew up in the 1950s, probably because older members had established cross-community contacts before the conflict erupted in the late 1960s.[34]

Whatever the reason there is little to suggest that being young in Northern Ireland necessarily goes hand in hand with holding more liberal perspectives on politics and society. Among twelve to seventeen year olds, for example, support for mixed religion schools and workplace has actually fallen in recent years.[35] Further, the NILT survey of 2004 (see Table 6) found that almost one third of eighteen to twenty-four year olds wished to grow up in neighbourhoods dominated by co-religionists rather than in any integrated or mixed space.

The level of entrenchment of the social divisions continues to have salience in the composition of physical segregation and dividing living patterns.[36] While segregation does not cause inter-group conflict, it plays a key role in maintaining conflict between the two communities.[37] Indeed, Brian Graham and Catherine Nash[38] demonstrate effectively how sectarian social differences remain deeply located in senses of space and place, while the symbolic differentiation of territory remains at the core of expressions of social difference.[39]

While sectarianism is far from confined to the working class, it is here that its effects remain most apparent and the connections between sectarianism and social deprivation most profoundly felt.[41] The sense of difference remains a core social construct, crucial to the maintenance of

Table 6: Preferred Neighbourhoods in Which to Live

Option	Age Group (%)				
	18–24	25–34	35–44	45–54	55 +
Own religion only	31	15	17	15	17
Mixed-religion neighbourhood	68	83	82	82	81
Other (specify)	1	1	1	2	1
Don't know	0	1	0	1	1

Source: Adapted from NILT Survey[40]

political and social identities across time, with everyday social interaction overwhelmingly concentrated and socially bonded within each community[42] reinforced by inward-looking social capital. The lived reality of this within loyalist communities has in part been revealed through a small but growing collection of biographies and oral histories of life in working-class Protestant areas.[43]

Such works begin to reveal how sectarianism is reproduced at both overt and banal levels within each community.[44] Sectarianism occurs in a society set against a background of difference and division, and where Protestants and Catholics have 'their own self-image and their own stereotypes' although neither 'corresponded very clearly to reality'.[45] What does this mean for the politics of loyalism? Graham suggests that working-class Protestant identity can best be understood as resting along two main, if somewhat schizophrenic, axes. He explains:

> An element of class politics does exist, reflected in radical unionist consciousness, which traditionally depended upon, as it continues to do, the alienation of the Protestant working class from its leaders. In general, however, that class consciousness has been at best diluted, at worst subsumed, by a sectarianism derived from the sacred sense of Protestantism.[46]

Within the value system of Protestant workers sectarianism and socialism are rarely constructed as polar opposites.[47] Indeed, as I have argued elsewhere, working-class loyalism is capable of, and often expresses a duality of, consciousness whereby both a basic understanding of socialism (or at least social democracy) and sectarianism run in parallel, at onetime intertwined, at another seen as in competition.[48]This involves the negotiation of a politics and sense of identity that for some includes expressions of sectarian consciousness, alongside those of leftist politics.

Hence, we need to use the term sectarianism with some precision. Unionist opposition to an all-Ireland state is not sectarian (although sectarian values may form part of the reason for opposition); not all Orange parades are sectarian; expressions of a 'sacred sense of Protestantism' are not sectarian; and not even all the actions of loyalist paramilitaries are necessarily sectarian. What is sectarian is the system of attitudes and beliefs, including the demonising of the others, that are associated by some with such events and which are used in constructing the Other.

UNIONISM'S DEFENCE: MYTHS AND MEMORIES

However, within the construction of the Other, sectarianism is only ever one variable in the structures and processes that go to make up unionist and loyalist identities. To fully understand this we must recognise how inter-related aspects of unionist identity (of which sectarianism may be a part) become bound together and woven into what Porter terms a 'grand cultural unionist narrative'.[49] In building a narrative meaningful to Protestants in Northern Ireland individuals draw on collective memories to construct political identities and to frame broader understandings of how best communities can relate to wider political issues and concerns. As John Brewer so rightly puts it:

> ... the past is continuously reconstituted on the basis of the present, so that present concerns affect how the past is recollected and understood. Tradition is the organizing medium of collective memory, interpreting the past and organizing it according to the concerns of the present.[50]

These political memories are usually expressed through folk know-ledge, and as common sense understandings of the world. Key to this are the ways in which constructed memories legitimise power relations, including sectarianism, and the ways in which these are seen to characterise and give continuity to Northern Irish society and the social and political forces within it. Thus, for example, the devastation and loss of life suffered in Belfast during the German Blitz of 1941 or the sacrifices at the Battle of the Somme[51] have been firmly established as key reference points in formulating contemporary unionist and loyalist identities.[52]

Hence, memories within loyalism help individuals and groups construct understandings of everyday life that are meaningful to them. This is done in part by recognising continuities (real or imagined) between the past and contemporary political happenings. There are important social processes at work here. As Peter Novick explains, people:

> ... choose to center certain memories because they seem to us to express what are central to our collective identity. Those memories, once brought to the fore, reinforce that form of identity.[53]

Unionist and loyalist group identities are framed and maintained through the understood legitimacy of these communal political-cultural memories. So why are the DUP increasingly seen by many unionists as the guardians of such political-cultural memories and as offering the clearest expression of contemporary unionist identity? The short answer is that the DUP have successfully framed what it is to be a unionist in a way that draws directly upon those common sense understandings and everyday discourses found across unionism.

In particular, the DUP continues to highlight the existence of an enemy that is always deceitful and double-dealing, albeit one that has moved its point of attack from the military to the cultural. In so doing the DUP links contemporary political concerns directly to a past that draws on everyday cultural memories and commemorations of defeat, victory and self-identity. Further, its members project the party as upholding traditional unionist values, and as offering the only secure bulkhead against the further dilution of the Union.

These notions have become central to the tale being told by the DUP. This framing was readily identifiable in the DUP's 2003 Assembly Manifesto, which projected an apocalyptic prophecy for Northern Ireland's future, including 'terrorists running the police', with the 'Irish language and Gaelic culture given prominence' and overall the creation of a society where 'British culture and identity [are] no longer in existence in many parts of the Province'.[54]

In response, the DUP placed itself, and importantly was seen to do so by others, as the only legitimate guardians against such incursions against the Union. Thus, there is continual emphasis by the DUP on the 'failures' of other unionists, especially the UUP, both historically and in the contemporary period. A key self-defined task for the DUP has been to achieve success in 'undoing the damage done by the UUP'[55] and to continue to put political pressure on republicans. This discourse is found throughout and across many of the political expressions of the DUP, as this statement from Peter Robinson makes clear:

> During the 'Trimble years' unionists watched, outraged and frustrated, as the government delivered a concession a day to the IRA. Unionists were left disadvantaged and while we have had some measure of correction under DUP leadership there is much more to be achieved before we reach fairness and equality.[56]

The DUP evidences a political process that has appeased republicanism.[57] As a result increasing numbers of unionists have bought into the claim that unless they fall directly in line with the DUP the UK government will continue to delude unionists, while blinding them to the eradication of 'all traces of ... British sovereignty'.[58] Moreover, many seem increasingly convinced by a discourse suggesting that it is only the DUP that can effectively guarantee the best deal for unionists and the existing constitutional position.

The strength of the DUP vote from 2003 onwards demonstrates that such discourses were still more than capable of mobilising unionist votes (although this in turn was challenged; see below and Chapter 8). The DUP legitimises its brand of politics around the projection of a revitalised and confident unionism able to resist whatever daily challenges unionism faces. The depth of this understanding within unionism and the claim of the DUP to represent the worldview of a large number of Ulster Protestants were again put to the test in the 2007 Assembly election.

SECURING THE PEACE FOR UNIONISM?

The 2007 Assembly results proved a resounding success for the DUP, confirming its position as the dominant party political force within unionism. Overall, the DUP further increased its share of the vote by 4.4 per cent, gained another six seats and took just over 30 per cent of all first preference votes (see Table 7). One of the loudest critics of the DUP before the election, Robert McCartney (who stood simultaneously in multiple constituencies), was swept aside. In North Down, previously seen as his power base, and where he had hoped to poll most strongly, McCartney secured only 1,806 votes, down nearly 6 per cent on his 2003 result.

More broadly within unionism, the overall UUP vote slumped yet again, dropping almost 8 per cent from the previous Assembly election in November 2003. As a consequence some key party members, such as Billy Bell in Lagan Valley and Esmond Birnie in South Belfast, lost their seats. The results raised further tensions within the UUP, with David Burnside, who held his seat, characterising himself as 'a hardline traditional Ulster Unionist, rather than a wee Free Presbyterian bigot', decrying the party's election slogan of 'For All of Us' as too glib, too liberal and arguing that the whole campaign had been ill-conceived.[59]

While the election confirmed broad patterns of voting preference within unionism, there were nuances within the broad trends. One notable feature was the high number of vote transfers to party colleagues (where that option was available). From DUP first preference winners, for example, some 83 per cent of transfers went to DUP running mates. The patterns were less clear among the UUP as most of its candidates were elected at the later stages of the count and were more likely to receive transfer votes rather than distribute them.

Despite some of the long-term tensions within unionism identified in this book, the election again confirmed the strength of intra-bloc voting

Table 7: Assembly Election Results, March 2007

Party	No. of Candidates	No. of Seats Won	Change from 2003	First Preference Votes	Percentage of First Preference Votes	Change from 2003
DUP	46	36	+6	207,721	30.1	+4.4
Sinn Féin	37	28	+4	180,573	26.2	+2.6
SDLP	35	16	-2	105,164	15.2	-1.8
UUP	38	18	-9	103,145	14.9	-7.7
Alliance	18	7	+1	36,139	5.2	+1.5
Green (NI)	13	1	+1	11,985	1.7	+1.3
PUP	3	1	0	3,822	0.6	-0.6
Independents	20	1	0	19,471	2.8	+1.9
UK Unionist	13	0	-1	10,452	1.5	+0.7
Others	32	0	0	11,741	1.8	+0.3
Totals255	108			690,213	100	

Sources: Adapted from ARK;[60] CAIN;[61] Electoral Commission[62]

with around two-thirds of DUP surplus votes going to the UUP and vice-versa (see Table 8). More broadly, while a majority of voters continued to express preferences after all the candidates from their top party had been elected or eliminated, this did not involve transfers across the main political divide.[63]

Following the results the question still remained as to whether or not Ian Paisley and the DUP would be prepared to cut a political deal involving sharing power with Sinn Féin. Throughout the campaign the DUP had managed to present an extremely clever public discourse, conveying a strong sense of duality on the point. On the one hand, there were suggestions that they might be ready to work with Sinn Féin in government; on the other, they constantly raised problems over issues such as policing, which suggested that they could still withdraw from any proposed deal.

After the all-party meeting at St Andrews, where the Agreement was reinvigorated and in part reworked, both the Irish and UK governments insisted that the elections were part of a timetable, whereby if devolved government were not agreed by 26 March 2007 then the whole venture would be scrapped. As Peter Hain put it, the choice was

Table 8: Vote Transfers in 2007 Assembly Elections

Party	Transferable Votes (%)	Main Beneficiaries
DUP	71	UUP received two-thirds
Sinn Féin	97	SDLP received 80 per cent
SDLP	92	Alliance and Sinn Féin
UUP	78	DUP received two-thirds

Source: Electoral Reform Society[64]

'devolution or dissolution'. While the DUP had participated in the multi-party talks, they remained the only party to refuse to sign up to the subsequent agreement and their readiness to share power remained uncertain. Even following the March election the DUP's direction was still unclear, although given the options offered by the secretary of state there was growing pressure upon them to confirm a power-sharing arrangement.

In the period immediately before the election the DUP had stressed the need for a total end to republican paramilitary activity and for Sinn Féin to confirm its support for the criminal justice system and the PSNI as its line in the sand. Following Sinn Féin's abandonment of its traditional policies and the softening of its line on policing, however, it became increasingly clear that the issues around which the DUP could legitimately position itself in opposition were becoming fewer.

Even so, when on Tuesday 8 May 2007 Ian Paisley and Martin McGuiness met with Tony Blair and Bertie Ahern to announce a power-sharing devolved administration, one long-term commentator described it as 'the closest thing to a miracle Belfast has seen'.[65] Not everyone was so impressed at the thought of sharing power with republicans, Dennis Kennedy describing the meeting as 'the triumph of cynicism and hypocrisy rather than reconciliation and understanding'.[66] Several DUP officials immediately resigned, the most prominent being the party's MEP, Jim Allister, who quickly began to organise co-ordinated opposition to the DUP position.

CONCLUSION

In its response to contemporary events the DUP has set about formulating its politics within what it constructs as the traditional frame of unionist values, presenting itself strongly as the force to carry the mantle as prime defenders of the Union. This is more complex than it may appear. Despite what the DUP might claim, there is no natural line of inheritance within unionism. Rather, the DUP has only been able to gain the position it has by aligning its political analysis with key public discourses and interpretations to dovetail with the existing meanings and everyday understandings that many unionists hold.

It is this alignment that provides the dynamic behind DUP politics and is reflected in how the DUP makes some issues particularly salient, through selecting aspects of a reality based on the perceived dangers of political and social decline within unionism and the very demise of the Union itself. Hence, much of the DUP's reaction to the Agreement has been framed in terms of crisis management and its belief in the existence of a Faustian deal between the UK and Irish governments, the republican movement and Irish America. What changed to allow the DUP to be part of such a pact, and does this mark disparity in how the DUP constructs its understanding of unionism?

1. Kane, A., 'Disillusionment may rob unionists of political victory', *News Letter*, 29 October 2005.
2. Mitchel, P., *Evangelicalism and National Identity in Ulster, 1921–1998* (Oxford: Oxford University Press, 2003), p.99.
3. *Northern Ireland Life and Times Survey 2005*.
4. Breen, S., 'Survey shows unionists divided over talks,' *Irish Times*, 11 September 1997.
5. *Belfast Telegraph*, 10 September 1997; *Irish Times*, 11 September 1997.
6. Hall, M., *The Death of the 'Peace Process'? A Survey of Community Perceptions* (Belfast: Island Pamphlets, 1997).
7. MacGinty, R., 'Unionist political attitudes after the Belfast Agreement', *Irish Political Studies*, 19, 1 (2004), pp.87–99.
8. Ibid.
9. See Boyd, N., 'Belfast Agreement's collapse inevitable', Northern Ireland Unionist Party press release (Belfast: NIUP, 11 April 2003); Vance, D., *Unionism Decayed, 1997–2007* (Milton Keynes: AuthorHouse, 2008).
10. Faith and Politics Group, *Transition*, p.1.
11. See Cairns, D., 'The object of sectarianism: the material reality of sectarianism in Ulster loyalism', *Journal of the Royal Anthropological Institute*, no. 6 (2000), pp.437–52; Heskin, K., 'Sectarianism: an optimistic prognosis', *Canadian Journal of Irish Studies*, 15, 2 (1989), pp.17–23; Irish Inter-Church Meeting, *Sectarianism: A Discussion Document* (Belfast: Inter-Church Group, 1993'); Kelly, B., 'Young people's views on communities and sectarianism in Northern Ireland, *Child Care in Practice*, 8, 1 (2002), pp.65–71; NIStudents.org, 'What is Sectarianism?'
12. Liechty, J. and Clegg, C., *Moving Beyond Sectarianism: Religion, Conflict, and Reconciliation in Northern Ireland* (Dublin: Columba Press, 2001), p.102.
13. Irish Inter-Church Meeting, *Sectarianism: A Discussion Document*.
14. O'Dowd, L., Rolston, B. and Tomlinson, M., *Northern Ireland: Between Civil Rights and Civil War* (London: CSE Books, 1980).
15. See Bryson, L. and McCartney, C., *Clashing Symbols* (Belfast: Queen's University Institute of Irish Studies, 1994); Buckley, A.D., '"We're trying to find our identity": uses of history among Ulster Protestants', in E. Tonkin (ed.), *History and Ethnicity* (London: Routledge, 1989); Heskin, K., 'Sectarianism: an optimistic prognosis'; Sugden, J. and Bairner, A., *Sport, Sectarianism and Society in a Divided Ireland* (Leicester: Leicester University Press, 1995).
16. See, for example, McKittrick, D., 'The enduring scar of sectarianism in Northern Ireland', *Belfast Telegraph*, 14 September 2009; Northern Ireland Assembly, 'Sectarianism and Sport in Northen Ireland', (research paper 26/01, October 2001) Sinclair, R. 'Voices Behind the Statistics. Young People's Views on Sectarianism in Northern Ireland (Seminar, Nuffield Foundation: National Children's Bureau, January 2005).
17. Darby, J. and MacGinty, R., 'Northern Ireland: long, cold peace', in J. Darby and R. MacGinty, *The Management of the Peace Process* (Basingstoke: Macmillan, 2000), pp.61–106.
18. Gébler, C., *The Glass Curtain* (London: Hamish Hamilton, 1991).
19. Burton, F., *The Politics of Legitimacy: Struggles in a Belfast Community* (London: Routledge and Kegan Paul, 1978).
20. Lysaght, K. and Basten, A., 'Violence, fear and the everyday: negotiating spatial practice in the city of Belfast', in E. Stanko (ed.), *Defining Violence* (London: Routledge, 2002).
21. Leonard, M., 'Building, bolstering and bridging boundaries: teenagers' negotiations of interface areas in Belfast', *Journal of Ethnic and Migration Studies*, 34, 3 (2008), pp.471–89.
22. Leonard, M., 'Teens and territory in contested spaces: negotiating sectarian interfaces in Northern Ireland', *Children's Geographies*, 4, 2 (2006), p.236.

23. Logue, K., *Anti-Sectarian Work: A Framework for Action* (Belfast: Community Relations Council, 1993).
24. McKittrick, D., *Endgame: The Search for Peace in Northern Ireland* (Belfast: Blackstaff Press, 1994).
25. Farrell, J., 'Apartheid', *New Statesman*, 28 November 2005, p.18.
26. See *Guardian*, 4 January 2002; *Guardian*, 7 January 2003.
27. Special EU Programmes Body, *Operational Programme for Peace III: Annex A – Socio-Economic Profile of Northern Ireland and the Border Region of Ireland* (Belfast Office, SEUPB, 2007), p.22.
28. Shirlow, P. and Murtagh, B., *Belfast: Segregation, Violence and the City* (London: Pluto, 2006).
29. Lister, S., 'Divided by 57 peace lines', *Belfast Telegraph*, 26 April 2007.
30. Jarman, N., 'Security and segregation: interface barriers in Belfast', *Shared Space*, no. 6 (2008), pp.21–33.
31. Hamilton, J., Bell, J. and Hansson, U., 'Segregation and sectarianism: impact on everyday life', *Shared Space*, no. 6 (2008), pp.35–49.
32. Ibid., p.48.
33. Hayes. B. and McAllister, I., 'Generations, prejudice and politics in Ireland North and South', in A.F. Heath, R. Breen and C.T. Whelan (eds), *Ireland North and South: Perspectives from Social Science* (Oxford: Oxford University Press, 1999), pp.474–5.
34. Shirlow, P., 'Fear, mobility and living in the Ardoyne and Upper Ardoyne communities', Mapping the Spaces of Fear Research Team, University of Ulster, Coleraine. Archived at: http://cain.ulst.ac.uk/issues/community/survey.htm
35. Schubotz, D. and Devine, P., 'What now? exploring community relations among 16-year-olds in Northern Ireland', *Shared Space*, 1, 1 (2005), pp.53–70.
36. Shirlow, P. and Murtagh, B., *Belfast: Segregation, Violence and the City* (London: Pluto, 2006).
37. Hewstone, Cairns, Voci, Paolini, McLernon, Crisp and Niens, 'Intergroup contact in a divided society'.
38. Graham, B. and Nash, C., 'A shared future: territoriality, pluralism and public policy in Northern Ireland', *Political Geography*, 23, 3 (2006), pp.253–78.
39. Brown, K. and MacGinty, R., 'Public attitudes toward partisan and neutral symbols in post-Agreement Northern Ireland', *Identities*, 10, 1 (2003), pp.83–108.
40. Adapted from *Northern Ireland Life and Times Survey 2004*.
41. McGrellis, S., 'Pushing the boundaries in Northern Ireland: young people, violence and sectarianism', *Contemporary Politics*, 11, 1 (2005), pp.53–71.
42. See Leonard, M., 'Social and subcultural capital among teenagers in Northern Ireland', *Youth and Society*, 40, 2 (2008), pp.224–44; McAuley, J.W., *The Politics of Identity: A Loyalist Community in Belfast* (Aldershot: Avebury Press, 1994); Neill, S., 'Wee warriors: youth involvement in the Northern Irish Troubles', *Humanities and Social Sciences*, 4, 1 (2008), pp.1–10.
43. See Beattie, G., *We Are the People: Journeys Through the Heart of Protestant Ulster* (London: Mandarin, 1993); Beattie, G., *Protestant Boy* (London: Granta, 2004); Boyd, J., *Out of My Class* (Belfast: Blackstaff Press, 1985); Harbinson, J., *No Surrender* (London: Faber and Faber, 1960).
44. See, for example, Conroy, J., *Belfast Diary: War as a Way of Life* (Boston: Beacon Press, 1995); Dawe, G., *The Rest is History* (Newry: Abbey Press, 1998); Dougan, D., *The Sash He Never Wore* (St Albans: Granada Publishing, 1974); Greacen, R., *The Sash My Father Wore: An Autobiography* (Edinburgh: Mainstream, 1997).
45. Arthur, P., *Government and Politics of Northern Ireland* (Harlow; Longman, 1984), p.49.
46. Graham, B., 'Ireland and Irishness: place, culture and identity', in B. Graham (ed.), *In Search of Ireland: A Cultural Geography* (London: Routledge, 1997), p.39.
47. Price, J., 'Political change and the Protestant working class', *Race and Class*, no. 37 (1995), p.61.
48. See McAuley, J.P., 'Loyalists and their ceasefire', *Parliamentary Brief, Special Issue on Northern Ireland*, 3, 1 (1994), pp.14–16; McAuley, J.P., 'Contemporary developments in a loyalist paramilitary group in Northern Ireland: back to basics ?', *Etudes Irlandaises*, 21, 1 (1996), pp.165–82; McAuley, J.P., 'The loyalist parties: a new respectability?,' *Etudes Irlandaises, Le Processus De Paix En Irlande Du Nord*, special volume on the peace process (edited by P. Joannon), 22, 2 (1997), pp.117–32; McAuley, J.P., 'Ulster loyalism and the politics of peace', in J. Goodman and J. Anderson (eds), *Agreeing Ireland: Political Agendas for Peace in Ireland's National Conflict* (London: Pluto Press, 1998), pp.193–210.
49. Porter, *Rethinking Unionism*, p.87.

50. Brewer, J., *Ethnography* (Buckingham: Open University Press), p.177.
51. See Brown, "'Our father organization": the cult of the Somme and the unionist "Golden Age"'; Graham, B., 'The past in the present: the shaping of identity in loyalist Ulster', *Terrorism and Political Violence*, 16, 3 (2004), pp.483–500; Graham, B. and Shirlow, P., 'The Battle of the Somme in Ulster memory and identity', *Political Geography*, no. 21 (2002), pp.881–904; Officer, D. and Walker, G., 'Protestant Ulster: ethno-history, memory and contemporary prospects,' *National Identities*, 2, 3 (2000), pp.293–307.
52. I am aware of various cross-community initiatives seeking to decontextualise the Battle of the Somme and in particular to highlight the number of Irish Catholic nationalists who fought alongside Ulster Protestants. For an excellent revisionist account see Grayson, R., *Belfast Boys: How Unionists and Nationalists Fought and Died Together in the First World War* (London: Continuum, 2009). Nonetheless, the Somme retains iconic status for most unionists. See, for example, the statement used by the DUP on 1 July 2009 entitled: 'Remembering the bravery and sacrifice of an earlier generation'. Archived at: http://www.dup.org.uk/Articles.asp?ArticleNewsID=996
53. Novick, P., *The Holocaust in American Life* (New York: Houghton Mifflin, 1999), p.5.
54. Democratic Unionist Party, *Fair Deal Manifesto* (Belfast: UDUP, 2003).
55. Dawson, G., 'Unionism making undoubted advances under DUP leadership'; Delanty, G., 'Negotiating the peace in Northern Ireland', *Journal of Peace Research*, 32, 3 (1995), pp.257–64.
56. 'Robinson addresses Conservative conference 2006'.
57. Donaldson, J., *The Northern Ireland Peace Process*.
58. Ian Paisley, cited in *Belfast Telegraph*, 11 June 2002.
59. Gordon, D., 'Burnside slams "glib" UUP slogan', *Belfast Telegraph*, 12 March 2007.
60. ARK, *Northern Ireland Election Results*.
61. CAIN, 'Results of elections held in Northern Ireland since 1968'.
62. Electoral Commission, 'Election results 2007'.
63. Electoral Reform Society, *STV in Practice: A Briefing on the Northern Ireland Assembly* (Election London: ERS, 2007).
64. Ibid.
65. McKittrick, D., 'The miracle of Belfast', *Independent*, 9 May 2005.
66. Kennedy, D., 'The case against the Belfast Agreement', in B. Barton and P.J. Roche (eds), *The Northern Ireland Question: The Peace Process and the Belfast Agreement* (Basingstoke: Palgrave Macmillan, 2009), p.263.

Chapter 8
Unionism and Loyalism in a Settled Peace?

It took six months for the Unionists to get pissed off with me.
They get pissed off with everyone from the British government eventually.

Mo Mowlam[1]

'Let me tell you something,' McClure went on. 'We're all
friends here, but the Protestant people have had enough so
they have. Enough talks about rights and all. There's a question of birthright being sold out here. Put that in your newspaper. We're the boys built the Empire and got a kick in the
arse for it. Write about that.'

Eoin McNamee, *Resurrection Man*[2]

As has been demonstrated throughout this book unionism and loyalism
have in recent times experienced political fragmentation, set in the context
of cultural and psychological turmoil and rapid demographic and economic change. Alongside this, contests surrounding the ideological fluc-
tuation and reinstatement of unionism have framed the main contours of
its response and reaction to contemporary events. In one sense, of course,
the politics of unionism still remain coherent, driven by the desire to
maintain Northern Ireland's constitutional position within the UK.

In other senses, however, there is a recognisable continuation of
trends towards the political fragmentation that began when Ian Paisley
mobilised against the existing unionist political hegemony in the late
1960s.[3] Party political unionism has largely remained convulsed and at
variance ever since. By emphasising many of the incompatibilities
within unionism, the peace process laid bare different understandings
of what it is to be a unionist, further exposing the different forces seeking to reshape unionism and the different strategic, ideological and
organisational bands within it.

Throughout the contemporary period, the DUP has articulated open suspicion of the motives of government, harnessed anxiety about unionism's social and political future and found conspiracy against the Union with every political development. In so doing the DUP frames a specific articulation of events that signals in a particular way to unionists and forms the basis for their support. In seeking to understand such processes, Hartman[4] usefully turns to Joseph Cappella and Kathleen Hall Jamieson, who present discursive framing as analogous to photography by suggesting that:

> A photographer frames her subjects by setting boundaries, choosing contexts, selecting and manipulating light. The act of framing determines what is included and excluded, what is salient and what is unimportant. It focuses the viewer's attention on its subjects in specific ways. The objects in the photograph are presented in a setting and illuminated to create visual effects. The photographer's act of framing binds its subjects together in a distinctive way; another photographer framing the same subject would produce a recognizably different picture.[5]

(RE) CREATING UNIONISM

So how has the discursive frame set by the DUP bound together unionism and determined what are the key political issues within this frame? Cathy Gormley-Heenan and Roger MacGinty suggest that the move of the DUP from self positioned 'outsiders' to the heart of devolved government should be understood in the context of ethnic outbidding and party modernisation, while still drawing on the traditional discourse of 'No Surrender'.[6] This is an important focus and it is important to build upon this to identify the forms of discourse constructed by the DUP to produce a recognisably different picture of unionism (see previous chapters).

Part of the DUP frame makes reference to frontiers between 'legitimate' and 'illegitimate' political aspirations.[7] Many of the discourses that continue to heighten and reinforce the core concerns of many unionists have increasingly gained credence in recent times. It is the DUP that provides a vital conjugate for the outlet of these views, as Ian Paisley makes readily apparent when he says:

> It is the destruction agenda of Ulster within the Union and the latest stage in the surrender process started by the Belfast Agreement. It has been designed by the government with the

assistance of Dublin and with the help of Mr Trimble to deliver the
Unionist people of Ulster further down the road of Irish unity.[8]

Underpinning all of this, therefore, is a discourse that draws heavily
on ideas of betrayal and the formation of a defensive politics by what
Boyce has characterised as the 'threatened community'.[9] This notion
was reinforced within DUP thinking from the mid-1980s and strengthened following the signing of the AIA, when the 'Irish dimension'
became an increasing reality for unionism. At a time when the UUP
and DUP had entered into an electoral pact, John Taylor noted the
move in support towards Ian Paisley was for many within unionism a
'natural' journey, suggesting Paisley 'scored because the Protestant
community felt under siege [because of the] IRA and lack of support in
London'.[10]

The notion of siege remains deeply engrained, and there is still a
widely held belief across unionism that the superstructure of the current settlement rests on a foundation of concessions to republicanism.
This has strong resonance, drawing as it does on an interpretative
frame that constructs an enemy that is always deceitful and double-
dealing.[11] Many unionists who reproduce this discourse do so in reaction to their perception that their contemporary political position is
being subverted.

One crucial question still needs to be answered, however. How did
the purveyors of such views come to such a dominant position within
unionist politics? John Darby makes the important proposition that in
any peace processes the primary goal of any political leadership is to
'deliver their own people'.[12] The DUP reacted strategically to expand
the definition of 'their own people' and sought to outbid others who
may compete for the leadership of unionism.[13]

To achieve this the DUP strategy was five-fold. First, they presented
the Agreement primarily through a discourse of concessions to republicanism and losses to unionism. Second, they made widespread and
repeated claims that other unionists had either betrayed or were likely
to betray the Union. Third, at least for much of the time, they placed
themselves outside of the processes and institutions of the peace
process. Fourth, while positioning themselves in this way, they built
anti-Agreement alliances and used electoral contests to reinforce their
standpoint. Finally, they claimed that they renegotiated the accord and
forced the republican movement onto the back foot, resulting in mainstream republicanism accepting partitionist institutions and being prepared to work within them.

While these strategies were successful for the DUP, it does not
explain why the party is seen as legitimate in doing so. To fully under-

stand this, we must recognise that the peace process brought about a crisis for unionism surrounding the fracturing of what Slavoj Zizek refers to as the existing symbolic order.[14] The subsequent 'dislocation' allowed alternative political discourses, such as those of new unionism or the PUP's emphasis on communality and the particular experiences of Protestant working-class communities, to be heard.[15]

In part at least, this marked an attempt to realign the frames of interpretation as new unionism sought to reposition its politics around a more inclusive form. For some time this alternative frame did gain a measure of credibility within unionism. New constructs of unionism, however, cannot be *forced* into a position of dominance, especially if the majority of those who claim unionism see this as an illegitimate articulation of their central beliefs. Thus, the fate of both new loyalism and new unionism was to remain at the margins of political life, seen by the majority as unable to represent unionism's core values.

More specifically the articulations of new unionism and new loyalism, promoting ideas of sharing responsibility and cultural pluralism, ran counter to the everyday understandings and experiences of many unionists. The DUP interpretation thus became more creditable within unionism because it drew directly on existing collective memories and broad cultural frames that are understood and believed by a majority of unionists.[16] This leads to the reinforcing of particular expressions of political identity and the perception of increased validity to the political stance of the DUP. To complete this positioning the DUP has also been able to convincingly portray the idea that it is the only grouping that has revealed the 'truth' about contemporary political events. Thus, the contemporary expressions of politics by the DUP are clearly located within the unionist discourses of perpetuity, to the exclusion of others such as the UUP.[17]

FRAMING PEACE THROUGH STRENGTH?

Further, the DUP has been able to convince voters that in return for their support it can guarantee some sense of symmetry in the political consequences of the settlement. Central in drawing support to the DUP position over the contemporary period has been its self-image as unwavering in its vigil against the enemies of Ulster. Moreover, it has consistently promoted the view that others, such as the UUP and the political representatives of paramilitarism, have proved unable to positively influence public perceptions of unionism.[18] Unionism has largely fallen in line behind the DUP, leading Gavin Robinson to claim that:

The internal unionist battle is well and truly over. All across the country the message being returned is that the DUP is on the march and they are getting it right. Over the coming weeks and months the electorate can have faith that whether they are being represented in negotiations or in government, the DUP will be leading the way forward.[19]

The upturn in electoral success for the DUP rested on the claim that it was the only political grouping to clearly recognise the overarching and devious challenge to the Union and to effectively resist this. The entire DUP political project is driven by the construction of discourses that place the DUP in the vanguard of Ulster's last stand,[20] that through the St Andrews meeting its representatives were able to renegotiate a more symmetrical settlement (at worst), and that in government the DUP is 'running rings around Sinn Féin in the Executive, blocking them at every turn on every major policy issue'.[21]

More broadly the DUP projects itself as a grouping that held out against the odds to secure a victory for the unionist people. Just how deeply this is embedded in DUP thinking is illustrated by the following from Peter Robinson:

Today it is the DUP that sets the political agenda in Northern Ireland. We got here not because we were weak but because we were firm; not because we caved in under pressure but because we stood up for what was right; not because we accepted other people's deadlines and diktats but because we insisted our own requirements be met.

... Who today would argue that we were wrong to hold out until republicans gave up their terror campaign and ended their criminality? We were told it would never happen, but we persevered until it did. Who today would argue that we were wrong to hold out until republicans gave up their illegal weapons? We were told it would never happen, but we persevered until it did. Who today would argue that we were wrong to hold out to ensure that accountability was introduced for Ministerial decisions? We were told it would never happen, but we persevered until it did. Who today would argue that we were wrong to hold out until Sinn Féin openly gave support to the police, the courts and the Rule of Law? We were told it would never happen, but we persevered until it did.[22]

THE DUP: SELLING OUT THE UNION?

It is important to recognise, however, that there is nothing natural about the leadership position currently occupied by the DUP. None of this is to say that the position of the DUP is now uncontested within unionism or that the categories used by the DUP to frame and make sense of the world are unchallenged within unionism. In late 2006, as Northern Ireland yet again inched towards the formation of a working devolved administration, the DUP found itself under sustained criticism from Robert McCartney for meeting with Sinn Féin, claiming that his 'unionist birthright' was being bartered 'for a mess of ministerial potage'.[23] Tensions rose to the point where Ian Paisley and other leading members of the DUP were forced to issue public denials that the party was split over the proposed move to government with Sinn Féin.[24]

At the time of the 2007 Assembly election the DUP, and Paisley in particular, came under challenge from other unionists for what they saw as his undue liberalism in even contemplating entering into government with Sinn Féin.[25] There was resistance from across the DUP's domain, brought to a head by a meeting between Ian Paisley and Gerry Adams in March 2007, which precipitated resignations from the Free Presbyterian Church ministry and notably Jim Allister, the DUP's sitting MEP, who openly questioned the political direction and judgement of Ian Paisley.

Allister later formed Traditional Unionist Voice (TUV), claiming that, for the DUP, the 'lure of office has clouded the Party's judgement'.[26] Hence the claim in the 2009 European Parliamentary election manifesto that a vote for the TUV would demonstrate that people 'reject terrorists in government'. It went on to suggest that this was the last chance for voters:

> ... to halt the Belfast/St Andrews Agreement conveyer belt to an all-Ireland Republic. If the DUP and their partner in government, Sinn Féin, succeed in their joint desire to snuff out Traditional Unionist opposition, then it will be full steam ahead.[27]

STRENGTHENING THE UNION: DEFENDING BRITISHNESS

So with the formation of a devolved government have the DUP and its supporters now been convinced that the situation has changed? Not really; rather what is different is that the DUP has been able to extend its interpretative frame to argue that because of them unionists have regained ground to the point where they can now negotiate from a position of strength. Moreover, they have been able to embed this in commonsense unionist interpretations of contemporary politics and society.

This thinking is clearly revealed in the following statement from Peter Robinson, claiming that the DUP has taken control of unionism's destiny, and that while it may now have the upper hand, there is continued need for vigilance:

> While there is good reason to be optimistic that after nearly forty years of terrorism the military conflict in Northern Ireland is over, the political battle between unionism and nationalism goes on. Republicans have not called a halt to aspiring to a United Ireland and we as unionists will tenaciously hold to the Union with Great Britain.
>
> The difference today is that unionism is in control of its own destiny, free from the threat of violence and possessing safeguards to protect the interests of the unionist community. Whereas for most of the last forty years decisions were taken over the heads of the unionist people, now we as unionists have control over our own destiny. Nonetheless unionists would be foolish if they were not forever vigilant in monitoring the character of Republican behaviour.[28]

This perspective is reinforced by the way in which the DUP draws on a particular form of constructed remembering,[29] which it consistently refers to as traditional unionism. This is used as a tool to construct an identifiable sense of belonging, part of which limits future political possibilities and reinforces contemporary political decisions by linking directly with a 'unionist past' and strengthens the certainty of contemporary identity. As Bhabha crucially reminds us, remembering 'is never a quiet act of introspection. It is a painful re-membering, a putting together of the dismembered past to make sense of the trauma of the present.'[30]

The DUP mines and articulates collective unionist memories and presents these in ways that are most meaningful for contemporary unionists.[31] Thus the DUP has succeeded in framing contemporary unionist politics and identity in ways that draw across a variety of major understandings of unionism as politicised Protestantism, of unionism as British identity, and of unionism as political expressions – the major building blocks of unionism highlighted throughout this book. Further, the DUP has convinced unionists that it was the party that negotiated the peace from a position of strength (and that only the DUP was capable of doing so) and that what was agreed at St Andrews ended republican appeasement and brought about a new period of unionist control.

This message is strongly projected by the DUP. Hence Paisley's part-ing claims as leader were that he had 'smashed Sinn Féin' because they had accepted 'the right of Britain to govern this country'[32] and that the DUP remained in pole position as 'the protector of British identity and culture throughout Ulster'.[33] Peter Robinson, who outlines what he sees as the contemporary agenda for unionism as follows, has readily taken up these themes:

> I have no doubt that most unionists would prefer if Sinn Féin were not in the Executive. But other than being in office what have they been able to achieve that has advanced by a single step their united Ireland agenda? Instead, for the first time in a gener-ation we as unionists have control over our own destiny.[34]

This current formation of unionist politics is, however, not fixed or permanent. The challenge to the DUP offered by the grouping coalesc-ing around TUV demonstrates this directly, particularly in its criticism of the DUP's willingness to administrate 'joint rule', that: 'props up a regime' with '[Martin] McGuinness as joint First Minister, and unre-pentant terrorists in other key posts'.[35] Indeed the claims of Jim McAllister and TUV were given some substance by the European elec-tion results, where in a three-way election contest between unionism, TUV polled a more than respectable 66,197 first preference votes (some 30 per cent of the unionist vote). This reflected almost directly the decline in first preferences for the DUP, whose first preference share fell from 32 per cent in 2004 to 18.2 per cent to total 88,346 votes, just ahead of the Ulster Conservatives and Unionists with 82,893.

For the moment, although undoubtedly vexed by the electoral chal-lenge of TUV and its claim that the DUP has 'squandered unreservedly the trust of a huge section of unionism',[36] the leadership of unionism remains under the guidance of Peter Robinson and Nigel Dodds, and the DUP continues the political and ideological dominance of contem-porary unionism. As the journalist Henry McDonald suggested imme-diately following the 2007 Assembly election results, the increased sup-port for the DUP essentially marked an insurance taken out by the unionist community.[37] There are now clearly those who regard others within unionism as better brokers of their security. Whether or not unionists ever feel that the policy needs to be cashed in, and who unionists see as offering the most direct route to protect the existing constitutional arrangements will determine much of the future direc-tion of politics in Northern Ireland.

NOTES

1. Mowlam, M., cited in A. Seldon, *Blair* (London: Free Press, 2005), p.355.
2. McNamee, E., *Resurrection Man* (London: Picador, 1995), p.151.
3. See, for various accounts, Cooke, D., *Persecuting Zeal: A Portrait of Ian Paisley* (Dingle: Brandon, 1996); Smyth, C., *Ian Paisley: Voice of Protestant Ulster* (Edinburgh: Scottish Academic Press, 1987).
4. Hartman, 'Talking the gun out of Irish politics'.
5. Cappella, J.N. and Jamieson, K.H., *Spiral of Cynicism: The Press and the Public Good* (Oxford: Oxford University Press, 1997), p.38.
6. Gormley-Heenan, C. and MacGinty, R., 'Ethnic outbidding and party modernization: understanding the Democratic Unionist Party's electoral success in the post-Agreement environment', *Ethnopolitics*, 7, 1 (2008), pp.43–61.
7. See E. Laclau and C. Mouffe, *Hegemony and Socialist Strategy: Towards a Radical Democratic Politics* (London: Verso, 1985); Howarth, D., Norval, A. and Stavrakakis, Y. (eds), *Discourse Theory and Political Analysis: Identities, Hegemonies and Social Change* (Manchester: Manchester University Press, 2000).
8. Paisley, I., 'Address by Ian Paisley at the centenary demonstration of the Independent Orange Institution, Ballymoney, 12 July 2003'. Archived at: http://www.dup.org.uk
9. Boyce, D.G., 'The suffering people and the threatened community: two traditions of political violence in Ireland', in A. O'Day (ed.), *Terrorism's Laboratory: The Case of Northern Ireland* (Aldershot: Dartmouth, 1995).
10. Taylor, J. cited in F. Millar, *Northern Ireland: A Triumph of Politics* (Dublin, Irish Academic Press, 2009), p.53.
11. See various essays in English and Walker, *Unionism in Modern Ireland*; Hanna (ed.) *The Union: Essays on Ireland and the British Connection*; Foster (ed.) *The Idea of the Union*.
12. Darby, J., *The Effects of Violence on Peace Processes* (Washington, DC: US Institute of Peace Press, 2001), p.120.
13. See Mitchell, P., O'Leary, B. and Evans, G., 'Northern Ireland: flanking extremists bite the moderates and emerge in their clothes', *Parliamentary Affairs*, no. 54 (2001), pp.725–42; Mitchell, P., Evans G. and O'Leary B., 'Extremist outbidding in ethnic party systems is not inevitable', PSPE working paper no. 6, 2006.
14. Zizek, S., *The Sublime Object of Ideology* (London: Verso, 1989).
15. Laclau, E. and Mouffe, C., *Hegemony and Socialist Strategy: Towards a Radical Democratic Politics* (London: Verso, 1985).
16. See Huyssen, A., 'Monuments and Holocaust memory in a media age', in A. Huyssen (ed.), *Twilight Memories: Marking Time in a Culture of Amnesia* (London: Routledge, 1995), pp.249–60; Misztal, B., *Theories of Social Remembering* (Maidenhead: Open University Press, 2003).
17. I have identified this directly in McAuley, J.W., 'Divided loyalists, divided loyalties: conflicts and continuities in contemporary unionist ideology', in J. Tonge and C. Gilligan (eds), *War or Peace: The Origins and Development of the Peace Process in Northern Ireland* (Aldershot: Ashgate Press, 1997), pp.37–53. I have developed the original idea in McAuley, J.W., 'Contemporary unionist understandings of the peace process', *The Global Review of Ethnopolitics*, 3, 1 (2004), pp.60–76.
18. Parkinson, A.F., *Ulster Loyalism and the British Media* (Dublin: Four Courts Press, 1998); Spencer, 'The decline of Ulster unionism', pp.45–63.
19. Robinson, G., 'Internal unionist battle is now well and truly over', *News Letter*, 10 March. 2007.
20. See Democratic Unionist Party, *Our Covenant with the Ulster People: Manifesto for the Forum Election 1996* (Belfast: DUP, 1996); Democratic Unionist Party, 'The tragedy of a false peace'. Archived at: http://www.dup.org.uk
21. *News Letter*, 19 July 2008.
22. Speech made by DUP leader Peter D. Robinson, MP MLA at the annual party conference 2008, Armagh.
23. McCartney, 'This is a situation hardly calculated to produce either clarity or truth'.
24. BBC News Online, 'Paisley denies power-sharing rift'. Archived at: http://newsvote.bbc.co.uk/1/hi/northern_ireland/6186154.stm; BBC News Online, 'Dodds denies internal DUP split'. Archived at: http://newsvote.bbc.co.uk/1/hi/northern_ ireland/6163703.stm

25. Heatley, C., 'DUP split will lead to new hardline party', *Sunday Business Post*, 16 September 2007.
26. McAdam, N., 'Republicanism "is being strengthened by DUP quitters"', *Belfast Telegraph*, 2 April 2007.
27. Traditional Unionist Voice, European parliamentary election, 4 June 2009, manifesto. Archived at: http://www.tuv.org.uk/files/electionmanifesto09.pdf
28. Robinson, P., 'Unionists are in control says deputy leader'.
29. See Middleton, D. and Edwards, D. (eds), *Collective Remembering* (London: Sage, 1991); Misztal, *Theories of Social Remembering*.
30. Bhabha, 'The managed identity', p.xvi.
31. See Paisley, I., 'God save Ulster', *Irish Times*, 1 December 1997; Paisley, I., 'Speech at the annual party conference', DUP press statement, 29 November 1997; Paisley, I., 'The fruits of appeasement', DUP press statement, 3 September 1998; Paisley, I., 'Statement by party leader', DUP 30th anniversary conference 2001; Robinson, P., 'Speech to DUP annual conference 1998'. Archived at: http://www.dup.org.uk
32. Paisley, I. 'I did smash Sinn Féin', BBC News Online. Archived at: http://news.bbc.co.uk/1/hi/uk_politics/7285912.stm
33. Dempster, S., 'DUP issues leaflet on its achievements', *News Letter*, 14 July 2008.
34. Robinson, P., 'First minister outlines the battle lines for next elections'. Archived at: http://www.dup.org.uk/articles.asp?ArticleNewsID=961
35. 'Allister hits out at DUP "joint rule"', *News Letter*, 19 July 2008.
36. Jim Allister, 'Hearts and Minds', BBC NI, 11 June 2009.
37. McDonald, H., 'Unionists have the whip hand but could still lose the game', *Observer*, 11 March 2007.

Chapter 9
Postscript – February 2010

This moment and this agreement belongs to the people of Northern Ireland, all of the people, and now more than ever before so does their future [it is] the last chapter of a long and troubled story and the beginning of a new chapter
>   (Gordon Brown, PM, 4 February 2010).

Ten years on from our first taste of Belfast Agreement devolution, some – who made careers and political advance out of denouncing the Good Friday deal – are now its chief operatives
>   (Jim Allister, TUV, 22 February 2010).

The main events of early 2010 strongly reinforced many of the broad political trends and patterns identified in this book. Perhaps the most positive was on Wednesday 6 January 2010 with the final act of UDA decommissioning of its weapons confirmed by the IICD, albeit over a decade after the signing of the Agreement, and 15 years following the UDA ceasefire. At the subsequent press conference held by the UPRG, it's main spokesperson Frankie Gallagher paid tribute those in the UDA: 'who had died or been imprisoned during the Troubles'. He went on to say:

> To all those in the community who have lost loved ones, we understand and we share in your sense of loss but we are determined and are willing to play our full part in ensuring that the tragedy of the last 40 years will never happen again.[1]

Undoubtedly the actions of some of those former members who remain politically active will find an outlet in collective community action designed at securing resources and strengthening the already high levels of social bonding demonstrated across loyalist working class communities. Involvement in creating and sustaining political dynamics that straddle communities remains limited, however, and it is only when, and if, such organizational structures are made concrete that the work of former paramilitaries and paramilitary prisoners will become fully embedded in the civil society of Northern Ireland.

More broadly across unionism, the opening months of 2010 saw the leadership role and political standing of the DUP questioned by emerging issues; two of which, in the demands by Sinn Féin for the completion of devolution and the continued political challenge of the TUV, were foreseen, the other much less so. Centred in the unpredictable were the events precipitated by the broadcasting of a BBC Spotlight programme[2] alleging financial and sexual impropriety on the part of Iris Robinson (an MP, MLA and local councillor) and wife of the First Minister.

The BBC documentary alleged that Mrs Robinson, well known for her fundamentalist views and conservative position on the family (once referring to homosexuality as an 'abomination'), had secured £50,000 from two business friends to help her then 19-year-old extramarital lover secure a deal to open a new café. As the details emerged, further allegations were made that Peter Robinson had also become aware of what had happened and the transfer of money, but had failed to inform the relevant authorities.

Following so closely as it did after the MP's expenses scandals in the Westminster parliament, the events had huge implications for the standing of the Office of the First and Deputy First Minister, and for confidence in politics more broadly. For a time the governance of Northern Ireland, (perhaps the entire political process itself) seemed in the balance. Sinn Féin claimed that the situation meant the first minister was now: 'hostage to right-wing elements in the DUP' and amidst several open calls for him to resign asked that he should consider his position.

The entire DUP leadership was thrown into political convulsion. In the short term, Peter Robinson was forced to take a short sabbatical, maintaining the DUP leadership, but being replaced in the role of first minister by party colleague Arlene Foster. Upon his return Robinson and the DUP faced two other issues that while more predictable were no less challenging. Prime amongst these was the issue of devolution of policing and security powers to the Assembly, broadly agreed as part of the Agreement, and later confirmed at St. Andrew's.

On 1 December 2009 a bill creating a justice department won cross-community backing in the Assembly, thus clearing the path for the full devolution of policing and security. The DUP immediately rejected the immediacy of the issue, prompting Martin McGuinness to talk of a forthcoming 'full-blown' crisis. This set the context for intense negotiations, which saw Sinn Féin and the DUP in deadlock. The direct involvement of both Irish and UK governments and 'shuttle diplomacy' between the main parties (mirroring the 1998 negotiations), failed to resolve the situation.

Even the hint of compromise drew forth recalcitrance from within ranks of the DUP, as 14 out of 35 of its Assembly members rebelled against proposals put by Peter Robinson. It was not until 4 February, after 10 days of near round-the-clock talks, that the blueprint for a deal was agreed, including the appointment of a justice minister with cross community support, working groups to consider reform of the Parades Commission and the functioning of the Assembly executive.

This did not mean, of course, that the proposed deal was accepted across unionism. Thus, a second major focus for the DUP remains how to counter disputes to their claims to represent the politics of 'real unionism'. Such claims were not made easier by the presentation of the new accord by the DUP's opponents as the concession of yet more ground to Sinn Féin. For Jim Allister and the TUV the creation of a new minister for justice executive merely gave more grist to his contention that Sinn Féin had been fully embedded at the centre of a coalition government, which he described as a 'deviant concoction of mutual vetoes for mutually exclusive political ideologies (which is) doomed to fail (and) the very antithesis of democracy'.[3] Moreover, for the TUV, the latest accord marked little more than 'another staging post in delivery of Sinn Fein's insatiable agenda'.[4]

Other concerns across unionism rested on the future of Orange parades and the 'right to march'. Initial exchanges did little to suggest that it would be an easy task for any new body brought about by the accord to make progress on the issue. Nelson McCausland of the DUP quickly accused the Garvaghy Road Residents Coalition of seeking to introduce a form 'cultural apartheid' into Northern Ireland, and it is clear that any support from the DUP for restrictions on marching will bring it into direct conflict with the Orange Order, which remains void of even any innuendo of movement towards what might be seen to compromise its physical or ideological space.

As the DUP sustains its journey from opposition to coalition government, the political space it occupies continues to be challenged, most directly by the TUV, but also by the UUP, which continues to reposition and rebuild its civic model of unionism through a closer working with the Conservative Party. More broadly, the real possibility of a three-way split in the unionist vote has led some to reconsider the captaincy of the DUP. The real possibility of the loss of two Westminster seats to Sinn Féin has refocused the leadership of the Orange Order to bolster its demands for a coalition, or at least an electoral pact, to secure the political representation of unionism.

Overall, while there is some evidence that the complex set of interrelated ideological and political strands upon which unionist identity is built has again begun to unravel, there is much counter evidence that unionism will reform and redefine as contemporary contingencies demand. The history of unionist politics demonstrates its ability to reorganise and reframe, especially when unionist perceptions of threat to the Union are seen to be high. In such circumstances the differing ideological and political strands identified throughout this book will re-assemble, perhaps in a somewhat different, but always recognisable form.

NOTES

1. UTV News (2010) 'UDA decommissioning confirmed'. Archived at: http://www.u.tv/NEWS/UDA-decommissioning-confirmed/ec5100f4-a391-4b49-86ac-b384e6f1749d; accessed 21 February 2010.
2. The programme was first broadcast on BBC NI on Thursday 7 January 2010.
3. Allister, J., 'Opinion', *News Letter*, 4 December 2009.
4. Harbinson, K. (2010) 'Harbinson Answers Foster On Hillsborough'. Archived at: http://www.tuv.org.uk/press-releases/view/553/harbinson-answers-foster-on-hillsborough; accessed; 21 February 2010.

Appendix 1
Westminster General Election 2005 Results:
Change by Constituency in Northern Ireland

East Antrim: Sammy Wilson (DUP) **DUP gain** (from UUP)

East Belfast: Peter Robinson (DUP) **DUP hold**

East Londonderry: Gregory Campbell (DUP) **DUP hold**

Fermanagh/South Tyrone: Michelle Gildernew (SF) **Sinn Féin hold**

Foyle: Mark Durkan (SDLP) **SDLP hold**

Lagan Valley: Jeffrey Donaldson (DUP) **DUP gain** (from UUP)

Mid-Ulster: Martin McGuinness (SF) **Sinn Féin hold**

Newry and Armagh: Conor Murphy (SF) **Sinn Féin gain** (from SDLP)

North Antrim: Rev. Ian Paisley (DUP) **DUP hold**

North Belfast: Nigel Dodds (DUP) **DUP hold**

North Down: Lady Sylvia Hermon (UUP) **UUP hold**

South Antrim: Rev. William McCrea (DUP) **DUP gain** (from UUP)

South Belfast: Alasdair McDonnell (SDLP) **SDLP gain** (from UUP)

South Down: Eddie McGrady (SDLP) **SDLP hold**

Strangford: Iris Robinson (DUP) **DUP hold**

Upper Bann: Alan Simpson (DUP) **DUP gain** (from UUP)

West Belfast: Gerry Adams (SF) **Sinn Féin hold**

West Tyrone: Pat Doherty (SF) **Sinn Féin hold**

Appendix 2
Northern Ireland Assembly 2007:
Executive Responsibilities

First Minister: **Ian Paisley (DUP)**

Deputy First Minister: **Martin McGuinness (Sinn Féin)**

Finance and Personnel: **Peter Robinson (DUP)**

Enterprise, Trade and Investment: **Nigel Dodds (DUP)**

Environment: **Arlene Foster (DUP)**

Culture, Arts and Leisure: **Edwin Poots (DUP)**

Education: **Caitríona Ruane (Sinn Féin)**

Regional Development: **Conor Murphy (Sinn Féin)**

Agriculture: **Michelle Gildernew (Sinn Féin)**

Health and Social Services: **Michael McGimpsey (UUP)**

Employment and Learning: **Sir Reg Empey (UUP)**

Social Development: **Margaret Ritchie (SDLP)**

Junior Minister – Office of the First and Deputy First Minister: **Ian Paisley Jr (DUP)**

Junior Minister – Office of the First and Deputy First Minister: **Gerry Kelly (Sinn Féin)**

Appendix 3
Northern Ireland Assembly 2008:
Executive Responsibilities

First Minister: **Peter Robinson (DUP)**
Deputy First Minister: **Martin McGuinness (Sinn Féin)**
Finance and Personnel: **Nigel Dodds (DUP)**
Enterprise, Trade and Investment: **Arlene Foster (DUP)**
Environment: **Sammy Wilson (DUP)**
Culture, Arts and Leisure: **Gregory Campbell (DUP)**
Education: **Caitríona Ruane (Sinn Féin)**
Regional Development: **Conor Murphy (Sinn Féin)**
Agriculture: **Michelle Gildernew (Sinn Féin)**
Health and Social Services: **Michael McGimpsey (UUP)**
Employment and Learning: **Sir Reg Empey (UUP)**
Social Development: **Margaret Ritchie (SDLP)**

Bibliography

Select Bibliography

Abrams, D., Marques, J. M. and Hogg, M.A. (eds) *The Social Psychology of Inclusion and Exclusion* (Philadelphia, PA: Psychology Press, 2005).

Adair, J. with McKendry, G. *Mad Dog* (London: John Blake, 2007).

Adams, G. *A Farther Shore: Ireland's Long Road to Peace* (New York: Random House, 2005).

Adams, G. *The New Ireland: A Vision for the Future* (Dingle: Brandon, 2005).

Alcock, A. *Understanding Ulster* (Armagh: Ulster Society, 1994).

Anderson, B. *Imagined Communities: Reflections on the Origin and Spread of Nationalism* (London: Verso, 1991).

Anderson, C. *The Billy Boy: The Life and Death of LVF leader Billy Wright* (Edinburgh: Mainstream Publishing, 2002).

Anderson, D. *14 Days in May: The Inside Story of the Loyalist Strike of 1974* (Dublin: Gill and Macmillan, 1994).

Anderson, J. and Goodman, J. *Dis/agreeing Ireland: Contexts, Obstacles, Hopes* (London: Pluto Press, 1998).

Arthur, P. *Government and Politics of Northern Ireland* (Harlow; Longman, 1984).

Arthur, P. *Special Relationships: Britain, Ireland and the Northern Ireland Problem* (Belfast: Blackstaff Press, 2000).

Atkinson, D. *Civil Renewal: Mending the Hole in the Social Ozone* (Studley: Brewin Books, 2004).

Aughey, A. *Under Siege: Ulster Unionism and the Anglo-Irish Agreement* (Belfast: Blackstaff Press, 1989).

Aughey, A. *The Politics of Northern Ireland: Beyond the Belfast Agreement* (London: Routledge, 2005).

Aughey, A. Burnside, D. Harris, E. Adams, G. and Donaldson, J. *Selling Unionism Home and Away* (Belfast: Ulster Review Publications, 1995).

Aughey, A. and Morrow, D. (eds) *Northern Ireland Politics* (London: Longman, 1996).

Bagguley, P. and Hearn, J. (eds) *Transforming Politics: Power and Resistance* (Basingstoke: Macmillan Press, 1999).

Bardon, J. *A History of Ulster* (Belfast: Blackstaff Press, 2001).

Barton, B. and Roche, P. J. (eds) *The Northern Ireland Question: Perspectives and Policies* (Aldershot: Avebury, 1994).

Barton, B. and Roche, P. J. (eds) *The Northern Ireland Question: The Peace Process and the Belfast Agreement* (Basingstoke: Palgrave Macmillan, 2009).

Bean, K. *The New Politics of Sinn Féin* (Liverpool: Liverpool University Press, 2007).

Beattie, G. *We Are the People: Journeys Through the Heart of Protestant Ulster* (London: Mandarin, 1993).

Beattie, G. *Protestant Boy* (London: Granta, 2004).

Beem, C. *The Necessity of Politics: Reclaiming American Public Life* (Chicago: University of Chicago Press, 1999).

Bell, D. *Acts of Union: Youth Culture and Sectarianism in Northern Ireland* (London: Macmillan, 1990).

Bell, G. *The Protestants of Ulster* (London: Pluto Press, 1976).

Benhabib, S. *The Claims of Culture: Equality and Diversity in the Global Era* (Princeton, NJ: Princeton University Press, 2002).

Bew, J. Frampton, M. and Gurruchaga, I., *Talking to Terrorists: Making Peace in Northern Ireland and the Basque Country* (London: Hurst & Company, 2009).

Bew, P. *The Making and Remaking of the Good Friday Agreement* (Dublin: Liffey Press, 2007).

Bew, P., Gibbon, P. and Patterson, H. *Northern Ireland 1921–1996: Political Forces and Social Classes* (London: Serif, 1995).

Bishop, P. and Mallie, E. *The Provisional IRA* (London: Corgi, 1988).

Bleakley, D. *Faulkner: Conflict and Consent in Irish Politics* (London: The Alden Press, 1974).

Bloomfield, K. *Stormont in Crisis: A Memoir* (Belfast: Blackstaff Press, 1994).

Borer, T. A., Darby, J. and McEvoy-Levy, S. *Peacebuilding After Peace Accords* (Notre Dame USA: University of Notre Dame Press, 2006).

Boulton, D. *The UVF 1966–73: An Anatomy of Loyalist Rebellion* (Dublin: Torc Books, 1973).

Bowyer Bell, J. *The Secret Army: The IRA 1916–1979* (Dublin: Academic Press, 1979).

Bowyer Bell, J. *Back to the Future: The Protestants and a United Ireland* (Dublin: Poolbeg Press, 1996).

Boyce, D. G. *The Irish Question and British Politics, 1868–1986* (Basingstoke: Macmillan, 1988).

Boyce, D. G. and O'Day, A. (eds) *Defenders of the Union: A Survey of British and Irish Unionism since 1801* (London: Routledge, 2001).

Boyd, J. *Out of My Class* (Belfast: Blackstaff, 1985).

Bradley, I. *Believing in Britain: The Spiritual Identity of Britishness* (Oxford: Lion Hudson, 2008).

Brewer, J. *Anti-Catholicism in Northern Ireland 1600–1998: The Mote and the Beam* (Basingstoke: Macmillan Press, 1998).

Brewer, J. *Ethnography* (Buckingham: Open University Press, 2001).

Brown, G. and Alexander, D. *Stronger Together: The 21st Century Case for Scotland and Britain* (London: Fabian Society, 2007).

Bruce, S. *God Save Ulster: The Religion and Politics of Paisleyism* (Oxford: Oxford University Press, 1986).

Bruce, S. *The Edge of the Union: The Ulster Loyalist Political Vision* (Oxford: Oxford University Press, 1994).

Bruce, S. *Paisley: Religion and Politics in Northern Ireland* (Oxford: Oxford University Press, 2007).

Bryan, D. *Orange Parades: The Politics of Ritual, Tradition and Control* (London: Pluto, 2000).

Bryan, D, Fraser, T. G. and Dunn, S. *Political Rituals: Loyalist Parades in Portadown* (Coleraine: University of Ulster, 1995).

Bryson, L. and McCartney, C. *Clashing Symbols* (Belfast: Queen's University Institute of Irish Studies, 1994).

Buckland, P. *Irish Unionism, 1885–1922* (London: Historical Association, 1973).

Burton, F. *The Politics of Legitimacy: Struggles in a Belfast Community* (London: Routledge and Kegan Paul, 1978).

Buscher, S. and Ling, B. *Máiréad Corrigan and Betty Williams: Making Peace in Northern Ireland* (New York: The Feminist Press, 1999).

Busteed, M., Neal, F. and Tonge, J. (eds) *Irish Protestant Identities* (Manchester: Manchester University Press, 2008).

Cairns, E. *Caught in Crossfire: Children and the Northern Ireland Conflict* (Belfast: Appletree Press, 1987).

Cairns, E. *Children and Political Violence* (Oxford: Blackwell, 1996).

Cappella, J. N. and Jamieson, K. H., *Spiral of Cynicism: The Press and the Public Good* (Oxford: Oxford University Press, 1997).

Carlton, C. (ed.) *Bigotry and Blood: Documents on the Ulster Troubles* (Chicago: Nelson-Hall, 1977).

Cash, J. D. *Identity, Ideology and Conflict: The Structuration of Politics in Northern Ireland* (Cambridge: Cambridge University Press 1996).

Catterall, P. and MacDougall, S. (eds) *The Northern Ireland Problem in British Politics* (Basingstoke: Macmillan, 1996).

Caunce, S., Mazierska, E., Sydney-Smith, S. and Walton, J. K. (eds) *Relocating Britishness* (Manchester: Manchester University Press, 2004).

Clayton, P. *Enemies and Passing Friends* (London: Pluto, 1996).

Coakley, J. (ed.) *Changing Shades of Orange and Green: Redefining the*

Union and the Nation in Contemporary Ireland (Dublin: University College Dublin Press 2002).

Cochrane, F. *Unionist Politics and the Politics of Unionism since the Anglo-Irish Agreement* (Cork: Cork University Press, 1997).

Cocker C. A., Olser, H. F. and Aall, P. (eds) *Turbulent Peace: The Challenges of Managing International Conflict* (Washington, DC: US Institute of Peace, 2001).

Coleman, J. S. *Foundations of Social Theory* (Cambridge, MA: Harvard University Press, 1990).

Conroy, J. *Belfast Diary: War as a Way of Life* (Boston: Beacon Press, 1995).

Cooke, D. *Persecuting Zeal: A Portrait of Ian Paisley* (Dingle: Brandon, 1996).

Coulter, C. *Contemporary Northern Irish Society: An Introduction* (London: Pluto 1999).

Coulter, C. and Murray, M. (eds) *Northern Ireland After the Troubles: A Society in Transition* (Manchester: Manchester University Press, 2008).

Cox M., Guelke A. and Stephen, F. (eds) *A Farewell to Arms? Beyond the Good Friday Agreement* (Manchester: Manchester University Press, 2006).

Crawford, A. and Newburn, T. *Youth Offending and Restorative Justice: Implementing Reform in Youth Justice* (Cullompton: Willan Press, 2003).

Crawford, C. *Inside the UDA: Volunteers and Violence* (London: Pluto Press, 2003).

Crawford, R.G. *Loyal to King Billy: A Portrait of the Ulster Protestants* (Dublin: Gill and MacMillan, 1987).

Cusack, J. and McDonald, H. *UVF* (Dublin: Poolbeg, 1997).

Darby, J. *Scorpions in a Bottle: Conflicting Cultures in Northern Ireland* (London: Minority Rights Publications, 1997).

Darby, J. *The Effects of Violence on Peace Processes* (Washington, DC: US Institute of Peace Press, 2001).

Darby, J. and MacGinty, R. *The Management of the Peace Process* (Basingstoke: Macmillan, 2000).

Dawe, G. *The Rest is History* (Newry: Abbey Press, 1998).

Della Porta, D. and Diani, M. *Social Movements: An Introduction* (Oxford: Blackwell, 1999).

De Paor, L. *Divided Ulster* (Harmondsworth: Penguin, 1970).

Deutsch, R. *Máiréad Corrigan/Betty Williams* (New York: Barron's Educational, 1977).

Diani, M. and Eyerman, R. (eds) *Studying Collective Action* (London: Sage, 1992).

Dillon, M. and Lehane, D. *Political Murder in Northern Ireland* (Harmondsworth: Penguin Books, 1973).

Dixon, P. *Northern Ireland – the Politics of War and Peace* (Basingstoke: Palgrave, 2001).

Dougan, D. *The Sash He Never Wore* (St Albans: Granada Publishing, 1974).

Downing, T. *The Troubles: The Background to the Question of Northern Ireland* (London: MacDonald Futura).

Dudley Edwards, R. *The Faithful Tribe: An Intimate Portrait of the Loyal Institutions* (London: Harper Collins, 1999).

Dunn, S. (ed.) *Facets of the Conflict in Northern Ireland* (Basingstoke: Macmillan, 1995).

Edwards, A. *A History of the Northern Ireland Labour Party: Democratic Socialism and Sectarianism* (Manchester: Manchester University Press, 2009).

Edwards, A. and Bloomer, S. (eds) *Transforming the Peace Process in Northern Ireland: From Terrorism to Democratic Politics* (Dublin: Irish Academic Press, 2008).

Edwards, M. *Civil Society* (Cambridge: Polity Press, 2004).

Ehrenberg, J. *Civil Society: The Critical History of an Idea* (New York: New York University Press, 1999).

Elliott, M. (ed.) *The Long Road to Peace in Northern Ireland* (Liverpool: Liverpool University Press, 2002).

English, R. *Armed Struggle: A History of the IRA* (Basingstoke: Macmillan, 2003).

English, R. and Walker, G. (eds) *Unionism in Modern Ireland* (Gill and Macmillan: Dublin, 1996).

Fanon, F. *Black Skins, White Masks*, translated by C. L. Markham (London: Pluto Press, 1986).

Farrell, M. *The Orange State* (London; Pluto, 1976).

Farrington, C. *Ulster Unionism and the Peace Process in Northern Ireland* (Basingstoke: Palgrave Macmillan, 2006).

Faulkner, B. *Memoirs of a Statesman* (London: Weidenfeld and Nicolson, 1978).

Fay, M. T., Morrissey, M. and Smyth, M. *Northern Ireland's Troubles: The Human Costs* (London: Pluto Press, 1999).

Fealty, M., Ringland, T. and Steven, D. *A Long Peace? The Future of Unionism in Northern Ireland* (Wimborne: Slugger O'Toole, 2003).

Feeney, B. *Sinn Féin: A Hundred Turbulent Years* (Dublin: O'Brien Press, 2002).

Fentress, J. and Wickham, C. *Social Memory* (Oxford: Blackwell, 1992).

Fisk, R. *The Point of No Return: The Strike Which Broke the British in Ulster* (London: Andre Deutsch, 1975).

Flackes, W. D. *Northern Ireland: A Political Directory* (London: Ariel Books, 1980).

Follis, B. *A State Under Siege: The Establishment of Northern Ireland, 1920–1925* (Oxford: Clarendon, 1995).

Foster, J. W. (ed.) *The Idea of the Union. Statements and Critiques in Support of the Union of Great Britain and Northern Ireland* (Vancouver: Belcouver Press, Canada, 1995).

Foster, R. F. *Modern Ireland 1600–1972* (London Penguin Books, 1990).

Frampton, M. *The Long March: The Political Strategy of Sinn Féin, 1981–2007* (Basingstoke: Palgrave Macmillan, 2009).

Galligher, J. F. and DeGregory, J. L. *Violence in Northern Ireland: Understanding Protestant Perspectives* (Dublin: Gill and MacMillan, 1985).

Garland, R. *Gusty Spence* (Belfast: Blackstaff Press, 2001).

Gébler, C. *The Glass Curtain* (London: Hamish Hamilton, 1991).

Geddes, A. and Favell, A. (eds) *The Politics of Belonging: Migrants and Minorities in Contemporary Europe* (Aldershot: Ashgate, 1999).

Gellner, E. *Nations and Nationalism* (Oxford: Blackwell, 1993).

Gibbon, P. *The Origins of Ulster Unionism: The Formation of Popular Protestant Politics and Ideology in Nineteenth-Century Ireland* (Manchester: Manchester University Press, 1975).

Gillespie, N. Lovett, T. and Garner, W. *Youth Work and Working Class Youth Culture: Rules and Resistance in West Belfast* (Buckingham: Open University Press, 1992).

Gilligan, C. and Tonge, J. (eds) *Peace or War? Understanding the Peace Process in Ireland* (Aldershot: Ashgate, 1997).

Gilroy, P. *After Empire: Melancholia or Convivial Culture?* (London: Taylor and Francis, 2004).

Godson, D. *Himself Alone: David Trimble and the Ordeal of Unionism* (London: Harper Collins, 2004).

Goffman, E. *Frame Analysis: An Essay on the Organization of Experience* (London: Harper and Row, 1974).

Goodey, J. *Victims and Victimology: Research, Policy and Practice* (Harlow: Longman Pearson, 2005).

Goodman, J. and Anderson, J. (eds.) *Agreeing Ireland: Political Agendas for Peace in Ireland's National Conflict* (London: Pluto Press, 1998).

Graham, B. (ed.) *In Search of Ireland: A Cultural Geography* (London: Routledge, 1997).

Greacen, R. *The Sash My Father Wore: An Autobiography* (Edinburgh: Mainstream, 1997).

Hadden T. and Boyle, K. *The Anglo-Irish Agreement: Commentary, Text and Official Review* (London: Maxwell and Sweet, 1985).

Hainsworth, P. (ed.) *Divided Society: Ethnic Minorities and Racism in Northern Ireland* (London: Pluto Press, 1998).

Hanna, R. (ed.) *The Union: Essays on Ireland and the British Connection* (Newtownards: Colourpoint Books, 2001).

Harbinson, J. F. *The Ulster Unionist Party 1882–1973* (Belfast: Blackstaff, 1973).

Hargie, O. and Dickson, D. (eds) *Researching the Troubles: Social Science Perspectives on the Northern Ireland Conflict* (Edinburgh: Mainstream Publishing, 2003).

Harrington, J. P. and Mitchell, E. J. (eds) *Politics and Performance in Contemporary Northern Ireland* (Amherst: University of Massachusetts Press, 1999).

Heath, A. F., Breen, R. and Whelan, C. T. (eds) *Ireland North and South: Perspectives from Social Science* (Oxford: Oxford University Press, 1999).

Hennessey, T. *A History of Northern Ireland, 1920–1996* (London: Macmillan, 1996).

Hennessey, T. *Dividing Ireland, World War One and Partition* (London: Routledge, 1998).

Hennessey, T. *The Northern Ireland Peace Process: Ending the Troubles?* (Dublin: Gill and Macmillan, 2000).

Hennessey, T. *Northern Ireland: The Origins of the Troubles* (Dublin: Gill and Macmillan, 2005).

Hickey, J. *Religion and the Northern Ireland Problem* (Dublin: Gill and Macmillan, 1984).

Hobsbawn, E. and Ranger, T. (eds) *The Invention of Tradition* (Cambridge: CUP, 1983).

Holland, J. *Hope Against History: The Ulster Conflict* (London: Hodder and Stoughton, 1999).

Hughes, E. (ed.) *Culture and Politics in Northern Ireland: 1960–1990* (Milton Keynes: Open University Press, 1991).

Hume, D. *The Ulster Unionist Party 1972–92* (Lurgan: Ulster Society Publications, 1996).

Hutton, S. and Stewart, P. (eds) *Ireland's Histories* (London: Routledge, 1991).

Hyndman, M. *Further Afield: Journeys from a Protestant Past* (Belfast: Beyond the Pale Publications, 1996).

Jacobs, S., Jacobson, R. and Marchbank, J. (eds) *States of Conflict* (London: Zed Books, 2000).

Jarman, N. *Material Conflicts: Parades and Visual Displays in Northern Ireland* (Oxford: Berg, 1997).

Jervis, J. *Transgressing the Modern: Explorations in the Western Experience of Otherness* (London: Blackwell, 1999).

Johnston, H. and Klandermas, B. (eds) *Social Movements and Culture* (UCL Press, London, 1995).

Jordan, G. *Not of This World?: Evangelical Protestants in Northern Ireland* (Belfast: Blackstaff Press, 2001).

Jordan, H. *Milestones in Murder* (Edinburgh: Mainstream, 2002).

Kaufmann, E. *The Orange Order: A Contemporary Northern Irish History* (Oxford: Oxford University Press, 2007).

Kavirai, S. and Khilnani, S. (eds) *Civil Society: History and Possibilities* (Cambridge: Cambridge University Press, 2001).

Kelley, K. *The Longest War: Northern Ireland and the IRA* (Dingle: Brandon, 1982).

Kennaway, B. *The Orange Order: A Tradition Betrayed* (London: Methuen, 2006).

Kennedy, D. *The Widening Gulf: Northern Attitudes to the Independent Irish State, 1919–1949* (Belfast: Blackstaff, 1988).

Kenny, A. *The Road to Hillsborough: The Shaping of the Anglo-Irish Agreement* (London: Pergamon, 1986).

Kerr, M. *Transforming Unionism: David Trimble and the 2005 General Election* (Dublin: Irish Academic Press, 2005).

Kingsley, P. *Londonderry Revisited: A Loyalist Analysis of the Civil Rights Controversy* (Belfast: Belfast Publications, 1989).

Knox, C. and Monaghan, R. *Informal Justice in Divided Societies* (Basingstoke: Palgrave Macmillan, 2002).

Laclau, E. and Mouffe, C. *Hegemony and Socialist Strategy: Towards a Radical Democratic Politics* (Verso: London, 1985).

Lanclos, D. *At Play in Belfast: Children's Folklore and Identities in Northern Ireland* (London: Rutgers University Press, 2003).

Lee, J. J. *Ireland 1912–85: Politics and Society* (Cambridge: Cambridge University Press).

Lennon, B. *Peace Comes Dropping Slow* (Belfast: Community Dialogue, 2004).

Lewis, P. *Young, British and Muslim* (London: Continuum, 2007).

Lister, D. and Jordan, H. *Mad Dog: The Rise and Fall of Johnny Adair and 'C Company'* (Edinburgh: Mainstream, 2003).

Lucy, G. and McClure, E. (eds) *Cool Britannia? What Britishness Means to Me* (Lurgan: Ulster Society, 1999).

Lyons, F. S. L. *Ireland Since the Famine* (London: Collins Fontana, 1982).

Mac anGhaill, M. *Contemporary Racisms and Ethnicities* (Buckingham: Open University Press, 1999).

MacDonald, M. *Children of Wrath: Political Violence in Northern Ireland* (Cambridge: Polity, 1986).

MacPherson, Sir W. *The Stephen Lawrence Inquiry: Report of an Inquiry by Sir William MacPherson of Cluny, advised by Tom Cook, The Right Reverend Dr. John Sentamu, Dr. Richard Stone, Cm 4262-I* (London: HMSO, 1999).

Mallie, E. and McKittrick, D. *The Fight for Peace: The Secret Story Behind the Irish Peace Process* (London: Mandarin, 1997).

McAuley, J.W. 'Cuchulainn and an RPG-7: The Ideology and Politics of the UDA', in E. Hughes, (ed.) *Culture and Politics in Northern Ireland* (Milton Keynes: Open University Press, 1991).

McAuley, J.W. 'The Protestant Working Class and the State in Northern Ireland since 1930: a Problematic Relationship', in S. Hutton and P. Stewart (eds) *Ireland's Histories* (London: Routledge, 1991).

McAuley, J.W. *The Politics of Identity: A Loyalist Community in Belfast* (Aldershot: Avebury Press, 1994).

McAuley, J.W. '"Not a Game of Cowboys and Indians"– the Ulster Defence Association in the 1990s' in A. O'Day (ed.) *Terrorism's Laboratory: The Case of Northern Ireland* (Dartmouth: Aldershot, 1995).

McAuley, J.W. 'From Loyal Soldiers to Political Spokespersons: A Political History of a Loyalist Paramilitary Group in Northern Ireland', *Etudes Irlandaises*, (1996) 21, 1, pp.165-182.

McAuley, J.W. '(Re) Constructing Ulster Loyalism: Political Responses to the "Peace Process"', *Irish Journal of Sociology*, 6 (1996), pp.127–153.

McAuley, J.W. 'Flying the One-Winged Bird: Ulster Unionism and the Peace Process' in P. Shirlow and M. McGovern (eds), *Who Are 'The People'?* (1997), pp.158–175.

McAuley, J.W. 'The Ulster Loyalist Political Parties: Towards a New Respectability', in P. Joannon (ed.) Le Processus De Paix En Irlande Du Nord, *Etudes Irlandaises* 22, 2 (1997), pp.117–132.

McAuley, J.W. 'Divided Loyalists, Divided Loyalties: Conflict and Continuities in Contemporary Unionist Ideology', in C. Gilligan and J. Tonge (eds), *Peace or War? Understanding the Peace Process in Northern Ireland* (1997), pp.37–53.

McAuley, J.W. (1998) 'Surrender?: Loyalist Perceptions of Conflict Settlement' in J. Anderson and J. Goodman (eds) *(Dis)Agreeing Ireland* (London: Pluto Press), pp. 193–210.

McAuley, J. W. 'Very British Rebels: Politics and Discourse within contemporary Ulster Unionism', in P. Bagguley and J. Hearn (eds) *Transforming Politics: Power and Resistance* (Basingstoke: Macmillan Press, 1999), pp.106–125.

McAuley, J. W. (1999b) 'Still "No Surrender"?: New Loyalism and the Peace Process in Ireland', in J. P. Harrington and E. J. Mitchell (eds) *Politics and Performance in Contemporary Northern Ireland* (Amherest: University of Massachusetts Press), pp. 57–81.

McAuley, J. W. 'Mobilising Ulster Unionism: New Directions or Old?', *Capital and Class*, 70, Spring (2000), pp.37– 64.

McAuley, J. W. 'Redefining Loyalism–An Academic Perspective', Dublin: Institute for British–Irish Studies, IBIS working paper no. 4. (2001).

McAuley, J. W. 'Ulster Unionism after the Peace', in J. Neuheiser and S. Wolff (eds), *Breakthrough to Peace? The Impact of the Good Friday*

Agreement on Northern Irish Politics and Society (New York and Oxford: Berghahn Books, 2002), pp.76–93.

McAuley, J. W. 'The Emergence of New Loyalism', in J. Coakley (ed.) *Changing Shades of Orange and Green* (2002), pp. 106–122.

McAuley, J. W. 'Peace and Progress? Political and Social Change Among Young Loyalists in Northern Ireland', *Journal of Social Issues*, 60, 3 (2004), pp.541–562.

McAuley, J. W. '"Just Fighting to Survive": Loyalist Paramilitary Politics and the Progressive Unionist Party', *Terrorism and Political Violence*, 16, 3 (2004), pp.522–543.

McAuley, J. W. 'Fantasy Politics? Restructuring Unionism After the Good Friday Agreement,' *Eire–Ireland*, 39, 1/2 (2004), pp.189–214.

McAuley, J. W. 'Whither New Loyalism? Changing Loyalist Politics After the Belfast Agreement', *Irish Political Studies*, 20, 3 (2005), pp.323–340.

McAuley, J. W. and Hislop, S. 'Many roads forward: politics and ideology within the Progressive Unionist Party', *Études Irlandaises*, 25, 1 (2000), pp.173–92.

McAuley, J.W. and McCormick, P. J. 'The Protestant Working Class and the State in Northern Ireland: The Loosening Bond', *Social Studies, An Irish Journal of Sociology*, 10, 1/2 (1989), pp.32–44.

McAuley, J.W. and McCormick, P. J. 'Hounds of Ulster and the Re-writing of Irish History', *Études Irlandaises*, 15, 2 (1990), pp.149–164.

McAuley, J. W. and Tonge, J. 'Over the Rainbow?: Relationships between Loyalists and Republicans in the Northern Ireland Assembly', *Études Irlandaises*, 28, 1 (2003), pp.177–198.

McAuley, J. W. and Tonge, J. '"For God and for the Crown": Contemporary Political and Social Attitudes among Orange Order Members in Northern Ireland', *Political Psychology* 28, 1 (2007), pp.33– 54.

McBride, I. *The Siege of Derry in Ulster Protestant Mythology* (Dublin: Four Courts Press 1997).

McBride, I. (ed.) *History and Memory in Modern Ireland* (Cambridge: Cambridge University Press, 2001).

McCann, E. *War and an Irish Town* (London: Pluto, 1972).

McCartney, R. *Reflections on Liberty, Democracy and the Union* (Dublin: Maunsel and Company, 2001).

McDonald, H. *Trimble* (London: Bloomsbury, 2000).

McDonald, H. and Cusack, J. *UDA: Inside the Heart of Loyalist Terror* (London: Penguin, 2004).

McDowell, J. *The Mummy's Boys: Threats and Menaces from Ulster's ParaMafia* (Dublin; Gill and Macmillan, 2008).

McGarry, J. and O'Leary, B. *Explaining Northern Ireland* (Oxford: Blackwell, 1995).

McGrath, C. and O'Malley, E. (eds) *Irish Political Studies Reader: Key Contributions* (London: Routledge, 2008).

McKay, S. *Northern Protestants: An Unsettled People* (Belfast: Blackstaff Press, 2005).

McKeown, C. *The Passion of Peace* (Belfast: Blackstaff Press, 1984).

McKittrick, D. *Endgame: The Search for Peace in Northern Ireland* (Belfast: Blackstaff Press, 1994).

McKittrick, D. *The Nervous Peace* (Belfast: Blackstaff Press, 1996).

McKittrick, D., Kelters, S., Feeney, B. and Thornton, C., *Lost Lives* (Edinburgh: Mainstream Publishing, 1999).

McKittrick, D. and McVea, D., *Making Sense of the Troubles* (London: Penguin Books, 2000).

McNamee, E. *Resurrection Man* (London, Picador, 1995).

Middleton, D. and Edwards, D. (eds) *Collective Remembering* (London: Sage, 1991).

Millar, F. *David Trimble: The Price of Peace* (Dublin: The Liffey Press, 2004).

Millar, F. *Northern Ireland: A Triumph of Politics, Interviews and Analysis 1998–2008* (Dublin: Irish Academic Press, 2009).

Miller, D. *Rethinking Northern Ireland: Culture, Ideology and Colonialism* (London: Longman, 1998).

Miller, D. *Queen's Rebels: Ulster Loyalism in Historical Perspective* (Dublin: Gill and Macmillan, 1978).

Miller, D. *Queen's Rebels: Ulster Loyalism in Historical Perspective* [reprinted with a new introduction by John Bew] (Dublin: University College Dublin Press, 2007).

Misztal, B. *Theories of Social Remembering* (Maidenhead: Open University Press, 2003).

Mitchel, P. *Evangelicalism and National Identity in Ulster 1921–1998* (Oxford: Oxford University Press, 2003).

Mitchell, C. *Religion, Identity and Politics in Northern Ireland: Boundaries of Belonging and Belief* (Aldershot: Ashgate, 2006).

Mitchell, G. J. *Making Peace. The Inside Story of the Making of the Good Friday Agreement* (London: William Heinemann, 1999).

Mitchell, P. and Wilford, R. (eds) *Politics in Northern Ireland* (Boulder, Co: Westview Press, 1999).

Modood, T. *Multicultural Politics: Racism, Ethnicity and Muslims in Britain* (Edinburgh: Edinburgh University Press, 2005).

Moloney, E. *A Secret History of the IRA* (London: Penguin, 2002).

Moloney, E. *Paisley: From Demagogue to Democrat?* (Dublin: Poolbeg Press, 2008).

Moody, T. W. *The Ulster Question, 1603–1973* (Dublin: Mercier Press, 1980).

Mooney, G. and Neal, S. (eds) *Community: Welfare, Crime and Society* (Maidenhead: Open University Press, 2009).

Morris, A. and McClurg Mueller, C. (eds) *Frontiers In Social Movement Theory* (New Haven: Yale University Press, 1992).

Morrissey, M. and Smyth, M. *Northern Ireland After the Good Friday Agreement: Victims, Grievance and Blame* (London: Pluto, 2002).

Moxon-Browne, E. P. *Nation, Class and Creed in Northern Ireland* (Aldershot: Gower, 1983).

Mudimbe, V. Y. (ed.) *Nations, Identities, Cultures* (Durham, NC: Duke University Press, 1997).

Mulholland, M. *Northern Ireland at the Crossroads: Ulster Unionism in the O'Neill Years, 1960– 69* (Basingstoke: Palgrave, 2000).

Murray, D. (ed.) *Protestant Perceptions of the Peace Process in Northern Ireland* (University of Limerick: Centre for Peace and Development Studies, 2000).

Nairn, T. *Pariah: Misfortunes of the British Kingdom* (London: Verso, 2002).

Nairn, T. *Gordon Brown: Bard of Britishness* (Cardiff: Institute of Welsh Affairs, 2006).

Nelson, S. *Ulster's Uncertain Defenders: Loyalists and the Northern Ireland Conflict* (Belfast: Appletree Press, 1984).

Neuheiser, J. and Wolff, S. (eds) *Peace at Last? The Impact of the Good Friday Agreement on Northern Ireland* (Oxford: Berghahn Books, 2002).

Nic Craith, M. *Plural Identities Singular Narratives: The Case of Northern Ireland* (Oxford: Berghahn, 2002).

Nora, P. and Kritzman L. D. (eds) *Realms of Memory: Rethinking the French Past. Vol. 1: Conflicts and Divisions* (New York and Chichester: Columbia University Press, 1996).

Novick, P. *The Holocaust in American Life* (New York: Houghton Mifflin, 1999).

O'Brien, B. *The Long War: The IRA and Sinn Féin* (New York: Syracuse University Press, 1999).

O'Day, A. (ed.) *Terrorism's Laboratory: Northern Ireland* (Dartmouth: Dartmouth Press, 1995).

Ó'Dochartaigh, N. *From Civil Rights to Armalites: Derry and the Birth of the Irish Troubles* (Cork: Cork University Press, 1997).

O'Dowd, L., Rolston, B. and Tomlinson, M., *Northern Ireland: Between Civil Rights and Civil War* (London: CSE Books, 1980).

O'Leary B. and McGarry, J., *The Politics of Antagonism: Understanding Northern Ireland* (London: Athlone Press, 1993).

O'Neill, M. (ed.) *Devolution and British Politics* (Harlow: Pearson, 2004).

Parekh, B. *Rethinking Multiculturalism: Cultural Diversity and Political Theory* (Basingstoke: Palgrave, 2000).

Parkinson, A. F. *Ulster Loyalism and the British Media* (Dublin: Four Courts Press, 1998).

Patterson, H. *The Politics of Illusion: A Political History of the IRA* (London: Serif, 1997).

Patterson H. and Kaufmann, E., *Unionism and Orangeism in Northern Ireland Since 1945: The Decline of the Loyal Family* (Manchester: Manchester University Press, 2007).

Peatling, G. *The Failure of the Northern Ireland Peace Process* (Dublin: Irish Academic Press, 2004).

Penrose, J. and Jackson, P. (eds) *Constructions of Race, Place and Nation* (London: UCL Press, 1993).

Porter, N. *Rethinking Unionism: An Alternative Vision for Northern Ireland* (Belfast: Blackstaff, 1996).

Powell, J. *Great Hatred, Little Room: Making Peace in Northern Ireland* (London: The Bodley Head, 2008).

Probert, B. *Beyond Orange and Green: The Political Economy of the Northern Ireland Crisis* (London: Zed Press, 1978).

Purdie, B. *Politics in the Streets: The Origins of the Civil Rights Movement in Northern Ireland* (Belfast: Blackstaff, 1990).

Purdy, A. *Molyneaux: The Long View* (Antrim: Greystone Books, 1989).

Putnam, R. D. *Making Democracy Work–Civic Traditions in Modern Italy* (Princeton, USA: Princeton University Press, 1993).

Putnam, R. D. and Goss, K. A. (eds) *Democracies in Flux: The Evolution of Social Capital in Contemporary Society* (Oxford: Oxford University Press, 2002).

Quinn, D. *Understanding Northern Ireland* (Manchester: Baseline Books, 1993).

Ridd, R. and Calloway, H. (eds) *Caught Up in Conflict* (Basingstoke: Macmillan, 1986).

Roberts, I. *Craft, Class and Control: The Sociology of a Shipbuilding Community* (Edinburgh: Edinburgh University Press, 1993).

Rosenbaum, S. *Against Home Rule: The Case for the Union* (London: Frederick Warne and Co, 1912).

Roulston, C. and Davies, C. *Gender, Democracy and Inclusion in Northern Ireland* (Houndmills: Palgrave, 2000).

Rowan, B. *Behind The Lines: The Story of the IRA and Loyalist Ceasefires* (Belfast: Blackstaff Press, 1995).

Rowan, B. *The Armed Peace: Life and Death after the Ceasefires* (Edinburgh: Mainstream Publishing, 2003).

Rowan, B. *Paisley and the Provos* (Belfast: Brehon Press, 2005).

Rowan, B. *How the Peace Was Won* (Dublin: Gill and Macmillan, 2008).

Ruane, J. and Todd, J. *The Dynamics of Conflict in Northern Ireland: Power, Conflict and Emancipation* (Cambridge: Cambridge University Press, 1996).

Ruane, J. and Todd, J. (eds) *After the Belfast Agreement: Analysing Political Change in Northern Ireland* (Dublin: University College Dublin Press, 1999).

Rutherford, J. (ed.) *Identity: Community, Culture, Difference* (London: Lawrence & Wishart, 1990).

Said, E. *Orientalism* (London: Routledge & Kegan Paul, 1978).

Sales, R. *Women Divided: Gender, Religion and Politics in Northern Ireland* (London: Routledge, 1997).

Seldon, A. *Blair* (London: Free Press, 2005).

Shirlow, P. and McGovern, M. (eds) *Who are 'The People'? Unionism, Protestantism and Loyalism in Northern Ireland* (London: Pluto, 1997).

Shirlow, P. and Murtagh, B. *Belfast: Segregation, Violence and the City* (London: Pluto, 2006).

Shirlow, P. and McEvoy, K. *Beyond the Wire: Former Prisoners and Conflict Transformation in Northern Ireland* (London: Pluto, 2008).

Shirlow, P., Tonge, J., McAuley, J. W. and McGlynn, C. *Abandoning Historical Conflict? Former Paramilitary Prisoners and Political Reconciliation in Northern Ireland* (Manchester: Manchester University Press, 2010).

Sims, J. Y. *Farewell to the Hammer: A Shankill Boyhood* (Belfast: White Row Press, 1992).

Sinnerton, H. *David Ervine: Uncharted Waters* (Dingle: Brandon, 2002).

Smith, J. *Making the Peace in Ireland* (London: Pearson Education, 2002).

Smyth, C. *Ian Paisley: Voice of Protestant Ulster* (Edinburgh: Scottish Academic Press, 1987).

Smyth, M. and Fay, M. T. (eds) *Personal Accounts from Northern Ireland's Troubles: Public Conflict, Private Loss* (London: Pluto Press, 2000).

Spencer, G. *The State of Loyalism in Northern Ireland* (Houndmills: Palgrave Macmillan, 2008).

Stanko, E. (ed.) *Defining Violence* (London: Routledge, 2002).

Stevenson, J. *'We Wrecked the Place': Contemplating an End to the Northern Irish Troubles* (London: The Free Press, 1996).

Stewart, A. T. Q. *The Ulster Crisis: Resistance to Home Rule 1912–1914* (Belfast: Blackstaff Press, 1997).

Stone, M. *None Shall Divide Us* (London: John Blake, 2004).

Stringer, P. and Robinson, G. (eds) *Social Attitudes in Northern Ireland: The Second Report 1991–1992* (Belfast: Blackstaff Press, 1992).

Sugden, J. and Bairner, A. *Sport, Sectarianism and Society in a Divided Ireland* (London: Leicester University Press, 1995).

Tarrow, S. *Power in Movement: Social Movements, Collective Action and Politics* (Cambridge: Cambridge University Press, 1994).

Taylor, P. *Families At War: Voices From The Troubles* (London: BBC Books, 1989).

Taylor, P. *Provos: The IRA and Sinn Féin* (London: Bloomsbury, 1997).

Taylor, P. *Loyalists* (London: Bloomsbury, 2000).

Teague, P. (ed.) *The Economy of Northern Ireland* (London: Lawrence & Wishart, 1993).

Tiernan, J. *The Dublin and Monaghan Bombings and the Murder Triangle* (Published by the Author, 2002).

Tilly, C. *Stories, Identities and Political Change* (Oxford: Rowman and Littlefield, 2002).

Tonge, J. *Northern Ireland: Conflict and Change* (London: Prentice Hall, 1998).

Tonge, J. *The New Northern Irish Politics* (Basingstoke: Palgrave, 2005).

Tonge, J. and McAuley, J. 'The Contemporary Orange Order in Northern Ireland' in M. Busteed, F. Neal and J. Tonge (eds) *Irish Protestant Identities* (Manchester: Manchester University Press, 2008), pp.289–302.

Townshend, C. (ed.) *Consensus in Ireland: Approaches and Recessions* (Oxford: Clarendon Press, 1998).

Van Til, J. *Breaching Derry's Walls: The Quest for a Lasting Peace in Northern Ireland* (Plymouth: University Press of America).

Walker, B. *Dancing to History's Tune: History, Myth and Politics in Ireland* (Belfast: Queen's University of Belfast, 1996).

Walker, B. *Past and Present: History, Identity and Politics in Ireland* (Belfast: Queen's University of Belfast, 2000).

Walker, G. *A History of the Ulster Unionist Party: Protest, Pragmatism and Pessimism* (Manchester: Manchester University Press, 2004).

Walker, G. and English, R. (eds) *Unionism in Modern Ireland* (Dublin: Gill and Macmillan, 1996).

Ward, P. *Unionism in the United Kingdom, 1918–1974* (Basingstoke: Palgrave Macmillan, 2005).

Ward, R. *Women, Unionism and Loyalism in Northern Ireland: From Tea-Makers to Political Actors* (Dublin: Irish Academic Press, 2006).

Ware, V. *Who Cares About Britishness? A Global View of the National Identity Debate* (London, Arcadia Books, 2007).

Watt, D. (ed.) *The Constitution of Northern Ireland: Problems and Prospects* (London: Heinemann, 1981).

Weiner, R. *The Rape and Plunder of the Shankill* (Belfast, published by the author, 1975).

Wertsch, J. *Voices of Collective Remembering* (Cambridge: Cambridge University Press, 2002).

Whyte, J. *Interpreting Northern Ireland* (Oxford: Clarendon Press, 1991).

Wichert, S. *Northern Ireland Since 1945* (London: Longman, 1991).

Wilford, R. (ed.) *Aspects of the Belfast Agreement* (Oxford: Oxford University Press, 2001).

Wilson, T. *Ulster: Conflict and Consent* (Oxford: Basil Blackwell, 1989).

Wood, I. S. *Crimes of Loyalty: a History of the UDA* (Edinburgh: Edinburgh University Press, 2006).

Wright, F. *Two Lands on One Soil: Ulster Politics Before Home Rule* (Dublin: Gill and Macmillan, 1996).

Zizek, S. *The Sublime Object of Ideology* (London: Verso, 1989).

Index